hyveth williams

Waiting

on tiptoes

for the

Lord

anticipation

Pacific Press® Publishing Association
Nampa, Idaho
Oshawa, Ontario, Canada

Edited by Tim Lale
Designed by Michelle C. Petz
Cover photograph by John Baker

Anticipation
by Hyveth Williams
Copyright © 2000 by
Pacific Press® Publishing Association
Printed in United States of America
All rights reserved.

ISBN: 0-8163-1789-5

00 01 02 03 04 • 5 4 3 2 1

Contents

Acknowledgments

This book is lovingly dedicated to God, who is the lamp that lit the torch of inspiration, illuminating my path to the insights and concepts recorded here. It is also devoted to my son, Steven, who lovingly allows me to continue using some of his experiences as illustrations, with one warning, "This one is gonna cost you *big*, Mom!"

A special note of thanks to my mother, Margaret Page (my father is deceased), my aunt, Vernetta, who cares for my mother so that I may pursue and fulfill my dreams. My sisters, Renita Taylor by birth and Ella Taylor by rebirth, and my brother, Trevor, whose return to the family circle is anxiously anticipated, are appreciated.

I could not have written this book without the assistance of Christy Robinson, editorial coordinator for the Loma Linda University School of Dentistry, who read and edited my first draft; Laura Kong, creative design director for Campus Hill Seventh-day Adventist Church in Loma Linda, California, whose computer and graphic design expertise were invaluable; Jim Carroll, acting business administrator for Campus Hill Church, who took the time to encourage and pray with me every day; Lillian Smith, my faithful prayer partner; and all of my staff who have surrounded me with grace as I tried to give birth to *Anticipation*.

I am especially grateful for the challenge to "put out into the deep," from the Pacific Press personnel, particularly Susan Harvey, Jerry Thomas, and Tim Lale, my editor. I hope everyone who reads this book will be blessed as I have been in preparing and presenting it.

Hyveth Williams

Foreword

Did you know that Jewish bridegrooms express their joy in a special dance, based on a legend of Abraham's reaction to the events described in Genesis 15:1-19? And did you know that, according to Luke 10:21, Jesus' rejoicing at seeing Satan fall from heaven is described using the same word for the dance of the bridegroom? Such is the jubilation of the Godhead in providing for our salvation. With such joy, we may anticipate the marriage supper of the Lamb, the Bridegroom, "who daily walks and talks with us, whispering sweet 'somethings' (not 'nothings') in our hearts to reaffirm and assure us that we are indeed His own." This is one of the many remarkable lessons from the book you hold in your hand.

It has been my privilege to know Pastor Hyveth Williams for almost three and a half years, she being the senior pastor of the Loma Linda Campus Hill Church and I, the pastor for Church Ministries. Hyveth Williams has become a household name in North America and throughout the world, in part because of her autobiography *Will I Ever Learn?* published around the time she joined the Campus Hill Church staff in 1996. Traveling widely, she is a popular speaker for weeks of prayer, convocations, and camp meetings. She is appreciated as a writer and recognized throughout the area east of Los Angeles for her dynamic weekly sermons broadcast by KSGN Christian radio. Many of the concepts Pastor Williams expresses in this volume have been shared in sermons, prayer meeting sessions, and university classes (she is an adjunct professor in the School of Religion of Loma Linda University). Her sermons are marked by enthusiasm, vivid illustrations, and constant reference to the meaning of words in the original Hebrew and Greek of the Bible. The reader will discover, however, that each chapter is much more than a sermon, with a thorough treatment of themes she is addressing.

In "Watching and Waiting," you'll find Pastor Williams's unforgettable account of a moment of exaltation turned into deep humiliation and embarrassment during a worship service at which she was speaking, as her skirt got caught on her shoe heel while she was kneeling for prayer! She displays her rich creativity and imagination in the recounting of her dream of being on trial in the judgment, dealing with the likes of Ordinary Joe (O. J.) Sinner, Judge N. O. Mercy, Attorney J. C. Son-Oman and Prosecutor Luce F. R. DeVille, in the chapter, "Don't Give Up!"

In 1998, Hyveth Williams received her doctoral degree from Boston University. Her dissertation entitled, "Theleia Theology—a Preaching Model for Women in Ministry," advocates a preaching model rich in a theology of hope and and one that elucidates the original meaning of biblical words and concepts. This educational background augments her natural giftedness in presenting scriptural lessons from a discernibly feminine perspective. Hope is the very essence of the present volume, and hope is reflected in most of the chapter titles.

Working with Pastor Williams on the staff of a university church and listening to her preach and speak often, I have found that she is an excellent communicator, an intelligent thinker, an outstanding and effective leader, and a powerful motivator. The hallmark of her ministry is the hours she spends counseling and visiting with people. She is a great problem solver and knows how to win over those who disagree with her.

The cross of Jesus Christ and the theme of salvation are central to all her communication. She takes great care to explain her understanding of salvation and justification by faith in the chapter, "Sleeping With the Enemy." Under her leadership the Campus Hill Church is very much alive and bustling with all kinds of activities and ministries and has become home for peoples of many nations, kindreds, tongues, and peoples. Acts 2:47 describes the dynamic of the New Testament church in these words, "And the Lord added to their number daily those who were being saved." This is currently happening at the Campus Hill Church under her pastoral care.

What is most significant, I believe, is her presentation of biblical truth from a woman's perspective—an angle that male preachers could not deliver no matter how they might try. In the chapter, "A Touch of Grace," Pastor Williams dares to address the forbidden subject of menstruation in the context of the woman with an issue of blood whom Jesus healed. And the story of Ruth becomes an allegory of women in ministry in the chapter, "Women in Waiting."

Often I am moved to tears by Pastor Williams' preaching. It is my hope that her ministry will flourish and that this book will introduce one fabulous woman preacher ordained by the Carpenter of Galilee. Perhaps my church will come to accept and appreciate the Spirit's work, and women, gifted by the Holy Spirit as she is, will be encouraged to take up ministry as the Lord lays it upon their hearts.

Larry Christoffel, Pastor for Church Ministry
Campus Hill Church, Loma Linda, California

Chapter 1

A-N-T-I-C-I-P-A-T-I-O-N

Several decades ago, Madison Avenue advertisers captured the imagination of Americans with one word—ANTICIPATION. It was as if they introduced that word into our vocabulary. As a result, generations of boomers and busters, mods and misfits, cannot look at a Heinz ketchup bottle without thinking of the phrase "Anticipation . . . it's making me wait," from the Carly Simon song that accompanied the television commercial.

Wait? That's almost un-American! We "will choose speed over depth every time," said George Barna in his book, *The Second Coming of the Church*.[1] He explains, "Because our time is limited and there are so many experiences we'd like to have, speed is attractive. We'll take the quick fix over the laborious renovation. We prefer immediate profits to building a strong financial base for the future. Loyalty is a thing of the past; we often relinquish long-term relationships in favor of new relationships that promise more immediate, higher quality results."

We are a nation hooked on speed. Not the drugs, but the drivenness that sends us hurtling fast-forward through time and space, through relationships and religions, even though we don't often know exactly where we are going. This addiction to speed makes it difficult for us to wait for anything.

So we've created fast-food restaurants, speedy car washes, souped-up cars and supermarkets to satisfy our addiction to speed. We have instant pain pills, a network of communication systems faster than the speed of light, superhighways on which motorists attempt to break the sound barrier. Even in our prayers we are pushy for quick responses. The Bible says, "Wait on the Lord." We say, "Lord, we need patience to wait, but give it now!"

The word *anticipation* has almost lost its meaning in today's society. *Anticipation* is the act of looking forward with pleasurable expectation. Although *anticipation* does not appear in biblical Hebrew or Greek, a close correspondent is the word *wait*, which means to look forward with eager expectation and steadfast endurance. It does not mean to push, as we are prone to do when we forget that good things come to those who wait. Neither does it mean to sit idly by.

To me, anticipation conjures up expectation and summons excitement. It transposes disappointments into declarations of hope. It causes one to linger, but not idly, as it calls forth action for believers to occupy 'til Jesus comes. Anticipation looks boldly into the future with pleasure because of the hope that will turn loss into gain. Anticipation is the gambler's concubine, the preacher's inspiration, and the people's pre-notion of grace. It leaves room for the dramatic visualization of things not seen with the naked eye, but felt with the passion of a pounding heart.

A-N-T-I-C-I-P-A-T-I-O-N . . . it's making me wait, not hopelessly, but expectantly for the promised mother lode of joy in the morning, according to Psalm 30:5. That joy is none other than the second coming of Christ.

David, the psalmist and youngest son of Jesse, was intimately acquainted with the experience of anticipation. Anointed the second king of Israel in a very public ceremony by the prophet Samuel, he had to wait and hope for several decades for the fulfillment of the promised dream. Instead of immediately ascending to the throne as expected after the anointing ceremony, David found himself running like a fugitive, hiding in the rocks and caves of the wilderness from his archenemy, Saul, the first king of Israel.

While anticipating the hope set before him, David penned the poignant Psalm 27, in which he revealed a spirit of absolute confidence in God despite the threats of his enemy. Called the tonic psalm because it is filled with concentrated strength and anticipation in God, it ends with verse 14: *"Wait for the Lord; be strong, and let your heart take courage; yes, wait for the Lord."*

In this verse, the word *wait* comes from the Hebrew word, *qavah,* which means to wait in eager anticipation. It is to literally wait on tiptoes, as *tikvah,* one of its derivatives, suggests.

I had the pleasure of witnessing this kind of waiting when I lived in Massachusetts. I had a Pomeranian pup, so precious there are no words to describe her love for me. She was a sable-colored dog with intelligent eyes and a most wonderful personality. We named her Foxy because not only was she a foxy lady, she looked like a fox. When I traveled, she cried so hard sometimes tears would come from her eyes. Even though dogs do not usually cry tears, this one could. I eventually gave her away because I was traveling so much, and it broke her heart and mine every time I left on a trip. I gave her to a homebound woman, a rich lady whose father invented coats, mitts, gloves, and booties for dogs.

That lucky dog—she went from my humble home into the lap of luxury, where her new owner put her in fur coats and leather gloves during the winter. She even got snooty as a result of her new status. One day I saw her walking with her new owner's caregiver. Foxy was dressed in her fineries. When I tried to get her attention, she stuck her nose in the air and just walked by as if she didn't know me. She's a dog, what more can I say?

When she lived with me, before she became too big for her custom-made britches, she could distinguish the sound of my car from any other. When I came home from a trip, as soon as she heard my car, I would see her bouncing back and forth like a rubber ball as she jumped as high as she could to get a glimpse of me through the window. She would stretch herself beyond her full height as she stood on her hind legs and strained to see me. She would be literally waiting on tiptoes in anticipation of my arrival. As I ran up the steps to the front door I could hear the pitter-patter of her paws on the wooden floor as she ran back and forth in a frenzy. She jumped around on tiptoes in anticipation to cover me with licks of love as she darted about, anxiously waiting to welcome me home.

That's what David was describing when he used the word *qavah* in his song. He had learned what we must learn—that the people of God are a people in waiting, as if on tiptoes, peering through the passage of time, anxiously anticipating Christ's response to our prayers and promised arrival in the Second Coming.

There are ladies in waiting, there are men full of anticipation in the world around us, but in the Scriptures the people of God are supposed to be the ones who wait, and are intimately acquainted with the true meaning of anticipation. Called out from the maddening pace of a planet spinning out of control and apparently addicted to speed, believers are commanded to *"Be still, and know that I am God!"* (Psalm 46:10, KJV). They are repeatedly reminded, in the words of the prophet Isaiah, that *"those who wait for the Lord will gain new strength; they will mount up with wings like eagles, they will run and not get tired, they will walk and not become weary"* (40:31).

The good people of God must wait for vindication from evil by the God who said *"vengeance is mine, I will repay"* (Romans 12:19). We are to anxiously anticipate the desire, the hope of all denominations, that light will consume darkness and good will triumph over evil. But, as time goes by, we discover that this will be in God's good time, and we must wait on God who said, *"I am the Lord; in its time I will do this swiftly"* (Isaiah 60:22, NIV).

On the other hand, non-believers are saying, "Give me my rights, now or not at all!" If our hearts are urging us toward immediacy, know that the heart has lost sight of the promise of God embodied in the word *tikvah*: wait, on tiptoes, for the Lord.

No one seemed to understand this concept of anticipation as well as three Hebrew men whose story is recorded in Daniel chapter 3. Daniel gives a clear comparison between the people of God who wait or anticipate His actions on their behalf, and the pagan people who are driven by immediacy, by speed, as they are tyrannized by the urgent. In 605 B.C., during his first Syrian campaign, King Nebuchadnezzar (ruler of one of the greatest empires in earth's history, extending from India to Ethiopia and far beyond) took Daniel and many other princes of royal blood captive, to train them for government service at his headquarters in Babylon.

Even though many believers today seem convinced that the word *Babylon* means confusion, it actually comes from the word *babel*, which means "the door of God." When the people of Shinar (see Genesis 11) tried to build the tower of Babel, they were attempting to make a religion based on the experience we popularly refer to as salvation by works, which would usurp the role of God in His plan of redemption. To accomplish that, they tried to make a way or door into the heavens. Consequently God caused them to speak in many hitherto unknown tongues, which resulted in the confusion of their common language. The name Babel therefore became a symbol of human attempts to usurp the place and power of God, which always leads to mass confusion. Among the Jews, the word *Babylon* became synonymous with these futile human attempts.

Before his conversion, the Babylonish attitude of usurpation was a strong trait in King Nebuchadnezzar's character. A good example of this, according to Dr. Jacques Doukhan, one of my seminary professors, is his attempts to usurp the role of God in the lives of the Hebrew captives on several different levels:

1. *The religious level*—by taking some of the articles from the house of the Hebrew God to the house of his gods (see Daniel 1:2) to communicate to the captives that his gods were much more powerful and had taken the place of theirs.

2. *The psychological level*—the king's attempt to re-educate the captives (see Daniel 1:4, 5). Teaching them the Babylonian language and literature, and how to "serve before the king"(NKJV), was religious training akin to a minister's training in a seminary. They would not only know how to worship their idols but also be able to teach others to do so.

3. *The level of identity*—through the changing of their names (see Daniel 1:7). To the Hebrews, names were not just a matter of personal identification, but especially emphasized the character of the bearer. For example, when the Scripture tells us to pray in the name of Jesus (see John 14:13, 14) it is not that we should simply tag the name "Jesus" to the end of our prayers, which even devils do and shudder (see James 2:19), but are still devils. Believers must pray in the character of Jesus, whose Hebrew name, Joshua, means "Yahweh (or God) saves." Thus many Hebrew names were *theophores* (meaning names that come from or have within them the name of God) to demonstrate that the person not only had the privilege of bearing the name of God, but also the potential of exemplifying His character in his or her life.

So, in order to usurp the place of God in their lives, the king decided to do what God alone can or should do (see Numbers 6:27; Deuteronomy 12:5; 1 Kings 9:3; 2 Chronicles 33:7). He would change the identity and destiny, spiritually and naturally, of the Hebrew captives. To accomplish this, Nebuchadnezzar "assigned" or gave them new names, Babylonian *theophores*, to indicate that their nature would thereafter reflect those of his pagan gods.

Hannaniah, which means "Grace of Yahweh," was changed to Shadrach, "Command of Aku," (the Sumerian moon god). Mishael, whose name meant "Who is what God is?" became known as Meshach, which means "Who is what Aku is?" Azariah, "Help of Yahweh," became Abed-nego, meaning "Servant of Nabu." Daniel, whose name means "My Judge is God," was absent during the events reported in this chapter, but his name was changed to Belteshazzar, which means "May Bel Protect His Life."

Later, Nebuchadnezzar had a dream in which he saw a great statue made of gold, iron, and clay. Daniel told the king that his kingdom represented the head of gold and that God had ordained that it would not last forever, but would be taken over by less powerful forces represented by iron and clay as time passed. The king, who was worshiped as a god, could not tolerate the idea that he would not live forever or that his kingdom would not last even longer. Thus, in the eighteenth year of his reign, in defiance of Daniel's interpretation of his dream, and with the mindset of his Babelian predecessors, Nebuchadnezzar ordered the construction of a huge golden image to represent his empire's universal and everlasting history. It was approximately the size of the Statue of Liberty without the pedestal, and the king had set it up on the plain of Dura, at the boundary of the province of Babylon, so that everyone who passed through the region could see it.

> Then Nebuchadnezzar the king sent word to assemble the satraps, the prefects and the governors, the counselors, the treasurers, the judges, the magistrates and all the rulers of the provinces to come to the dedication of the image that Nebuchadnezzar the king had set up (Daniel 3:2).

The princes were rulers over satrapies, the largest divisions of the empire. Governors administered provinces into which satrapies were divided. After them came, in this order, captains, judges, treasurers, counselors or lawyers, sheriffs or police officers, and finally rulers or officials of lower importance. The Chaldeans, mentioned in verse eight, were native Babylonians of royal parentage, from among whom leaders, close associates, and wives of the king were usually chosen. Some of the captains were Assyrians, while others were Jews taken into captivity (see Daniel 1:13), including Daniel and the three men. This was perhaps the first Million Man March on a state capital and, if one included the women and children, the numbers would triple.

> *Then the satraps, the prefects and the governors, the counselors, the treasurers, the judges, the magistrates and all the rulers of the provinces were assembled for the dedication of the image* (verse 3).

Notice that Nebuchadnezzar did not send an invitation saying, "Come worship the statue." He summoned them to a dedication or *Hanukkah*. In the time of the author of this ancient book, no one used italics or underlines to highlight a point. Instead, writers used the grammatical construction of repetition and poetic parallelism to underscore what was important. Thus Daniel repeated the word *dedication* so that centuries later readers would not miss this important point in the story.

This is significant. Although the theme of this chapter is the usurpation of the heavenly King's role and rights by an earthly monarch who was worshiped as a god, no other statue or person could be worshipped in Nebuchadnezzar's presence. This command performance was therefore a dedication, a *Hanukkah*, not a worship event for the image Nebuchadnezzar had created. Yet, the herald of the king, knowing the egotism of his master, introduced a new order of things when he loudly proclaimed,

"To you the command is given, O peoples, nations and men of every language, that at the moment you hear the sound of the horn, flute, lyre, trigon, psaltery, bagpipe, and all kinds of music, you are to fall down and worship the golden image that Nebuchadnezzar the king has set up. But whoever does not fall down and worship shall immediately be cast into the midst of a furnace of blazing fire" (verses 4-6).

There must have been some royal amazement at this proclamation. The king probably scratched his head, wondering, "when did I sign that decree?" Had he really signed it, it would have been issued with the summons, for that's how those kings operated.

Perhaps the herald turned to the king with a knowing smile that conveyed his self-satisfaction in having been smart enough to come up with that idea. The king was caught off guard, yet he sat there, basking in the glory of the moment and the grandeur of the herald's proclamation. He may have thought that the declaration made him look very good. The herald banked on the king's egotism to prevent the king from contradicting the veracity of his proclamation, and it worked. Emboldened by the king's silent approval of his proclamation, the herald declared death as the only response to disobedience of this edict.

"Therefore, at the time, when all the peoples heard the sound of the horn, flute, lyre, trigon, psaltery, bagpipe, and all kinds of music, all the peoples, nations and men of every language fell down and worshiped the golden image that Nebuchadnezzar the king had set up" (verse 7).

All except Shadrach, Meshach, and Abed-nego. The herald and some of the captains and Chaldeans planned to entrap these three men because they were very popular with the king. He trusted them implicitly. Thus the herald and his cohorts conspired to entrap the three men. The Hebrew men refused to succumb to pressure and persuasion to follow in the footsteps of other Hebrews who had compromised their commitment to God by participating in the Babylonian religious rites. Perhaps if Shadrach, Meshach, and Abednego had heard, in the original summons, that this was an event to worship the idol, they would have excused themselves through the proper channels so as not to publicly defy the order of the king and embarrass him. But it was obviously a secret plan on the part of their enemies to get them in trouble and trap them by way of that last-minute declaration.

For this reason at that time certain Chaldeans came forward and brought charges against the Jews (verse 8).

It is very interesting to me that the Hebrew word for "charges" means "to devour pieces of" or "to gnaw at someone or something." Their accusations were so intense it was as if they were eating the flesh of their victims or were gnawing at them as they complained to the king.

Have you ever had someone betray you in that way? Didn't it feel as though your flesh was being gnawed and your heart being devoured? This is especially so when a family member or a close trusted friend betrays you. It is the same kind of feeling you would get if someone in your place of employment, your church, or your neighborhood jealously accused or gossiped about you.

Know this, that when you stand for the Lord there is always someone, used by the enemy of our souls, to gnaw at our last nerves. For example, I was once working with a woman who became very angry with me because I would not make her my absolute, exclusive best friend. She tried to discourage me from having so many friends. Of course, being sanguine, I believe the more the merrier! Also, at my age, it is very difficult to get into the best-buddy business. She was not pleased with my response, which was to carry on as I normally do, loving everyone and drawing them into friendship.

So she decided to teach me a lesson. She repeated some confidential information I had shared, embellished with her own edits and additions. When I discovered what she had done, it made my stomach do flip-flops. My flesh felt as though it was being gnawed, and my bowels felt as though they were being devoured. The lies, mingled with enough truth to make it too complex to deny with a simple "I did not say that," stung so deeply that it took days of praying and fasting to get over them. It was a good thing I did not follow my passion and take revenge, because very shortly after that, the poor miscreant showed herself to be what she really was—a jealous, mean-spirited gossip. She was like the devil and those wicked Chaldeans who

> *responded and said to Nebuchadnezzar the king:* "O king, live forever! You yourself, O king, have made a decree [notice how they lie like the devil] *that every man who hears the sound of the [symphony] and all kinds of music, is to fall down and worship the golden image. But whoever does not fall down and worship shall be cast into the midst of a furnace of blazing fire.* [Now the accusation:] . . . *There are certain Jews whom you have appointed over the administration of the province of Babylon, namely Shadrach, Meshach and Abed-nego. These men, O king, have disregarded you; they do not serve your gods or worship the golden image which you have set up*" (verses 9-12).

Imagine that moment. The king had the herald blow the horn to begin the dedication ceremony. The attendants were standing by the statue ready to rip off the covering to reveal the beauty of that golden creation as it shone in the sun, when the Chaldeans and captains, including some very jealous Jews, interrupted everything with their lies and accusations. I imagine that the king must have been very happy up until that point as everyone, as far as he could see, bowed down and worshiped his statue of gold. He was very pleased with the proceedings until the Chaldeans opened their mouths and pointed to the dissidents who were none other than his own favorite high officials.

Then Nebuchadnezzar in rage and anger gave orders to bring Shadrach, Meshach and Abed-nego; then these men were brought before the king (verse 13).

On the biggest day of his fairly new reign, the king had called all of the top officials to a dedication of a golden sculpture that he had constructed in defiance of a divine edict about his tenure as ruler of the greatest empire on earth. His celebration was rudely interrupted by members of his cabinet complaining about the behavior of their colleagues.

Previously, nothing involving the king could be stopped or interrupted once started. Everything was immediate. If there was an emergency, it had to wait until the king's passion or desires were fulfilled. That pagan king did not know how to wait. It was not part of his royal culture, yet here he was kept waiting because of the behavior of a few Jews who refused to worship his golden statue. Nebuchadnezzar must have gotten visibly edgier and angrier as the moments ticked by, while he waited for the three Hebrew men to be brought immediately into his presence.

It appears that the three men were not standing close to the king because he had to send for them to be brought to his presence. By the time they got there his anger seemed somewhat abated. Perhaps he realized that these were three of his highest, most diligent, and trustworthy officials. It is important for believers not to panic and respond immediately in rage and anger, when they discover a betrayal or accusation because panic always causes us to do the wrong things, even if the motives are right. The people of God must wait for His vindication and vengeance. All eyes were on him, watching to see how he would handle the situation. Nebuchadnezzar calmed down enough to at least appear regal in his response.

Nebuchadnezzar responded and said to them, "Is it true, Shadrach, Meshach and Abed-nego, that you do not serve my gods or worship the golden image that I have set up?" (verse 14).

His tone was conciliatory, even compassionate. He seemed hesitant as he spoke. I imagine that he descended from his great seat, that temporary throne on which he sat for the dedication ceremony, then walked down the steps to the level where the three men were standing. He beckoned for them to come closer and as they came, he may have met them part way. Then, standing in their midst, he may have put his arms around them in a fatherly gesture, or in the manner of a benevolent master who was trying to influence them to do what they did not want to do. As I imagine it, the king said patronizingly, "Is it true, Shaddy baby?" [Well, that's at least how I would say it!] "Is it true, Meshie honey? Abed-nego, my favorite friend, tell me, you wouldn't defy the king now, would you?"

I believe that the king squeezed their shoulders in a friendly gesture as he spoke, but it soon became a painful pinch as he pressed them for the answer he wanted and expected. The manner in which the question was asked begged only one response, a firm denial, even if they had to lie to save his face. He knew what these Jews would have said, having been previously presented with their absolute commitment to their God and their determination to not worship and or serve any other gods, be they earthly monarchs or idols made by them. He understood all of that. Yet he asked the question because he did not want any other answer but a clear and firm "No." When they did not comply with his wishes, the king said,

"Now if you are ready, at the moment you hear the [symphony]

and all kinds of music, to fall down and worship the image that I have made, very well" (verse 15a).

The king's voice changed to a threatening tone as he emphasized his power of death to those who disobeyed his edicts. He may have been standing before them by then, staring in their eyes, glaring angrily at them, his hands lifted in a threatening gesture as he said:

"But if you will not worship, you will immediately be cast into the midst of a furnace of blazing fire; and what god is there who can deliver you out of my hands?" (verse 15b).

It was to be the clash of the titans. The king had thrown down the gauntlet. It was no longer a battle between the Babylonian king and three Hebrew men, but the great controversy between God and Satan or good and evil. And since the king thought he was the "badder," if not bigger, he threatened their immediate demise. Shadrach, Meshach and Abed-nego paused for a moment, in anticipation. They did not respond to the king's threat at once because they were a people in waiting for directions from God before being engaged by that man who thought he was God. When the moment was right and ripe they said to the king:

"O Nebuchadnezzar, we do not need to give you an answer concerning this. If it be so, our God whom we serve is able to deliver us from the furnace of blazing fire; and He will deliver us out of your hand, O king. But even if He does not, let it be known to you, O king, that we are not going to serve your gods or worship the golden image that you have set up" (verses 16-18).

They spoke to the king with great respect for his royal position, as dignified men of God ought to do. "O your Royal Highness," said they, "we do not have to give you an answer. We know anticipation. We have learned to wait on tiptoes for our God who can deliver us out of your furnace and even out of your hands, O king." Their response demonstrated that we don't have to be rude when we deny a request or defy a demand that goes against divine dictates.

The implication was that even though the king thought he was God, they knew, from a personal and intimate experience, that there was a greater God than he. Perhaps they had this promise impressed on their minds: "*When you walk through the fire, you will not be scorched, nor will the flame burn you. For I am the Lord your God*" (Isaiah 43:2, 3). They were not afraid of the furnace, so they accepted the king's challenge. They were willing to step into the furnace and wait on God. Even if He *did not* rescue or save them immediately, they were *not* going to serve the pagan gods or worship the golden image set up by the king. What holy defiance!

Too often, we human beings, especially believers living after the cross and before the second coming of Christ, when threatened with a furnace of fire, even before we feel the heat of it, give up on God and recant our prior praise and prayers. We scream and cry against God and even accuse Him of not keeping His promises to always protect and provide for us. We are so tyrannized by the immediate that we cannot wait and see that the Lord is good. God hardly ever has the opportunity to show, in public displays, that He still stands with us, that He is still Emmanuel—God with us—because we give up too soon.

This reminds me of the time I spoke at a camp meeting in Australia. A group composed of mostly disgruntled former church members, had edited some of my tapes to say what they wanted them to, so that they could charge me with heresy. They demanded that the conference president rescind his invitation to me, or there would be trouble at the camp meeting at which I was scheduled to speak.

On the first evening I was threatened with bodily harm if I persisted in fulfilling my speaking engagements. The president provided me with a personal bodyguard, who accompanied me on the campgrounds. I preached that week, as a woman possessed by God. At the end of the week-long meetings many people committed and rededicated their lives to the Lord. Many of my critics came and apologized for prejudging me, adding that they had seldom, if ever, heard the gospel preached with such clear tones. Other critics, however, were not pleased with the progress of the meeting and composed a ten-page document with slanderous statements they believed would undermine my reputation and ruin my credibility with the people. They threatened to blanket the more than 4,000 attendees with this document unless I would step aside and not speak for the final Sabbath morning service.

I didn't, and they did. The last day of the camp meeting was a Sabbath evening, and, oh, what a glorious, Spirit-filled meeting that was. Just as the devil does his most dastardly deeds under the cover of darkness, they carefully wrapped this document in plastic and placed one at every tent during the night. Their intent was that when people woke up they would discover the material and become repulsed by the image and word picture the author had painted of me.

Early Sunday morning when I was due to leave for my long, thirteen-hour trip home, a woman brought a copy of the document to me. I am glad I had not seen it before I spoke the previous Sabbath morning. I felt as though I was being devoured and gnawed at by the disgusting accusations reported in that paper. I ran into the restroom and sobbed as I accused God of failing to protect me in the way He had promised. I was sick at heart and overcome by my desperate need for immediate, public vindication to counteract what I perceived was an awful public humiliation. Being very dramatic, I swore that I would never preach again. I could not take that kind of treatment anymore from God, who was apparently silent, nor from His out-of-control people, who were so harsh.

Every joyous spiritual blessing from the week seemed to flee from my mind. Friends tried to remind me of the many people who gave their lives to the Lord, those who recommitted themselves to Christ and His church, the children who were touched and transformed, but nothing could drag me out of the fiery furnace that burned me inside and out. I was far from home, a woman weeping like a wimp in a toilet where I wished I could just flush myself out of sight. If I had access to a public forum at that very moment, I am sure I would have impulsively, verbally or by body language, retracted my commitment to Christ and His gospel.

I wish I had had the resolve of the three Hebrew men then as I do now. I wish I had remembered their courage. Perhaps it would have saved me the guilty feelings that followed. For while I was whining about being betrayed by people and abandoned by God, He was busily taking care of business.

Shortly after sequestering myself in the restroom, there was a knock on the front door. I almost refused to open it, but the person was persistent. I dried my tears and was still hiccuping from the trauma as I peered through the crack I had opened in the door. The conference president and his wife were standing there with a big smile, like a cat that had just had the last lick of delicious cream. Did they know? Had they read the document? Why were they smiling and chuckling? What was so funny when my world was crashing around me? I really didn't want to face them, but I decided I needed to be polite. After all, I was their guest. So I opened the door to invite them in when the president held up a giant garbage bag. He told me there was a knock on his door early that morning. When he opened it, someone had left the garbage bag filled with the tracts, still rolled up in plastic, and carefully fastened with a rubber band. Apparently, all of the tracts, thousands of them, except the one given to me, had been picked up by the stranger and taken to the president for his disposal.

I burst out crying again, but that time it was with tears of joy. God had not forgotten me. He had not abandoned me to my enemies but had done a miracle and rescued me out of a furnace of fear, in His time!

A few months later, after I returned to the safety of my church and security of my home, I received letters of apology from some of those who had protested my participation in that camp meeting. The president also wrote me several pages describing the positive responses he was still receiving from many who had been blessed by my ministry. He underscored the fact that not only was this one of the most well attended camp meetings, but also one of their most successful.

I am now embarrassed to admit that I did not display the faith and commitment the three Hebrew men did. Thank God, I have since learned to not only wait on the Lord's vindication and vengeance, as they did, but also to be considerate of this generation addicted to speed when they are seeking sanctification by the second.

Can you imagine what happened when the Hebrew men declared, "We are not going to give in to your pressure, O king?" The crowd must have gasped in consternation at their bold, public defiance of the king's demands. But those godly men were not moved. They were not intimidated by his threats to *immediately* put them to death. They said, "We're not going to do it," and didn't. The sound of the whispers of those million or more men and women who were shocked by what they heard, as they passed the words of defiance along, must have been nerve-racking for the king. It must have driven him crazy. The text says:

> *Then Nebuchadnezzar was filled with wrath, and his facial expression was altered toward Shadrach, Meshach and Abednego* (verse 19a).

The king was filled with so much fury it contorted his facial expression into a painful grimace, or as one translation described, "the form of his visage was changed," that is, distorted with rage. His face and personage were changed, from a smiling patron filled with gratification at seeing his favorite officers, to that of an evil demagogue intent on revenge. In essence, Nebuchadnezzar was exhibiting a wrath akin to God's wrath against sin, which results in the judgment that places those who refuse to be separated from sin in the lake of fire created for Satan and his fallen angels (see Revelation 20:14, 15).

The great controversy is heating up—literally! God's plan is to destroy Satan and sin in that lake of fire at the end of time, but Satan decided to create his own furnace of fire into which he planned to destroy God's people right then. Through the egotistical king Nebuchadnezzar, Satan (the father and founder of the immediate) determined not to wait until the end of time, but to do it immediately as Nebuchadnezzar gave orders to heat the furnace *seven times more than it was usually heated* (see verse 19b). I'd like to know what temperature the furnaces normally burned at to create the bricks for their pyramids, their holy high places. Two hundred degrees would kill a person. One thousand degrees or 7000 degrees is overkill! And so it was. The number seven had more of a religious meaning to the Jews than to the Babylonians. It represented completeness, especially from a divine perspective. The king's use of it was not to convey a measurable increase in the heat of the furnace (after all, fire is fire), but to demonstrate that his own godly power was as great or greater than their God was. Nebuchadnezzar's furnace of fire would equal or outdo the promised lake of fire. It was the king's intent to so intimidate those men that they would shudder in fear and give in to his demands.

The devil used the same strategy with Jesus at the cross. He tried to overwhelm Him with the threat of the second death and the eternal distance it would create between Him and His heavenly Father, in the hope that Jesus would give up and give in. But He did not, and neither did those men. So the king

commanded certain valiant warriors who were in his army to tie up Shadrach, Meshach and Abed-nego, in order to cast them into the furnace of blazing fire (verse 20).

You're toast, Shaddy baby! You're vapor, Meshie honey! You've defied the royal edict—now you must burn, the king must have thought sarcastically to himself as his anger raged like the fierce fire in the furnace. Then he commanded warriors, men of great might in his army, to cast them into the blazing fire.

Nebuchadnezzar was ready to declare that his divine powers were above any human effort. Yet, it is obvious that he chose those strong and courageous men instead of a few ordinary men among his leaders because they would be able to bind up the three helpless Jews and cast them in the blazing fire.

So the mighty men grabbed them just as they were, before they could escape and clothe themselves in specially medicated robes that could withstand fire. The three were bound in their sandals, hats, and other flammable garments, which makes the coming miracle even more incredible. Then the soldiers cast them into the middle of the kiln, not near the edge where they might have escaped the fierceness of the heat, but into the place where the furnace was blazing the hottest.

> *For this reason, because the king's command was urgent and the furnace had been made extremely hot, the flame of the fire slew those men who carried up Shadrach, Meshach and Abednego* (verse 22).

Notice that Nebuchadnezzar's command was urgent, immediate. It is also interesting that the word for urgent comes from a root which means to show insolence, indicating the attitude of the king toward the three men and their God. The marvel of this entire episode is that the men who carried them up to the furnace and were slain included some of the accusers, while the *"three men [who] fell into the midst of the furnace of blazing fire still tied up"* were not even scorched or singed.

> *Then Nebuchadnezzar the king was astounded and stood up*

in haste; he responded and said to his high officials, "Was it not three men we cast bound into the midst of the fire?" They answered and said to the king, "Certainly, O king." He answered and said, "Look! I see four men loosed and walking about in the midst of the fire without harm, and the appearance of the fourth is like a son of the gods!" (verses 24, 25).

While their accusers and those who bound and cast them in the furnace were dropping like flies from the heat, the three men were walking confidently about and singing praises to God because they realized they were not alone. What an incredible testimony of faith, to be singing in the midst of the fiery furnace! Emmanuel was with them. The One who promises that He will be with us always, even to the end of the age, stood with them in the fiery furnace, and they were not burned. In fact,

the fire had no effect on the bodies of these men nor was the hair of their head singed, nor were their trousers damaged, nor had the smell of the fire even come upon them (verse 27).

This miracle must have blown away the onlookers! Fire was the element of their god Iz-bar. Babylonians believed that once he started a fire, no one could put it out or save a cinder from its fury. It was where he had his greatest power. Yet, the God of the three Hebrew men was able to deliver them in such a miraculous way that the cords that tied them up were consumed, yet their clothes were not burned, their hair was not singed, and not even the smell of fire was on them.

The Babylonians had conquered Jerusalem, the city of God. They had burned His temple and taken His treasures under the power of their gods such as Iz-bar. When those who waited on the Lord were thrown into the very element that represented the power of their heathen god, it had no power over Jehovah's people, but burned the servants of Iz-bar to death. Iz-bar could not defend or rescue them. As great and radical as that miracle was, it became even more profound when Nebuchadnezzar put *his* head at the door of the oven and survived, making it four, not three, men who were saved when they saw God that day.

A-N-T-I-C-I-P-A-T-I-O-N—it made them wait, and they were miraculously rescued. When we wait with God, He stands with and for us. When we run before Him, when we fall into the trap of the immediate and are driven by the urgent, we lose sight of the power and authority of God. Whatever furnace you may find yourself being cast into by the enemy of our souls, get into it knowing that God has a plan for your life. Remember His promise that you will not be scorched.

As the people of God we know two things: first, that when we follow Him, the devil creates a furnace seven times hotter than the one waiting for him at the end of this evil age. Second, our God will stand with us, and we will not be scorched. So stand in the midst of your fiery furnace and praise God so that the rest of the nonbelieving world will see that your God stands with you.

A few years ago, I saw a television documentary of a trial of a man who had murdered his neighbor. This man had been released from prison, and when he could find no place to live, nor any person to hire him, he became a vagrant. He began to hire himself out as a handyman, and an elderly Christian woman eventually helped him get back on his feet. She also helped him get his life back on track so that he could readjust to society. She found him a place to live and work to do.

Unfortunately, the man went back to his old ways of abusing alcohol and other drugs, and he returned to a life with the gangs. One day he needed money for drugs and asked the elderly lady, who refused to honor his request. He became angry and beat her as he tried to force her to give him what he wanted. But instead of giving in, she prayed. That made him even angrier. Finally he threatened to kill her if she did not immediately give him what he wanted.

As he told his story through tears, I was moved beyond description. He told how he was so frustrated when she began to pray, "Our Father . . ." He described how he went into her kitchen and took a knife and slit her throat. He described in vivid details how the blood gushed out like a fountain, splattering over his face and hands and the floor. He told how he tasted her blood as it sprinkled on his lips when he stuck his tongue out at the same time. He told how he screamed at her to shut up, to deny God, but she kept on praying. He said even after her throat was cut her voice kept coming through the open esophagus, saying that same prayer that was to haunt him in prison until he surrendered his life to her Father in heaven. She died.

It was astonishing to me as I watched that man, moments away from a death sentence for his heinous crime, confessing his faith in Christ as he stood on the witness stand, saying, "I will and must be punished for what I did. But when I die, I will not die alone. I will be with the God of that woman who is standing with me even now in this, my fiery furnace. As I sat waiting for my trial in that prison cell, I was haunted by the scene and the sight of that woman whose life I took, but her confidence in God became my hope for forgiveness. I now have the assurance that I have been forgiven, so I can wait until that final judgment comes. I can wait, for the God of that woman is with me."

A-N-T-I-C-I-P-A-T-I-O-N . . . is it making you wait? Then wait on the Lord, for that is the hope of the people of the soon second coming God!

---

1. George Barna, *The Second Coming of the Church* (Word, 1998), 44.

Chapter 2

three women in
waiting

Legend has it that while teaching his disciples, a wise old rabbi asked them how one knows when it is dawn. After a few tense, contemplative moments, one brave student stood up and asked, "Rabbi, is it dawn when one can look at a distant hill and tell that a tree is a fig and not an olive?"

"No, my son," replied the rabbi. Soon another student ventured to answer, nervously saying, "Is it dawn when one can peer through the morning fog at a faraway field and know that an animal is a dog and not a wolf?"

"No, my child," said the rabbi patiently as his disciples tried for several minutes without success to figure out what they thought was an impossible riddle. Finally the rabbi interrupted and explained, "My children, we can tell it is dawn when we can look into the eyes of another and know that she or he is a sister or brother."

Even though I have had the privilege of seeing the amber rays of hope penetrating the horizon of our nation as more and more people who look like me are represented in leadership, as long as there exists the need for Black History Month programs, it is not yet dawn. Even though I see the Son of Righteousness splashing golden hues of salvation over Christian denominations, as long as there's a need for Women's Day events, it is not yet dawn. As long as those considered by society as poor and powerless are marginalized and excluded from benefits and opportunities in the Christian church and ministry, as long as we struggle for unity and equality in the diverse body of believers, it is not yet dawn.

Dawn will come, but only when our company of committed saints, who are urged by the apostle Paul to *"have the mind of Christ"* (1 Corinthians 2:16), take hold of the gospel of truth and love one another in the same way Jesus loves us. Then we will be able to look into each other's eyes and no longer see color, race, or gender, but see a sister or brother, a child of our heavenly Father, and be able to embrace each other as such, in Christ, according to Galatians 3:28.

All who are waiting for that dawn—anyone who is anticipating the end of the evils of segregation, separation, racism, and genderism for the new thing God is about to do, according to Isaiah 43:19— will draw many profound lessons from the following trilogy of women in waiting.

Waiting for Attention
(Matthew 15:21-27)

The first story takes us to the time when Jesus was at the peak of His ministry in a dazzling three years of unprecedented popularity. The unusual dignity of His personality, the divine authority of His words, the singular originality of His teaching, the penetrating power of His preaching, propelled this man from Nazareth into the forefront of public recognition throughout the region of Judea. No one seemed able to prevail against Him as thirsty throngs drew near to drink in His every word and devour His daily discourses. It was as if there could be no failure in His work, no discouragement in His experience, no deterrents to His meteoric rise to fame as multitudes followed this man from Galilee. Life was just a steady stream of successes, but things were about to take a sudden turn.

The most sought-after rabbi had stirred up the intense jealousy of the Pharisees, the ire of the scribes, and the indignation of the Sadducees. His perfect life and unconditional love for everyone threatened their authority, exposed their false pride, and diminished their influence over the people. They decided that the only way to redeem their crumbling credibility with the crowds that gathered to see and hear Jesus would be to kill Him.

They began by barring Him from the synagogues of Judea and Galilee, forcing Him to preach and teach in the open fields and on the mountainsides where He would be an easier target of their assassins. On one of those occasions, Jesus discovered their plot to kill Him, and in what initially appears as a rare act of self-preservation, fled with His disciples to a heathen country. We pick up the story in Matthew 15:21-27.

In reporting this event, Mark 7:24 says that Jesus wanted to keep His whereabouts a secret, but since this was the peak of His popularity, there was no escape from being recognized, even in a pagan place. Thus, while He was sequestered in the secular twin cities of Tyre and Sidon, a certain woman heard that Jesus was there, and she came seeking His help.

She was no ordinary woman. Besides being a very intelligent, articulate woman, she was a Gentile of Syrophoenician race (according to Mark). Matthew, whose Gospel was written to the Jews, described her as a Canaanite woman, to remind readers that she was from the race of Israel's ancient enemies, whose land the Jews captured and annexed for their Promised Land at the end of their Exodus from Egypt.

She was also a woman of color, a fact that is most important to this generation rife with racial and religious struggles. The Canaanites were descendants of Ham, one of the sons of Noah, whom Bible scholars point to as the father of the Black race. It also appeared that she was a single parent, perhaps a widow, but more likely the mother of an illegitimate child that she left at home alone. There was no man to speak on her behalf for the child's deliverance from demon possession. She was also nameless, so she truly represents women of all ages who are likewise disenfranchised, powerless, and marginalized and desperately in need of the liberating love of our Savior.

Whatever her circumstances, she came to Jesus because He was known even among the heathens as the great Healer, the one able to destroy prejudice and set devil-possessed people free. And as Providence would have it, she found Jesus walking down the streets of her hometown and fell at His feet, crying out, *"Have mercy on me, O Lord, Son of David; my daughter is cruelly demon-possessed"* (Matthew 15:22).

She had tried everything before coming to Christ that day. Just as we sing well-known choruses such as "I must tell Jesus of all my troubles" but only call on Him after we've tried everything else and failed, so had she. The woman had exhausted every incantation and exorcism, every ghastly séance, every ghoulish sacrifice, and healing method of her heathen nation, but nothing worked. Now her mother's heart was full of disappointment and sorrow for her only child, who was wasting away under the wicked wiles of the devil. She was at her wits' end and in her desperation cried out to Jesus, *"Have mercy on me, O Lord, son of David!"*

In her book, *The Desire of Ages*, Ellen White wrote:

This woman had heard of the prophet, who, it was reported, healed all manner of diseases. As she heard of His power, hope sprang up in her heart. Inspired by a mother's love, she determined to present her daughter's case to Him. It was her resolute purpose to bring her affliction to Jesus. He must heal her child. She had sought help from the heathen gods, but had obtained no relief. And at times she was tempted to think, what can this Jewish teacher do for me? But the word had come, He heals all manner of diseases, whether those who come to Him for help are rich or poor. She determined not to lose her only hope.[1]

But to her amazement, her urgent pleas were met with silent resistance, as Jesus seemed to ignore her. She was shocked! His long silence became distressing. She couldn't understand the reason for it. Was not this the One about whom people said, He has the Spirit of the Lord on Him in a mighty way? Was not this the One who proclaimed that He was anointed by God to bring good news to the afflicted, the One sent to bind up the broken hearted, the One called to preach liberty to captives and freedom to prisoners? Wasn't this the rabbi from Galilee who proclaimed that He was willing to leave ninety-nine sheep safe in the fold to search for one lost sheep? And here she was, that lost one, entangled and troubled, powerless and in pain, seeking deliverance for her daughter, and He was silent!

For a moment, she thought that perhaps He was deeply absorbed in sacred meditation and did not hear her appeals, so she mustered all her courage and cried out again in a loud, shrill voice, energized by the vivid memory of her daughter dying alone at home. But He still did not answer. Even as His disciples begged Him to order her to leave, He remained silent, according to Matthew 15:23. She was driving them to distraction with her shouts for help. When they tried to physically remove her from their presence, Jesus seemed unmoved by her emotional outbursts as she shouted and struggled and wriggled to free herself from the iron grip of the disciples who were determined to push her away.

They wanted her gone because they were afraid that the commotion she created would attract a crowd and draw the attention of the local authorities. The authorities, for a bribe, would quickly disclose the group's whereabouts to the Pharisees and bring about their immediate arrest as fugitives from the law. But most of all, they wanted to remove her defiling, pagan, Canaanite, womanish presence because of their deeply ingrained racial and religious prejudices, which Jesus seemed to encourage with His prolonged silence.

The best of us would have stormed out in a huff! Sometimes when we pray earnestly and there is no voice, no immediate answer, we forget that the silent, dark night of the soul is usually a prelude to the filled-up, pressed-down, and running-over cup of experience. At other times, when the waiting period is rather long, we fail to recognize that there are many reasons for the delay, such as the enduring impact the answer will have on us as well as on others. So often, we walk away too soon because we do not realize the thoughtful love and holy wisdom in God's silence. Silence, in this case, He deployed to destroy the power of prejudice in the hearts of the disciples, to liberate that woman from its cruel consequences, and release her absent daughter from the control of the enemy.

On the other hand, some, like the disciples, misread or misunderstand the silence of God. For example, many seem to misread God's silence or slowness to respond to the debate over the full integration of women in all phases of ministry as a sign that He is on the side of those who are against this. But perhaps He has allowed and is allowing this debate to develop to expose a fatal flaw in our theology of unconditional equality, which He will correct in His good time to save both opponents and proponents of this issue.

All of us need to learn to wait on the Lord for His answers and actions, for, as Ellen White points out,

Christ knew this woman's situation. He knew that she was longing to see Him, and He placed Himself in her path. By ministering to her sorrow, He could give a living representation of the lesson He designed to teach. For this He had brought His disciples into the region. He desired them to see the ignorance existing in cities and villages close to the land of Israel. The partition wall which Jewish pride had erected shut even the disciples from sympathy with the heathen world. But these barriers were to be broken down.[2]

Too often we walk away from God—give up easily—when we need to hang in and plead on. In the words of the prophet Isaiah, *"You who call on the Lord, give yourselves no rest, and give Him no rest, till He establishes Jerusalem"* (Isaiah 62:6, 7, NIV). He will answer in His good time, because He has a plan for our lives and a master plan for breaking down barriers!

And plead that woman did, crying to Jesus, saying, *"Have mercy on me O Lord!"* Still, when the answer came, it seemed worse than His silence for *"He answered and said, 'I was sent only to the lost sheep of the house of Israel'"* (Matthew 15:24).

In that simple statement, Jesus seemed to reject her by reciting His résumé of religious pedigree and privileged position—that of being a minister only to the lost sheep of Israel. If nothing else, that should have shut her up, right? Wrong! His apparent arrogance, steeped in historical hatred of heathens, did not deter her for one second. We are told that in that very moment she came closer to Jesus and began to bow in submission before Him, to worship Him like a penitent slave, as she begged Him saying, *"Lord, help me!"* Her actions seemed to say, "I know your God is no respecter of persons, be they male or female, Gentile or Jew! He is not inhibited by human customs and culture nor is He confined by boundaries set by nations or denominations, so please help me!" But again her appeals were met with rough rejection as Jesus answered, *"It is not good to take the children's bread and throw it to the dogs"* (verse 26).

Every time I read this story, especially this statement, my heart aches for that poor woman, and a lump forms in my throat. She must have been devastated when she heard those words, at least momentarily, before the reality of His response dawned on her mind and broke into her aching heart. She didn't have the benefit of time to instantly know, as we do now from extensive study, that Jesus was not rejecting her. In reality, He was working toward totally liberating her and His disciples from the power of racial and religious prejudice so carefully engineered and fostered by the enemy of our souls.

Most of us, especially people of color and women, know from experience how demeaning and dishonoring ethnic, racial, or gender prejudice can be, especially when it happens in the presence of prejudiced people. So it's not too difficult to imagine how this woman felt in the presence of twelve men who did not consider her to be among their peers under any circumstances. But don't linger too long in that frame of reference, where it is so easy to get lost in how debilitating racial and gender prejudice are. And they really are!

How difficult it must have been for Jesus to play the role of a bigoted, arrogant person. Never before had He used such stern, cold words to someone pleading for help. Never had He ever spoken so roughly and rejected a request from anyone, much less a woman weeping for the deliverance of her demon-possessed child! Yet, throughout this harsh verbal exchange, Jesus hoped that the Syrophoenician woman had ears to hear and courage to claim the key to His response, which would unlock the storehouse of goodness God had prepared for her that day. And she did! Suddenly she caught a glimpse of the slim thread of hope and grabbed it!

In almost every translation of this text, Jesus is reported to have used the word *dogs* to address her. I am sure, like the translators, the disciples heard the Greek word *kuon*, their common word for "dog." This word described the wild, scavenging, savage animals that roamed the roads of their cities, devouring every kind of filthy garbage, ravaging each other to greedily feed on the carcasses of dead animals. This was the same word that the Jews used to describe Gentiles in a derogatory, prejudiced manner. The word best expressed their disgust for the Gentiles' pagan religious rituals. The Jews felt that Gentiles were like those dogs—spiritual scavengers, savages who worshipped many gods, ingesting every kind of doctrinal garbage, ranting and raving as they greedily devoured the dead words of their heathen prophets. As a matter of fact, when a Jew called a Gentile a dog in those days, it had the same negative impact as when a person of color is called the "N" word today.

For decades, theologians have missed the point in their commentaries. Feminists have rejected Jesus on the basis of their perception that He referred to that woman, and therefore all women, as "dogs." Recently I heard a well-educated, popular radio evangelist ask, "How would you like to be called a dog by Jesus?" intimating that was what Jesus said and meant.

But wait! That wasn't what Jesus said. He used the Greek words *ta kuneria*, which means "little dogs" and describes cute, loveable, huggable, pretty pups that rich Jewish parents bought for their children to keep indoors as pets to play with, since there were no Toys-R-Us stores.

Wow! What a difference a word makes. As soon as she heard Him say that, a renewed hope swelled in her heart. It burst upon her mind and blew out of her mouth. Then she said, *"Yes, Lord, but even the little dogs, the pretty little pups, feed on the crumbs that fall from their master's table, and all I'm asking for is my share of the crumbs from your vast reservoir of grace!"* (verse 27, paraphrased).

Then Jesus, elated by her response, said to her, *"O woman."* Notice the term of endearment, which immediately shows that she too was a daughter of Abraham, not by physical birth, but by spiritual rebirth and great faith. He continued, *"Your faith is great; be it done for you as you wish."*

I have imagined this scene a thousand times. I picture Jesus standing tall and majestic, while His disciples cringed in horror in a corner as that despised pagan woman forced her way toward Him, fell at His feet, grabbed the fringe (see Matthew 14:36) of His outer garment, and pleaded for help. When the disciples heard Jesus say,

"It is not good to take the children's bread and throw it to the dogs,"
they must have smiled with assurance that Jesus was endorsing their
prejudice. But when the woman heard those same words, she
discovered grace as she lifted her eyes to Him who spoke worlds
into existence at the beginning of time. Their eyes must have locked
in a lingering gaze in a millisecond of silence, which seemed to her
like a millennium of sacredness, before He broke the trance by gently
taking her hand to raise her from her knees. Then He could wrap
His strong, heavenly arms around her as He pulled her to His bosom.
He must have lifted her with a cry of joy before he danced her
about, shouting in ecstasy like Henry Higgins in *My Fair Lady*,
saying, "By George, she's got it!" And in that instant, her daughter
was healed!

What a totally different ending this story would have had if that
Syrophoenician woman had not waited for a response to her appeal.
Because she waited, the record remains to teach us the following
lessons.

First, the authors of this story did not name the woman, perhaps
because she became an integral, public, prominent part of the early
church and they did not want to embarrass her or allow later believers
to make an icon of her. To me, the fact that she is nameless means
that she represents all women who are marginalized because of their
race, gender, or religious affiliations. Her story becomes our story
no matter what generation we may live in. And just as Jesus liberated
her socially, politically, and spiritually, so are we also liberated by
His sacrifice on the cross and are, under no circumstances,
marginalized in His invisible kingdom, even though some try to
make us feel as such in the visible church.

A second and most important lesson is for parents, particularly
mothers, whose children are possessed by the power of the enemy
so that they do not follow the faith of their parents. If your child is
possessed by the demon of alcohol or other drugs, materialism, or
bitterness over your experience of betrayal by a church, wait for

Jesus' attention to your request for deliverance for your child. Take comfort in this, that just as that mother threw herself on the mercy of Jesus and instantly her daughter was made well, so you, too, must throw yourself on His mercy and believe that He will give you the desire of your heart. And He will. Your children will return to the faith in which you raised them.

As I write, I do so from a mother's heart that waited decades for attention to the prayers offered to God for the deliverance and salvation of my only son. He was never a raging lunatic like the child in this story. He is a smart and successful young man who was under the devil's influence and control for more years than I care to mention. On one occasion, the situation was so desperate that I begged God for relief. He assured me then that my son was not only His but would one day preach the good news of salvation. After decades of waiting without the expected results, I began to seriously doubt whether I had heard God correctly. I spent a lot of time and emotional energy praying and appealing to other believers to pray for my son. When I studied this story, it impacted me in such a powerful manner that I stopped wringing my hands while waiting for God's response or asking others to pray as though their prayers could push God into doing what I wanted.

I had written a different end to this story, because then I was still waiting. But before this manuscript was finished, I had a telephone call from my son. He was nervous and hesitant to share that he had recognized that God was calling Him. He wanted to know what to do, how to respond, where to go. I am delighted to say that having given birth to him, I am now being used by God to assist in his rebirth and delivery as one of His sons.

Today, I am an ambassador of hope appealing to parents of children who have not surrendered their lives to Christ in the way they hoped. I have the assurance, from personal experience, that God will also deliver your sons and daughters out of the hands of our enemy, the devil. He will liberate your children out of the hands of the demons of this day! Just you wait and see the miracles that God will do for those who wait patiently on Him. In the words of the apostle Peter, *"Gird your minds for action, keep sober in spirit, [and] fix your hope completely on the grace to be brought to you at the revelation of Jesus Christ"* (1 Peter 1:13).

Waiting for Answers
(Luke 18:1-8)

Some days I just feel like bragging. For example, when I read the biographies of great women and their contributions to the political advances of our nation and especially the spiritual growth of the Christian church in the world, I just want to stick my chest out and shout: *"Yessss!"* Being sanguine in temperament, I am quite a mistress of boasting. Yet, I know of no adult who can brag the way children do. Three little girls were playing during recess at their elementary school and were overheard boasting about their parents. The first little girl said, "My daddy is a doctor and he is *soooo* good, all the movie stars in Hollywood call him to come and see them in their homes." The second girl boasted that her father was the CEO of one of the largest and fastest growing companies in the country, adding, "He is so rich, every year we get to meet presidents and prime ministers from all over the world." As they spoke, the third girl, being a poor pastor's daughter, had to think hard as to how she could compete with any amount of success. When her turn came, she threw her shoulders back and said, "That's nothing, my mother is a minister and she owns all of hell!"

"No way," protested her two friends, "no one can own hell." They scoffed and bristled under the realization that they were being outdone. "You're lying!" one girl charged, attempting to intimidate the minister's model daughter into backing down. But she held her ground and insisted, "It's true—my mom never lies—and last night I heard her telling Dad that the elders of our church took her aside and they all gave her hell—so there!"

There's hardly any woman, especially those in ministry who are longing for a resolution and waiting for an earthly and heavenly answer to the injustice of inequality, who could not truthfully testify they were the recipient of that gift. But I would like to draw your attention to a story in which Jesus puts a different spin on this experience by noting that the recipient of this ungracious gift was none other than a judge who was given this gift by a woman.

He was a very dignified judge who had difficulty keeping his propriety because a certain widow was persistent in stalking his every step. No matter how he tried he could not get away from her. She was at his door in the morning, confronted him at noon in the marketplace, interrupted his conversation with esteemed associates, disrupted his judgments at the city gate, and waited to harass him when he got home at night. Her appeal was always the same: "Avenge me against my adversary!" In other words, "give me justice or legal protection from my opponent."

This was an almost unbelievable situation—a woman demanding legal rights in a society where women, especially widows, had few if any rights in those days. To show how few rights they had, the rabbis prayed daily, saying:

"Blessed art thou who hast not made me a Gentile,
Blessed art thou who hast not made me an uneducated man,
Blessed art thou who hast not made me a woman."[3]

Although this threefold prayer "is not found in the authoritative Mishnah but in the Tosephta, the competitive Mishna which did not gain authority"[4] among the leading rabbis, it was so popular among the people that it was generally the first introduction of Gentiles to Judaism. Some scholars suggest that this prayer is demonstrative of beliefs that women, Gentiles, and men uneducated in the Torah were inferior to those who are students of the law. Others report that it was more a sign of "a love for the opportunity to study the law than a depreciation of Gentiles, slaves, and women."[5] Be that as it may, this prayer, which had its Greek counterpart with thanksgiving for being "born a human and not a beast, a man and not a woman, a Greek and not a barbarian," was the source of the apostle Paul's strong response and negation of this prejudice in Galatians 3:27, 28.

Disparagement of women's character and nature are forthrightly asserted in extra-biblical literature known as Apocrypha. For example, Romans 5 reports that sin entered into the world through one man, Adam. But one of the most negative statements attributing the origin of sin to women is found in the apocryphal writings in Ecclesiasticus 25:33, which says, "From a woman came the beginning of sin, and by her we all die." The spread of this idea, along with many other derogatory statements about women found in that chapter, caused many in ancient Israel to believe that a woman could only be saved through childbirth. One would hardly expect to encounter this in the inspired Word of God, but this concept is reiterated even by the apostle Paul in the New Testament: *"For it was Adam who was first created, and then Eve. And it was not Adam who was deceived, but the woman being quite deceived, fell into transgression. But women shall be preserved through the bearing of children if they continue in faith and love and sanctity with self-restraint"* (1 Timothy 2:13-15).

To show the persistent negative attitude toward women, disagreeable characteristics are not only highlighted, they are enumerated in the Old Testament. Women are described as contentious, noisy, indiscreet and unintelligent (see, for example, Proverbs 9:13; 11:22; 25:24). Micah seems unable to avoid adding to and reflecting this negative portrait and attitude toward women by inserting this assertion in his warning against lying: *"Do not trust in a neighbor; do not have confidence in a friend. From her who lies in your bosom guard your lips"* (Micah 7:5).

Although many Hebrew laws were written with the intent that men and women were equals and should be so treated, the common, accepted practice was to marginalize women from almost all areas and functions of social, political, and religious experience. In his book, *Jerusalem in the Time of Jesus*, Joachim Jeremias quoted R. Eliezer (ca. A.D. 90), a tireless upholder of the old traditions of the Jews, who declared impressively, "If a man gives his daughter a knowledge of the law it is as though he taught her lechery."[6] Jeremias also noted that women were forbidden to teach and "bear witness because it was concluded from Genesis 18:15 that she is a liar."[7] This was based on Sarah's denial that she laughed when the Lord said she would become pregnant at her advanced age (see Genesis 18:11-15).

Jesus broke with these traditions when He included women's activities in parables (see Luke 15:8-10), to demonstrate that the gospel was available to all, regardless of gender. His attitude toward women was exactly opposite to most of His contemporaries. It was not only radical, it was refreshing and intriguing. Not only did He heal many women (see Matthew 8:14, 15 and Mark 5:21-43), He allowed some to follow and watch over Him during His brief ministry on earth (see Mark 15:40, 41). He taught them the Torah (see John 11:20-27) even though they were exempt from its study because they were considered inferior to men.

Women's inferior status in their society was reflected in the practice of laws such as those found in Leviticus 12:1-5, which stated that a daughter was less desirable than a son was. From these, it becomes clear that valuation of a man was much different than that of a woman. The Bible accurately reports her position in ancient society as subordination to her father, husband, son, and all males who had the legal right to rule over her. So you can imagine the attitudes toward old women and widows. It was so prejudiced and alienating that God had to remind them repeatedly of their divinely appointed responsibility to look after widows as well as orphans and other socioeconomic outcasts.

Yet this judge, known as a hard, impervious man who constantly re-fortified his self-image by declaring that he did not fear God or respect any man, was afraid of this poor widow woman in Jesus' parable found in Luke 18:1-8.

The incongruity is laughable! True, she was no retiring, self-effacing burden on society's benevolence. True, she was a tough lady who knew her rights, few as they were, and was not about to let up until the judge recognized them. The contradiction between the judge's articulation of his authority and his growing fear of the widow must have also struck the funny bone of the disciples when Jesus said, *"And for a while he was unwilling; but afterward he said to himself, 'Even though I do not fear God nor respect man, yet because this widow bothers me, I will give her legal protection, lest by continually coming she wear me out'"* (verses 4, 5).

Lloyd John Ogilvie commented on this passage in his book *Autobiography of God*:

> *The humor is found in a more accurate translation of the phrase "wear me out." Actually, this phrase is rooted in a bit of slang, which means "hit under the eye." Translators have tried to suggest that Jesus would never have used slang, and that it meant shadows under the eyes or fatigue; thus, "wear me out." Not so! I think He quoted the judge as fearing that the woman would give him a black eye. "Lest she come and beat me" is a literal interpretation of the Greek.[8]*

Whenever I speak at women's events, invariably I hear a testimony of a church's fear that when women gather together it is to hatch ideas of beating up on our men folk. Whenever women meet to discuss the role of women and the Word, it is generally suspected that our agenda is to demand recognition of the few rights we have in order to give the church a black eye. But it is my privilege to report and promote the fact that instead of giving hell (the same gift the little girl in our opening story said was bequeathed to her minister mom) to those who hold back benefits from women, we offer hope. Instead of giving a black eye (what Jesus said the judge in this parable was afraid of receiving from the widow) to leaders who lack the courage to provide legal protection for women in the Word, we importune God on their behalf. Women called by God are lifting up the church and its leaders to Christ while waiting for answers that will cause justice to eventually roll down like rivers of waters.

Even though our lot has significantly improved, as God gives answers to our prayers and melts the hearts of some of His recalcitrant men who continue to refuse to open the doors of opportunity in ministry to His women, we cannot become complacent. We, like the widow, must continue to seek justice through powerful preaching of the Word, peaceful practice of a life lived in Christ and through confident, authoritative administration of God's work. At the same time, I also pray that the great judges of the church will give us our rights before, as Jesus said in this parable, *"God Himself comes to speedily bring about justice"* for us. For come He will. And woe to the ones He finds forgetting to be faithful to females and little children. In the words of Jesus, *"Whoever causes one of these little ones who believe in me to stumble, it is better for him that a heavy millstone be hung around his neck, and that he be drowned in the depth of the sea"* (Matthew 18:6). This also means, on the other hand, that the chosen women of God must be responsible to the church and accountable to Christ for the treasures entrusted to them.

In addition to the many lessons that can be drawn from this parable, the central theme is about how God answers our prayers. Dr. Luke introduces this parable on this topic with the following statement, *"Now He [Jesus] was telling them a parable to show that at all times they ought to pray and not to lose heart"* (Luke 18:1). Carnally conditioned by our human nature to fight or take flight when faced with the pressures of a crisis, Christians tend to faint rather than exhibit the faith and patience that always and ultimately moves the Hand of grace.

The doctrine of delay, waiting for answers from God, should be a very prominent one among Christians who struggle with this age-old problem. Through the long pilgrimage in this sinful world, through war and struggles, through blood, sweat and tears, through heroism that often seemed fruitless and useless, through sacrifices that seemed like spilt milk, the great challenge of divine delay and its long disappointments has induced deep despair. But to those who strive for a consistent relationship with God, divine delay becomes the polished instrument of God that is marked by the depth of the relationship and the height of the Creator's purpose in that believer.

The joy that comes in the morning, echoed in the cry of the psalmist in Psalm 30:5, is sharpened and illumined by the long night of weeping endured and from which it springs. We should never lose heart in what appear to be God's delays. Speed, after all, is a relative term. There is more love in God's slow methods, so pray on. Strive on, casting all doubts (and the devil who inspired them) out of your mind, believing that the love which never mocks us will give us the desires of our hearts—in His good time! While you are waiting, remember the prophet Isaiah's words:

> *Yet those who wait for the Lord*
> *Will gain new strength;*
> *They will mount up with wings like eagles,*
> *They will run and not get tired,*
> *They will walk and not become weary (Isaiah 40:31).*

The following comments on this passage by Chuck Swindoll are most appropriate. He said:

From this verse we learn that four things happen when we wait:
First, we gain new strength. We may feel weak, even intimidated, when we turn to our Lord. While waiting,

amazingly, we exchange our weakness for His strength. Second, we get a clearer perspective. It says we "will mount up with wings like eagles." Eagles can spot fish in a lake several miles away on a clear day. By soaring like eagles while waiting, we gain perspective on what we are dealing with. Third, We store up extra energy. "We will run and not get tired." Notice, it's future tense. When we do encounter the thing we have been dreading, we will encounter it with new strength—extra energy will be ours to use. Fourth, we will deepen our determination to persevere. We "will walk and not become weary." The Lord whispers reassurance to us. He puts steel in our bones, so to speak. We begin to feel increasingly more invincible . . . All that happens when we wait.[9]

All who are waiting on the Lord, this is your legacy!

Waiting for Acceptance
(Ruth)

The book of Ruth is an engaging, intriguing story. Some scholars say it was written to establish ethnic openness in national Israel, but I have been fortunate to find many other important lessons in it. It is set early in the Old Testament, but I can never find it because I am always looking for it later among the ancient books of the Bible. God's name is seldom mentioned, yet this book is one of the noblest explorations of what theologians call "theodicy," the ways of God with humankind in the face of evil.

It is the account of a Jewish family—a husband, his wife, and two sons who migrated to the land of Moab from their native home, Bethlehem of Judah, because of a severe famine in their land. As Americans whose ancestors migrated from communities of hardship to this land of promise, as believers moving in faith toward the hope of the coming of the Son of Righteousness, we can all associate with this family's move from familiar surroundings to a strange, new land.

But our focus is on the true tale of three women, Naomi, Ruth and Orpah, and one woman's anxious anticipation for acceptance.

They were brought together by God in an unusual bond of love, because Naomi was a Jew and her daughters-in-law were descendants of one of her nation's fiercest enemies, the Moabites, offspring of one of the sons of Lot and his daughters' incestuous unions. Yet, I find this story refreshing and welcome in contrast to the numerous other Bible stories that portray women competing against each other for status, power, and men—such as the stories of Hagar and Sarah, Rachel and Leah, and Miriam against Moses' wife, to name a few.

Ruth's story is one of the oldest testimonies of female connectedness and bonding. It is a legacy of love that survives the test of time despite the odds against women as individuals, as friends and as females living with and without men. The Hebrew woman, Naomi, is introduced through her husband Elimelech (Ruth 1:2). A famine forced him to take his wife and their two sons, Mahlon and Chilion, from their homeland in Bethlehem of Judah to an unknown city in Moab, presently southwest Jordan, where food was plentiful in those days. As children always do, the boys grew up, left the protective care of their parents and married, not Jewish princesses, but two Moabite models of beauty named Ruth and Orpah.

Shortly after the nuptials, Naomi's husband died. Ten years later, her two sons also passed away, leaving their women childless and alone to live with their mother-in-law. Most of us cannot imagine that situation working out. We tell jokes that begin, "Let me tell you about my mother-in-law," followed by negative statements or humorous anecdotes. In fact, the mother-in-law caricature is such a standard centerpiece of ridicule and comedy in this country, and perhaps the world, that most of those rough relationships are more fulfillment of funny stories than incompatible in-laws. But in the book of Ruth, this mother-in-law was loved, appreciated and totally accepted by her foreign daughters-in-law in a home where three widow women lived, bound by their mutual love for each other and fond memories of their husbands. Someone once said that two queens cannot reign on a throne, but they proved that three widows and one God could live in a hut in harmony.

Now, the only thing worse than being a woman was being a widow in those days, because they were taken advantage of or totally ignored. Widows were almost always poverty stricken, abandoned, and isolated from their community. So the three widows pooled their resources to live with their losses as we pick up the story in Ruth, chapter 1, verse 6. Even though they were living in relative comfort and were good company for each other, when Naomi *"heard in the land of Moab that the Lord had visited His people in giving them food"* in Bethlehem of Judah, she immediately decided to go home. *"So she departed from the place where she was, and her two daughters-in-law with her; and they went on the way to return to the land of Judah"* (verse 7).

Can you imagine the excitement as those three women packed and planned for their journey to Judah? But somewhere between Moab and Bethlehem, Naomi suddenly came to her senses—she remembered the Bethlehem she had left behind, the religious and racial prejudice that pervaded that proud city—and she panicked. She couldn't take these devoted daughters there, and she couldn't tell them the truth, so she pulled them in a loving embrace and said:

> *"Go, return each of you to her mother's house. May the Lord deal kindly with you as you have dealt with the dead and with me. May the Lord grant that you may find rest, each in the house of her husband." Then she kissed them, and they lifted up their voices and wept* (verses 8, 9).

When words fail, tears always flow. This is one of the most unforgettable scenes in Scripture. The widow, Naomi, was ready and willing to undergo whatever uncertainties and hazards might be involved in returning to her homeland, but she loved her Moabite daughters-in-law, Ruth and Orpah. It seemed that she loved them so much that she could not expose them to the prejudices they would encounter and certain privations they'd experience in Judah. So she embraced them and begged them to go back to their Moabite parents. This suggestion implies safety and security in their motherland instead of the potential prejudice in Naomi's nation.

> *And they said to her, "No, but we will surely return with you to your people."*
>
> *But Naomi said, "Return, my daughters. Why should you go with me? Have I yet sons in my womb, that they may be your husbands? Return, my daughters! Go, for I am too old to have a husband. If I said I have hope, if I should even have a husband tonight and also bear sons, would you therefore wait until they were grown? Would you therefore refrain from marrying? No, my daughters; for it is harder for me than for you, for the hand of the Lord has gone forth against me." And they lifted up their voices and wept again; and Orpah kissed her mother-in-law, but Ruth clung to her* (verses 10-14).

Orpah thought about the words Naomi had said three times: "Return my daughters." She could have rejected that appeal, but when Naomi said, "God is against me," that was the straw that broke that camel's back. She could face prejudice and privation with her in-laws as long as God was with Naomi, but without Him, she knew she didn't have a chance. Perhaps she decided that it was better to hang on to God in a pagan land she knew, than to be among strangers without Him. Thus she decided to do exactly as her mother-in-law suggested and after much weeping and loud wailing, after they lifted up their voices in unison, after one of the most poignant partings in human history, that winsome woman Orpah slipped away into the silence of the Word of God. She slipped away to be forever maligned by many commentators as one who, in the biting criticism of her mother-in-law, "has gone back to her people and her gods." But Ruth clung to her mother-in-law as Naomi wept, saying, in a fourth and final appeal: *"Behold, your sister-in-law has gone back to her people and her gods; return after your sister-in-law."* (verse 15).

As I study the Bible, I am more and more convinced that the greatest need in our time is to return to the essential teaching methods of our Master, who used real, earthly stories to give heavenly meanings in what we recognize as parables and allegories. These simple tales drawn from daily life paint an incredible portrait of God and His gracious dealings with people. They are often the most unforgettable lessons learned. As they yield their inner secrets and outer substance to draw us closer to God, we discover practical answers and spiritual truths for our lives.

Thus I present the story of Ruth as an allegory for women and men and children who are waiting for acceptance.

Naomi's husband, Elimelech, whose name means "God is King," epitomizes the founding fathers of our faith who forged their way into foreign lands to develop churches and enlighten people with the Word of God. When there was a famine for the Word, they exercised faith in God their King and left the familiar domain of established denominations to go on a spiritual quest as Abraham did. They went not knowing where, yet realized that God was with them.

The two sons, Mahlon, whose name means "sickly," and Chilion, whose name means "wasting away," represent the good-old-boy male-dominated ministry—the old guard—that is sickly and wasting away with the integration of more women in ministry.

The widow woman, Naomi, whose name means "my sweetness," represents the Christian church in general, and our church in particular, especially in her relationship with her daughters-in-law, Ruth and Orpah. In the beginning she welcomed them into her life. She lived for years in a loving, engaging relationship with them. She even invited them to go with her to the land of promise, but when she remembered the prejudice of her own people she pleaded with them to go back to their own land, because she knew that her land held no potential for them.

I was born in Jamaica, but I've been gone so long, and I've become such an acculturated American, that I no longer fit easily in my own native country. So, whenever I return, I am treated like a tourist. That's how it would have been for the two women who had assumed the culture and customs of their Jewish husbands for so long. So, instead of standing with her beloved daughters-in-law, Naomi was willing to sacrifice their relationship, just as the church often does with some women in ministry, whose call from God she ought to be affirming.

To hide the truth that should have been buried with her dead sons, to cover her lack of courage to face those old prejudices and fight for her precious daughters-in-law, Naomi whined and wailed about God's hand having gone forth against her. Instead of avenging the women she called "daughters" against the adversary of age-old alienation, this woman, whose name means "my sweetness," begged that her name be changed to Mara, "bitter." Notice verse 20: *"And she said to them, 'Do not call me Naomi; call me Mara, for the Almighty has dealt very bitterly with me.' "*

Didn't Ruth sacrifice everything to be with her, as some of us have done to serve the church? But listen to the ingratitude of a sweet woman who becomes bitter when she is spurned by the "apple of her eye" and is left with only the one she simply tolerates. " *'I went out full, but the Lord has brought me back empty. Why do you call me Naomi, since the Lord has witnessed against me and the Almighty has afflicted me?' "* (verse 21).

That must have hurt Ruth terribly as she realized that Naomi loved Orpah more and was reeling under the reality that she was the one who had left her. In the same way that Naomi failed to readily recognize the commitment and companionship of Ruth, so the church, in these last days, is failing to acknowledge the commitment of women who refuse to leave in spite of the hardships they may face in ministry.

The two women, Ruth and Orpah, are symbols of two seasons in the lives of women who are called to serve. Notice that they both loved their mother-in-law. They both willingly left their native land to follow her to her homeland. They were both pressed to go back to their mothers' house. One returned, and one remained. First, Orpah, whose name means "neck (swan-like) girl with a full mane (lots of hair cascading down her shoulders) and rain cloud (promise/ potential)." To me she represents gifted women who start out in ministry but quit for one reason or another, mostly because their mother-in-law, the church, convinced them to go back. Yet when they do, they are criticized with caustic comments, like the bitter words of Naomi which so vividly describe "that they have gone back to their people and their gods" like a dog returning to its own vomit, according to Proverbs 26:11.

After studying this passage I have come to realize that Orpah's leaving, like so many women who have left the ministry, was not a lighthearted decision. It was as poignant, painful, heart-wrenching a parting for them as it was for her. Not only are we told she wept uncontrollably, but the Hebrew suggests that she literally "tore herself from the warm embrace and security of Naomi's arms" to reluctantly return to something she no longer knew and was not really sure existed in the purple hills of Moab.

Maybe Orpah served God faithfully and maybe she did go back to her gods—we don't know. So please, let us no longer use the words of a bitter old woman, for those are not God's words, to condemn Orpah or women who leave the ministry to go back to their former or different professions after being pushed away by the church. Instead, let us prayerfully wait on tiptoes and watch for their return as the patient prodigal father in one of Jesus' most powerful parables.

Second, Ruth, whose name means "contracted from" and "companion," represents a breed of women for all seasons who cling to the church, no matter how they are pushed away or pressed to go. After being told four times to go, Ruth said,

> *"Do not urge me to leave you or turn back from following you; for where you go, I will go and where you lodge, I will lodge. Your people shall be my people, and your God, my God. Where you die, I will die, and there I will be buried. Thus may the Lord do to me, and worse, if anything but death parts you and me"* (verses 16, 17).

These words are uncompromising in their commitment. They are so resolute in their pledge, they embarrass this "love me and leave me" generation and should put to shame men and women who stand in the way of those who are called by God to cling to Christ and His church. They are not, as we have adapted them, words spoken between a woman and a man pledging faithfulness to each other in holy matrimony. They are words of fidelity from a woman—a marginalized, alienated, disenfranchised foreigner—to a woman who had a place of belonging among the chosen people of God. They are the words of a younger woman pledging herself to the older, more experienced in a testimony of sisterhood as she committed herself to serve, to care for, and to stand by that older woman, no matter what.

That Moabite girl, that alien child of the hills, that foreigner, that woman in a society of devalued women and oppressed widows, stood by her mother-in-law in loyalty to love and dedication to duty. For her unselfish commitment, God accepted her as a partner in the covenant of grace so that her name is numbered in the genealogy of His Son. It will stand there as long as the stars shine, as long as the ocean moves, as long as the breezes blow, because she found that which is the most precious thing in the world, a place in the Covenant of Grace and the household of faith. And if you look in the first chapter of the book of Matthew today, there her name still stands as the mother of Obed who became the father of Jesse, who became the father of David, in whose lineage we find Jesus Christ, our Lord and Savior of the world.

This powerful parable ends in a profound way in chapter 4, verses 13-15:

> *So Boaz took Ruth, and she became his wife, and he went in to her. And the Lord enabled her to conceive, and she gave birth to a son. Then the women said to Naomi, "Blessed is the Lord who has not left you without a redeemer today, and may his name become famous in Israel. May he also be to you a restorer of life and a sustainer of your old age; for your daughter-in-law, who loves you and is better to you than seven sons, has given birth to him."*

Notice that Ruth married Boaz, whose name means "a quick-witted, sprightly lord of strength," and who is a symbol of Christ to women waiting for acceptance. He is also a sign to women in ministry that we cannot bear the Son of God into this barren world without a Boaz—a brother in ministry—and vice versa.

It was also said that Ruth became better to Naomi than seven sons! Who could have imagined that God would choose to use a humble foreign woman in such a way? No one, because God's ways are not our ways!

Many people, especially me, are also still in awe that God should use this Jamaican-English-American woman, who was born out of time, in the way He has in the last few decades. Yet some of us are still trying, even now, to choose who should preach and teach God's Word. It's to our shame that we do so at the expense of the glorious gospel of Jesus Christ given through the nurturing eyes of women.

It's to our shame that we prefer our prejudices above God's choice of servants in His sacred plan of salvation. It's to our shame that we will dishonor our Lord and misrepresent grace if we miss the message in this book named after a woman of priceless worth in the kingdom of God.

The message to the church in the story of Ruth is, beware how you pressure and push people away from God, from His church and His work, for we might lose some like Orpah who are full of potential and promise. Or you, dear mother-church might even overlook others like Ruth, righteous women waiting for acceptance who, in the end, may be better to you than seven sons!

---

1. Ellen G. White, *The Desire of Ages.*, 400.
2. Ibid.
3. See Palestinian Talmud Ber. 136b.
4. Aída Besançon Spencer, *Beyond the Curse* (Hendrickson, 1993), 65.
5. Ibid., 64.
6. Joachim Jeremias, *Jerusalem in the Time of Jesus* (Fortress Press, 1979), 373.
7. Ibid., 375.
8. Lloyd John Ogilvie, *Autobiography of God* (Regal Books, 1981), 182, 183.
9. Charles Swindoll, *Esther: A Woman of Strength and Dignity* (Word, 1997), 98.

Chapter 3

sleeping with the enemy

He was new in town. After checking out several churches he decided to join one. But, unbeknown to him, this church was notorious for its exclusiveness. One morning after church, Jim told the pastor that he wanted to join his congregation, but to his surprise the minister tried everything to dissuade him. After Jim pressed the issue much more than the pastor expected, the poor exasperated man finally told him to go, reflect more carefully on the matter, and pray for guidance.

The following week, to the pastor's surprise, Jim showed up again in church. This time he eagerly repeated his original request.

"Well, did you pray about this?" asked the minister with a hint of frustration in his voice as he attempted to again evade the issue.

"Yes, sir! I prayed, and the Lord asked me why on earth I wanted to join your church," Jim replied, watching the minister's expressions as he continued. "When I told Him the reason was that your church is near my home, God laughed and said, 'You'll never get into that church. I've been trying for years to get in, and they won't let me in!' "

The Roman church was becoming as exclusive as that one when the apostle Paul wrote to them in A.D. 57. Founded by Jews who had come to Christ at Pentecost (see Acts 2), the church in Rome experienced rapid growth for a while. The excitement that the charter members brought from Pentecost pulled people in by the hundreds, but by the time Paul planned to visit Rome, the church was losing its focus on *sola fide, sola Christos* (only faith, only Christ). After a brief introduction, Paul presented them with the facts of the gospel in Romans 1:16, 17:

> *For I am not ashamed of [scandalized by] the gospel, for it is the power ["dunamis" or dynamite] of God for salvation to everyone who believes, to the Jew first and also to the Greek [Gentile]. For in it the righteousness of God is revealed from faith to faith; as it is written, "But the righteous man shall live by faith."*

Here Paul declared his allegiance to the gospel before he continued to build an airtight case, like an intelligent, articulate attorney, for the lost condition of mankind and the necessity for God's intervention to save them. In chapter 2, he presents the good news that salvation is available to everyone, regardless of identity, heritage, culture, or customs.

Then in chapter 3, from a Jewish perspective, Paul raised and responded to objections to his assertions, before nailing the point of justification by faith, like a perfect gymnastic move. In that chapter, verses 21-31, the aging apostle confidently declared that only through Christ alone could we be justified before God.

Whether we are Jews or Gentiles, Orientals or occidentals, God treats us all the same, and that is good news. No matter who we are, we are justified by faith, not works, lest we should boast about our accomplishments. We are justified by faith in a Person, Jesus Christ our Redeemer.

Because the Jews were proud of their parentage, especially the fact that they were the direct descendants of Abraham, Paul used Abraham in chapter 4 as a good example of one saved by faith:

> *What then shall we say, that Abraham, our forefather according to the flesh, has found? For if Abraham was justified by works, he has something to boast about; but not before God. For what does the Scripture say? "And Abraham believed God and it was reckoned to him as righteousness." Now to the one who works, his wage is not reckoned as a favor, but as what is due. But to the one who does not work, but believes in Him who justifies the ungodly, his faith is reckoned as righteousness* (Romans 4:1-5).

When I was a little girl, I knew a song that I thought was a church song. It goes something like this: "If salvation was a thing that money could buy, the rich would live and the poor would die." Thank God that it isn't so! Thank God for preserving Romans chapters 4 and 5 so that we can be reminded today and for every generation that it is not so. I am especially glad that it will never be the case. The precious gift of salvation is free for those who do not work or try to buy their way in, but who *believe* in Christ, the One who justifies the ungodly whether they are rich or poor.

This whole idea of righteousness by faith is a much-debated one. When I first became a Christian, I didn't know there could be any other righteousness except that by faith. But as soon as I got involved with organized religions I discovered that there were debates and disputes over this doctrine. But isn't righteousness by faith the only biblical way to go? So what's the big fuss about? Why are these debates so intense? Why are there so many volumes and popular polemics written about righteousness by faith versus righteousness by works, when Paul makes it so plain in his letter to the Romans that it is by *faith* alone—*sola fide*?

First, let us define the word "faith." The Greek word *pistis* primarily means a firm persuasion, a conviction based upon hearing and an assurance, a certainty in God or spiritual things. It is possible to have faith in non-spiritual and ungodly things, but we are here defining faith from a biblical perspective. Now notice that in Romans 4, it is the word *pisteuo,* "believe" from the same root as "faith," but it means to be persuaded, to place confidence in, to trust, to place reliance (not mere credence) on something that is used repeatedly. Sometimes the two words are used interchangeably in the Bible.

Regardless of which of these two words are used, the idea is that biblical faith or belief is not what our modern secular society defines it to be. For example, the contemporary meaning is that faith is something that is hopefully true—possible, but not certain; belief is something you can accept passively and not do anything about it.

Biblical faith and belief demands a response. It is certain, it is sure, and if you believe something, you must obey its requirements or act on its instructions.

The word "reckoned" means to be counted or imputed. It was originally used in connection with the keeping of accounts. Thus, Abraham's faith was reckoned or counted in the books of heaven as righteousness. The word righteousness means the character or quality of being right or just. It was originally spelled "rightwiseness" which clearly expresses the meaning "to be right with wisdom." It was not Abraham's ability to do the right things, or being right, that was set down in the ledger of his life, but his believing in God that caused him to be counted as rightwise by the Great Accountant. It is believing, and keeping on believing in God that justifies the impious, impervious, irreverent one who repents, and is taken just as he or she is, to be pardoned by faith. To the one who does not work, nor tries to do his or her own thing to be saved, but believes that no matter where they've been or what they've done, his or her faith is reckoned as righteousness. Isn't that good news, especially to those of us who have tried to work for our salvation by doing or being good to gain God's favor? I must confess that I have tried to work for my salvation, and it is very difficult. I never seem able to get it right. Thank God I've finally given up trying!

By emphasizing the importance of faith, Paul was not saying that God's law is insignificant, and neither should we. A popular philosophy that many are teaching and preaching says that the law, meaning the Ten Commandments, was nailed to the cross. Some base these beliefs on the following passage:

> *Having canceled out the certificate of debt consisting of decrees against us and which was hostile to us; and He has taken it out of the way, having nailed it to the cross* (Colossians 2:14).

Because the word *decrees*, which refers to ordinances and laws, appears in the same statement about what has been "nailed to the cross," some have assumed that this is referring to the Ten Commandments, while others think it refers to the ceremonial ordinances. In his *Word Pictures in the New Testament*, Archibald Thomas Robertson translates "the certificate of debt consisting of decrees against us," as "the bond written in ordinances that was against us *(to kath' hemon cheirographon tois dogmasin)*."[1] He comments that "the late compound *cheirographon* (*cheir*, hand, *grapho* [write]) is very common in the papyri for certificate of debt or bond," and that many originals translate it as handwriting.[2] In essence, "the signature made a legal debt or bond as Paul says in Philemon 19: 'I Paul am writing this with mine own hand, I will repay it.' Many of the papyri examples have been 'crossed out' thus *X* as we do today and so cancelled. . . . It is striking that Paul has connected the common word *cheirographon* [handwriting] for bond or debt with the Cross of Christ"[3] to indicate that Jesus bore or took away the debt or sin of the world (see John 1:29). Clearly it was not the ceremonial ordinances that were canceled, and not the Law "nailed to the cross," but the debt of sin.

The Bible does teach that our Savior and His death certificate, according to Roman jurisprudence, an inscription written in Hebrew and Greek which said "JESUS THE NAZARENE, THE KING OF THE JEWS" (John 19:19), were nailed to the cross on Calvary. How do we get the Ten Commandments or even the ceremonial law out of that, I will never be able to figure. I have read this in as many translations and versions as possible, and I find nothing about the law being nailed to the cross and our responsibility to the law done away with. I have come to the conclusion that this was an excuse used to give those who refuse to obey the prompting of the Spirit regarding obedience to every aspect of God's commandments, a way out if they reject some commands.

The emphasis on faith is not a denunciation of grace, for grace without law is cheap just as law without grace is legalistic. But when law and grace meld, they are divine. The design of the apostle was to show that we cannot be saved by law or works, which was the primary attitude among ancient Jews toward the plan for their redemption imparted by God at Sinai. Their attitude was a legalistic one. They believed that no one could be justified through righteousness by faith. They believed they had to work for salvation. When God gave them the Ten Commandments at Sinai, they did not say, "We will believe and let You do it in us," rather they confirmed the covenant with God in one voice saying, *"All the words which the Lord has spoken we will do!"* (Exodus 24:3c and 7b). Thus they missed the point of justification by faith and thereafter became doers of the Word rather than "livers" of grace, transformed by the power and presence of the incredible work of grace and law. Justification, as you and I well know, is by faith and faith alone.

When some people learn that they are saved by faith, they worry. I have had people say to me, "Do I have enough faith? Is my faith strong enough to save me?" If you are among them, you are missing

3—A.

the point that the apostle Paul preached so diligently. He was informing, educating and instructing us to believe that it is a Person, Jesus Christ alone, who saves us. Not our feelings, actions, words, or works. Faith is only an instrument, a mere instrument that God has been pleased to appoint as a condition by which we may all be treated as righteous. Faith expresses a state of mind that demonstrates love to God, affection for His cause and character, reconciliation with Him, and friendship with one another. Faith is that state through which God has promised pardon and acceptance through the blood or life (see Deuteronomy 12:23) of Jesus Christ, which is strong enough to save us no matter how weak our faith may be. So then, salvation, as we well know, even though we take it for granted, is a grace gift from God, not because we earned it through our powerful faith, but because Jesus paid for it with His life.

What, then, is the role of faith? Faith is believing, trusting, and obeying Jesus Christ. Faith is reaching out to accept His wonderful gift of grace, especially when we don't feel or believe we deserve it. Faith is effective whether it is great or small, timid or bold, because God loves us. Nothing we do can change that.

God loves us! Romans 5 says that while we were sinners, enemies of God, Jesus Christ died for us. God loves us, no matter what!

That's why I find it offensive when we tell children, in stories or otherwise, that if they are good enough or if they behave a certain way, God will love them. They ought to be told the raw fact that God loves them any way they are. If He allows His rain of grace to fall on the just *and the unjust* adults who often are far from deserving, how much more will He do for His little children? We should tell them that because God loves them unconditionally, their loving response should be to do their very best to listen and follow the prompting of the Holy Spirit, so that they and all of us may be reckoned as righteous.

Now, what about the faith that was reckoned to Abraham as righteousness, which makes this passage relevant for us today? The answer is in the Word of God, where I find some scriptures that fight me, that wrestle me to the ground and lay me out. This was one of them! I have read and reread oodles of books, commentaries of every class and kind, versions and paraphrases. You should have seen my study as I prepared to write this chapter: it was strewn with books as I wrestled with this passage. But I want you to know that faith pays off in the end, because I have learned some lessons and want to share them with you.

One lesson was that Abraham (then called Abram) renounced self, even before his name was changed, and that's why his faith was reckoned as righteousness. Let's look at what he did, as recorded in Genesis 15:1-6:

> *After these things the word of the Lord came to Abram in a vision, saying, "Do not fear, Abram, I am a shield to you; Your reward shall be very great." And Abram said, "O Lord God, what will You give me, since I am childless, and the heir of my house is Eliezer of Damascus?" And Abram said, "Since you have given no offspring to me, one born in my house is my heir." Then behold, the word of the Lord came to him, saying, "This man will not be your heir; but one who shall come forth from your own body, he shall be your heir." And He took him outside and said, "Now look toward the heavens, and count the stars, if you are able to count them." And He said to him, "so shall your descendants be." The he (Abram) believed [trusted] in the Lord; and He reckoned it to him as righteousness.*

Notice that God opened the conversation with Abram by saying that although he had already started to be afraid, he should stop. Whenever religious people attempt to gain their salvation by works, guilt and fear always accompany their effort.

For those of us who turn to Jesus Christ, the Bible promises that the perfect, unconditional love of God casts out all fear (see

1 John 4:18) when accepted by faith. And God goes so far as to make sure that everyone who is born into this world, whether they believe in Him or not, are given a measure of faith (see Romans 12:3).

Thus we do not have to conjure up faith willingly activated by the wooing presence of the Holy Spirit. For it is He who propels us into renouncing guilt and fear (the enemies of faith) so that we can accept the gift of salvation, paid for in full through the sacrifice of God's only begotten Son, Jesus Christ our Lord.

Abram was in a rut. He wanted something from God, and he realized that he could do nothing about it. So he cried out to God. He didn't complain and say, "God, everyone else around me has an heir, and I don't, even though I do everything to please you." He did not pity himself, saying, "I deserve an heir, and if God does not give me one then I must be guilty of some secret sin for which I am being punished." If you have been given a promise from God and it is not being fulfilled in the time and way you expected, "beware of saying, 'Oh well, I must have misinterpreted what God meant.' We have to build in absolute confidence on God. There is nothing more heroic than to have faith in God when you can see so many better things in which to have faith . . . the whole discipline of the life of faith is to mix together the light of heaven and the sordid actuality of earth."[4]

There is a wildness in God's expectations of Abraham's faith. He took His friend, who was faithful and authentic enough to reveal the depths of his heart, outside and showed him the stars He had created in the heavens. He said to him, "If you believe that I really made those and hung them there and that nothing on earth can shake them out of their path, then believe that I can provide you with an heir out of your own body, when I am ready, no matter what shape your body may be in." And *"Against all hope, Abraham in hope believed"* (Rom. 4:18, NIV) God, who wants us to have similar faith in His promises. But it is a big stretch of our meager measure of faith. That is why I find help in Oswald Chambers's commentary on this passage. He said, "If only He [God] had told us to hitch our wagon to a mule, we could see how it might be done; but to tell us to hitch our natural lumbering wagons to the star of Almighty God makes us wonder whether we have understood Him aright. Faith sticks to the wagon and the star; fanaticism jumps from the wagon to the star and breaks its neck."[5] Why? Because fanaticism always tries to reach for and grasp by works what God promises is ours by faith alone.

Our wagons of hope must be hitched to the stars of God. No matter what the vision that God has given us, we must avoid every instinct, desire, or interpretation of our own destinies, for it is the soul of fanaticism to accomplish these things in our own strength and understanding. Too often, desire, passion and eagerness—the fanaticism of faith—cause us to jump off from the safe place provided by God to try to reach what He has promised is ours by faith. We must remember that *"it is not by might, nor by power, but by My Spirit"* that these things are accomplished, said the Lord (Zechariah 4:6). We can do this only by renouncing self, which holds against us our past actions and failures and will not allow us to even look up at the stars, much less try to hitch our wagons to them. Self tells us that our lot is to live in the dumps where we are hostages to the immediate. It pushes us ahead of God's purpose. Consider Moses, who was eager to deliver his people 40 years earlier than God's plan for his life. Self urges us to attempt reaching our goals hastily and expediently, saying, "Hurry up and get what God has promised." Just as God made Moses wait on His timing, so must we also learn to wait on the Lord.

Again, Oswald Chambers speaks to the believer's dilemma of rushing ahead of God's plan, saying "living in the dumps and living in a hurry are worse than the Devil and are both excessively culpable. Living in the dumps is an absolute slur against God; I won't look up. I have done all I could but it is all over, and I am in despair.

Hurry is the same mood expressed in the opposite way: I have no time to pray, no time to look to God or to consider anything; I must do the thing. Perspiration is mistaken for inspiration, and we drive our miserable little wagon in a rut instead of hitching it to a star and pulling according to God's plan."[6]

So what is your wagon? What vision did God give you? When I was first converted, God said to me, "I want you to tell the world what I have done for you." When I heard that, I couldn't wait to go out and tell, and even though I had nothing to say, I hurried to create something. Instead of waiting for God to give me the words, to send me to my Arabia, as He did Paul in Galatians 1:15-17, I went out and bought myself a long green gown and stationed myself on one of the busiest street corners in Hartford, Connecticut. There, where I was well known as the executive assistant to the mayor, I began to shout, "Jesus saves, Jesus saves!" In retrospect, I realize that the friends who came and quickly bundled me in their car before the press got wind of my situation, were actually sent by God. It took several years of deep studies, a lot of remonstrance from the Holy Spirit, and the incredible grace-filled patience of God to keep me from repeating that fanaticism. So when I ask, what is your wagon and how are you handling it, I'm doing so from a profound place of experience. Have you been jumping off on your own and finding that with each move you are breaking your proverbial neck? What rut have you been stuck in because of that? Is it a religious or spiritual rut?

Sometimes when I travel to speak at different churches, one of the many outrageous stories I am told is that there are people who will come to church and leave because they oppose the person, gender, race, or history of the speaker. What a rut their wagon is in because God can speak to us through children, through elderly men and women, through the young and gifted people who populate our land. And if all those refuse to be used of God, He can use a donkey (see Numbers 22:28) or stones (see Luke 19:40)! What a rut it must be, that we cannot hitch our earth-bound wagons on God's heavenly stars and see the enormous possibilities that He can or will fulfill with this generation!

Who do we think we are hurting when we angrily or proudly get up and walk out of a worship service where God is present and is being lifted up in songs and sermon? We're not hurting the worship participants or the God-called presenters, for even if I disagree with someone being there, if God allows it, then that's who *should* be speaking. When we walk out, we are not hurting the worship participants or even the speaker, for often she or he is not aware of that action until they are told much later. Instead, we are blaspheming God, for that is a human, political protest and not a divinely directed response. We can learn an important lesson from the story in 1 Samuel 16:5-14, especially verse 7, which says, *"Do not look at [the] appearance or at the height of [the] stature ... for God sees not as man sees, for man looks at the outward appearance, but the Lord looks at the heart."*

In order to get our wagons out of the rut, like Abram, we must look up at the stars God showed him. In order for us to look up at the stars, we must renounce self, that enemy of faith, and believe God. We must remember that the fanatic's motivation is to always *do something,* while faith is called upon by God to *wait* for the movement of Providence.

Another lesson I gleaned from my study of Romans 4:3 is that Abraham learned to rely not on self but on God. Wherever there is reliance on self, there is pride. And wherever there is pride, the Lord must inevitably be put to open shame. That was a powerful and painful lesson for Abraham, according to Genesis 16, where we are shown that the fanatic, passionate desire to hurry up and fulfill God's will led him into desperate error. He and his wife, Sarah (then called Sarai), leaned on their own understanding of what God said, instead of trusting God to provide the answers and insights. Even after God took him outside and showed him the stars, even after he believed

God and it was reckoned to him as righteousness, Abram allowed his wife to influence his natural, carnal desires instead of remembering God's promises, according to Genesis 16:1-5:

> *Now Sarai, Abram's wife had borne him no children, and she had an Egyptian maid whose name was Hagar. So Sarai said to Abram, "Now behold, the Lord has prevented me from bearing children. Please go in to my maid; perhaps I shall obtain children through her." And Abram listened to the voice of Sarai. And after Abram had lived ten years in the land of Canaan, Abram's wife Sarai took Hagar the Egyptian, her maid, and gave her to her husband Abram as his wife. And he went in to Hagar, and Hagar conceived; and when she saw that she had conceived, her mistress was despised in her sight. And Sarai said to Abram, "May the wrong done me be upon you. I gave my maid into your arms; but when she saw that she had conceived, I was despised in her sight. May the Lord judge between you and me."*

The first thing I noticed was that Abraham believed God before he had fully turned over his life to Him. Notice that both he and Sarai were following the divine directives as well as the cultural customs of their day, much like when we walk with one foot in the church and the other in the world. The other telling thing is that their heathen names (Abram, which means, "the father is high" and Sarai, "mistress"), were not yet changed by God to Hebrew names that represented their transformed characters. Abram became Abraham (see Genesis 17:5). This means, "father of the faithful" and "friend of God." Sarai became Sarah, meaning "princess," after they had entered fully into a covenant relationship with God, which we now recognize as conversion—when justification is accepted by faith and the soul is transformed by God's Spirit.

Hagar, whose name means "flight" or "emigration," was a

princess by birth, being one of the daughters of the Pharaoh and one of his concubines, who was given to Abraham as a gift (Genesis 12:16). Hagar was later used by the apostle Paul to represent the natural life (see Galatians 4:21-31), when it gets out of place and attempts to take precedence over the spiritual life.

"Our natural life must be in subordination and under the absolute control of the spiritual," warned Oswald Chambers, who also said, "The natural must be turned into the spiritual by obedience, whatever sword has to go through its heart. The characteristic of the natural life is the independent passion for free dominion over itself. Thus, it is not only sin that produces the havoc in life; it is also the good opposing the best—the natural inclination and determination to 'boss the show' for God and everyone else."[7]

Sarah, on the other hand, represents the spiritual life that is still under the influence of fanaticism and does not have complete trust in God. She represents the person who believes and thus allows God to answer, but when He does not answer soon enough, they think that a little help from His friends won't do much harm. But the rest of the story in Genesis tells us otherwise. The natural "Hagar" life and the spiritual "Sarai" life are always in conflict. It is a mortal combat that one must win. The spiritual fanaticism always treats the carnal or natural life harshly (see Genesis 16:6b), which evidences itself in legalism's strict rules and regulations to keep the carnal in its place. This struggle is an example of the way in which we wound our own souls and injure other lives when we try to take God's providence in our own hands.

It reminds me of a story I heard about John Wesley, the great man of faith and founder of the Methodist church, as well as one of the greatest preachers and believers in righteousness by faith who has ever walked among the human family. It was said that as he performed his ministry, he became more and more convicted that God did not want him to live alone, that God wanted him to be married. He believed God, and in every other promise, he had demonstrated an incredible patience by waiting on God to fulfill it, except in this one.

Instead of waiting on God, he chose a woman and married her. It is said that he had one of the most miserable marriages known to humanity. There are legends that he wore out a place on the wooden floor of his study where, long after his death, one could see the indentation of his knees from his long hours of prayer to God for deliverance from such a miserable marriage.

John Wesley wrote volumes in his diaries about everything relating to the practical Christian life, but there was only one mention of his wife. There's hardly anything known about her except a terse sentence in his diary saying, "My wife died today," which gives expression of his taking the opportunity to finally exhale in peace.

When we take things in our own hands, when we rely on ourselves and our own knowledge to accomplish a dream or a vision given to us by God, most of the time we end up in desperate error and cause a lot of trouble for ourselves and for others. We must always be aware of the error of being more eager to do God's will than He is for us to do it.

The remarkable lesson we can learn from the life of our Lord Jesus Christ is that He was not only eager to do His Father's will, but He was earnest in waiting on His directives as to when and how to do it. Oswald Chambers also noted that even when Jesus had the vision and it was clear to Him, He waited on His Father's instruction before acting on them. He never put His holy hands to the plow, or his fingers across the threads of His father's providential orders and gave it a tug saying, "I know what this is all about; let me give Him a hand because He's so slow." Jesus simply obeyed, leaving His Father's wisdom to arrange all for Him, and that's what God wants from us, to give up our reliance on self and rely on Him. But, instead, like Sarai and Abram, we rush in and say, "I see that God wants me to do this or that and I will help Him." We end up injuring others as we make a lie of the truth that Jesus paid it all and did it all for us.

We also rely on self, wounding our souls, as we continue sleeping with that enemy.

Abraham learned to wait on the reservations that were made for him by God. At first, God said to Abraham, "I will make you," but he was too anxious for the reality of that vision, so he and Sarah went out and tried to make the reality of that vision for themselves. Too late, they learned this lesson and had to live thereafter with the consequences of their haste (see Genesis 21). After Abraham received his vision, according to Genesis 15, horror and great darkness fell upon him, and instead of waiting for the darkness to pass, he tried to fix things, to do things for himself because he didn't understand that he should *wait* when the darkness comes. There is nothing worse than being given a very clear vision and being told to sit, wait, and do nothing about it, especially through the long, dark night of wrestling with one's inner desire to accomplish by works what God bestows to us by faith.

It appears to me that when God gives us a vision, He hides us in the shadow, in the cleft of His hands, where we can't see and it appears to be dark. At that time it is our duty to be still, to listen and wait for His divine "go." But too often, like Abraham in Genesis 16, in the dark night of anticipation we seek the good advice of our families and friends, and rather than waiting for God to send His marvelous light in the morning, we try to do something about it. But, just as there is an eerie calm before a great storm, so there is darkness before the coming of light that illumines the life and soul of every human being. Throughout history, there has always been a dark period of depravity before the light of redemption. Perhaps it is so to allow us to see the contrast more clearly. Too often we mistake the darkness for rejection or refusal by God to grant us our wishes, instead of accepting it as a time to prepare for the grand manifestation of the limitless love of God through unprecedented miracles.

As Americans, if not as adventists—a people anxiously anticipating the promised second coming of Christ—we are a nation of doers. We are not slothful; neither are we waiting for the pie-in-the-sky heritage. We get out there, roll up our sleeves and get on with the job that needs to be done to accomplish our dreams and visions. As a result of this nature, I find God perplexing or at best frustrating when He gives us a clear call and tells us to wait. Then months and sometimes years go by, and you eventually have to do something about it! God often seems to give the vision first, then after a long, long time of hard days and nights, through the deep valleys of humiliation and the high mountains of anticipation, He brings the results and realities.

When God gives us a vision and darkness follows, we shouldn't panic. We should pray and wait. For if God has given us a vision, He will bring the reality of it in our lives and experience. It is, of course, our inalienable right to try to accomplish on our own what comes to our mind to do. But God wants us to surrender that right to Him and ignore the dangers that often come with good advice, for in the end we will discover that waiting on the Lord is the right way to go.

There's a whole year missing in my life and ministry because I, too, did not understand that the darkness was a prelude to God's remarkable delivery out of a predicament. I also didn't understand the importance of waiting on the reservations made by God. I remember when God called me again, years after the first call, to tell others what He had done for me, I refused to follow His plan of preparation to preach. He wanted me to go to school, but I refused to follow that plan, and instead of going at the time when He directed, I stayed at home sulking.

One whole year I couldn't find any work as a professional administrator. Prior to that, I had been wooed by the Washington D.C. headhunters. I had been offered positions on Capitol Hill and with some of the major corporations in America. Yet, there I was, unemployed and no one would have me because I was infringing on God's reservation for my life. I finally took a job as a maid rather than wait, and it was the only job from which I have ever been fired.

I wasn't doing a poor job, but I was trying to work out the vision by myself. I was following the good advice of my own mind, which had convinced me that God wouldn't call a woman into ministry, particularly *this* woman. I had been taught that God would never do this, and when He insisted that I obey *His* call to preach and teach the gospel, I had already painted myself into an impossible corner and could not find a way out. One whole year of frustrated sulking went by before I repented. One year when I could have been used by God. One year when I could have been healed by Him. One year of injuring my own soul and hurting others by sleeping with the enemy called self. In the end, like Sarai, I had to deal harshly with that carnal nature until I accepted God's grace of justification by faith.

So, my friends, wait on the Lord. Don't let the clear vision on your Mount of Transfiguration hurry you into helping God in the days of darkness that often follow. The times when God seems to be sending us through the doldrums are often the most positive and most powerful times of our experience if we use them to strengthen our weak faith by deliberately practicing being in His presence. Don't rush through it, for according to one of my favorite Christian authors, all of God's commands are His enablings. If He commands you to go through the darkness, ride the wave with Him, because a shout of joy will come in the morning.

Remember, wait on the Lord. Even though for most believers the biggest danger is to reach God's destination in our own time, in our own power, we must learn like Abraham to wait on the Lord. Wait on the Lord, so that we, too, may emerge out of the discipline of darkness with one determination, to always allow God's way with our lives. Then we will be able to prove ourselves to be true children of Abraham—those whose faith is reckoned as righteousness.

Otherwise, we can be like Jerry Jones, who was a he-man with an "I" problem. Not the kind of eye problem that an ophthalmologist can cure, but that disease described by Chuck Swindoll, in his book, *Second Wind For Those Struggling To Get Up Again*, as "ingrownius eyeballitus" or "ingrown eyeballs." Swindoll says that we are all familiar with this disease because it strikes all of us at one time or another, in some subtle or dramatic ways. It is the stubborn enemy of our souls that makes us paranoid people who are more absorbed with self than salvation. When it is raging out of control, "ingrownious eyeballitus" is evidenced by a constant ringing of sour (as opposed to sweet) nothings in our inner ears and hearts, reminding us, as one Christian author noted, of how unappreciated and ill-treated we are; how gifted yet ignored; how important, yet overlooked; how brilliant, yet eclipsed; how valuable, yet unrewarded.

Jerry Jones had a bad case of this disease, and to overcompensate for its haunting presence, he did some of the most outrageous acts to shock people and draw attention to himself. He lived in New England, where winters are very cold and icy, yet he paraded his well-proportioned, muscle-bound, six-foot-six frame in shorts, walking about bare-chested, bare-legged, barefooted, even bare-minded, during the coldest, ice-storm days. He used to boast about how absolutely ineffective the cold was on him, but nothing was as demonstrative of his exhibitionism as what he did one summer.

He frightened all of the staff in the mayor's office, where I served as executive assistant, when he showed up with a huge boa constrictor wrapped around his well-formed, tattooed, bare arms and chest. He boasted that his pet python was so tame that he could kiss it on the mouth. He would stroke its head, the boa would put its fangs out, and Jerry would draw its face to his and kiss that monstrous menace. We women, and I dare say some of the men in the office, jumped on our desks screaming as though there was a mouse in the house.

The terror he created seemed to inspire Jerry, who insisted that the boa was so gentle he slept with it wrapped around his body. No amount of warnings about the power of that python and the danger in which Jerry placed himself by sleeping with a natural enemy made any difference to him. Everyone told Jerry Jones that his boa constrictor could not think, that it did not have human rationality, and would instinctively act out its typical behavior and while sleeping he might unknowingly arouse its killer instincts. But no amount of warnings seemed to worry or impress Jerry Jones. One night, as Jerry slept with the snake wrapped around his body, his pet boa constricted and squeezed the life out of its master. He died a crushed man, so to speak.

Today, the memory of that man who lost his life while sleeping with the enemy serves me well. He serves as an object lesson for those who are called by Christ but are crushed while sleeping with the enemy. That enemy is not only Satan, but also our inner, original, rebellious nature, on which the devil hooks his temptation, so that he can drag us down and crush the eternal life out of us.

This enemy with whom we are sleeping is generally presented in two forms, or classifications, in the Bible. The first and most lethal of the two is widely recognized as the original sin, the inherited sin, which operates in us as the carnal nature and is traced to our fore-parents, Adam and Eve, and has affected every one of their descendants thereafter. The apostle Paul speaks of it in this fashion:

> *Therefore, just as through one man (Adam) sin entered into the world, and death through sin, and so death spread to all men because all sinned—for until the Law sin was in the world; but sin is not imputed when there is no law. Nevertheless death reigned from Adam until Moses, even over those who had not sinned in the likeness of the offense of Adam, who is a type of Him who was to come* (Romans 5:12-14).

Although Paul was referring, in one sense, to the death of sleep, he was really addressing the second death, that perishable predator that takes away our eternal life. Only one, Jesus Christ, could rescue us out of that dilemma, and he could do it only as a relative, a *goel* (kinsman-redeemer), through the cruel death of crucifixion. Jesus was also the sacrificial Lamb that was given from the foundation of the world (see Revelation 13:8). His type is modeled in the animal killed by God to cover Adam and Eve immediately after they had sinned and come short of the glory of God (Genesis 3:21).

According to John 1:29, when John the Baptist saw Jesus he said *"Behold the lamb of God that takes away the sin of the world,"* and I'm sure you've heard that he used the word for "lamb" that referred to the sacrificial *Lamb*. Not just any lamb, but the lamb without blemish that is usually sacrificed. He referred to Jesus as the sacrificial Lamb, the One that God would take and lay on the altar and take His life. And John said, behold the Lamb of God that takes away the *sin* of the world.

Many passages point us to the fact that the death of Jesus Christ on the cross was to eradicate the original sin (see John 1:29) so that the fruit of personal, individual acts of sin that grow out of the root or original sin may also be daily eliminated.

Most of the time, believers apply the blood of Jesus Christ to the eradication of the fruit before we understand that the blood of Christ eliminates the root first. The idea is that if the root is eliminated, the tree, the carnal nature, will die day by day (see 1 Corinthians 15:31), so that the tree eventually dies and cannot bear any more fruits. That's God's plan to take care of the carnal nature, which Paul addresses in Romans 5:12-18. In the words of Paul, in Romans 6:11-14, sin no longer reigns, or as John Wesley once said, sin remains, but no longer reigns.

The truth is that in our ignorance, we have been sleeping with the enemy who is at the root, instead of applying the blood of Jesus Christ to take care of that. The grand instrument Jesus chose to effectuate the removal of sin, the radical surgery that must be done in human beings, is justification by faith. The instant we are justified, the radical surgery happens and the root, or nature of sin, is removed and replaced by the holiness of God that produces the new fruit of the Spirit (see Galatians 5:22, 23). Of course, the old fruits, the acts of sin, continue, and sanctification takes care of them day by day.

It is significant to note that the word *justification* comes from the same Greek word as righteousness (rightwiseness). This is why justification by faith is used interchangeably with righteousness by faith. They have just a hair of difference in meaning but are the same. Justification is a forensic term that is used to describe the basic diagnosis of the human problem—the original sin recognized in our carnal nature and the divinely provided solution for it, which we call Jesus' sacrifice on the cross, that we receive and understand by faith (see Romans 3:21-26).

Now faith is not just something possible or hopefully true. According to the Bible, belief is certain—an active assurance, something absolutely trusted and immediately accompanied by action. For example, suppose I invite you to sit in one of my 100-year-old antique chairs, and I convince you that it will not fall apart under your weight. If you say that you believe me, but hesitate or avoid sitting in it, would you be communicating that you believed what I said? Absolutely not! Moreover, if you wait to see the result of anyone sitting in that chair, it definitely proves to me that you have no faith in what I said.

In his book *Not Knowing Where*, Oswald Chambers said that "the very nature of faith is that it must be tried; faith untried is only ideally real, not actually real. Because faith is not rational, it cannot be worked out on the basis of logical reason; it can only be worked out implicitly by living obedience."[8] In essence, faith says, "When you hear it, act on it whether anyone else has acted on it or not!" That's what this is all about. So when God said that in Christ's death on the cross salvation has been given instantly to those who believe and accept His only begotten Son as Savior, even though you may not see any signs of that transaction, you have to believe and act upon the promise. Then, day by day, sanctification will come to cleanse you and clarify this whole procedure.

Paul painted a wonderful portrait of justification by faith when he penned the following about the results, rewards, and resources of justification by faith, rendered here in Eugene Peterson's popular paraphrase, *The Message:*

> *By entering through faith into what God has always wanted to do for us—set us right with him, make us fit for him—we have it all together with God because of our Master Jesus. And that's not all: We throw open our doors to God and discover at the same moment that he has already thrown open his door to us. We find ourselves standing where we always hoped we might stand—out in the wide-open spaces of God's grace and glory, standing tall and shouting our praise.*
>
> *There's more to come: We continue to shout our praise even when we're hemmed in with troubles, because we know how troubles can develop passionate patience in us, and how that patience in turn forges the tempered steel of virtue, keeping us alert for whatever God will do next. In alert expectancy such as this, we're never feeling shortchanged. Quite the contrary—we can't round up enough containers to hold everything God generously pours into our lives through the Holy Spirit! (Romans 5:1-5, The Message).*

We immediately note that justification by faith, according to this passage, is a Trinitarian task that Paul said liberates those who exercise faith or belief in the death, resurrection, and redemption of Jesus Christ on the cross from the presence, the power, and penalty of sin. His writings are rich with this information. In Romans 6:23 he stated that the wages of sin (the root or original sin and not the fruit or acts of sin) is death, the second death. But the amazing grace-gift of God is eternal life because He removes that penalty of death through His death, so that none should perish (see John 3:16) but all should have eternal life. So that none should be sleeping with the enemy, but all should be resting with our friend and Savior, Jesus Christ our Lord—if we fully exercise our faith in God's astounding act of justification by faith.

Isn't that awesome? That puts it into perspective for me! I believe Paul was saying, in essence, *"therefore, having been justified by faith"* we have three things:

First, the rewards, which he underscored when he said *"we have peace with God through our Lord Jesus Christ."* Having peace with God now suggests that there was a time when we did not have it. It points to a time when we were hostile God-haters. Some of us can still remember those bad old days because it was not so long ago when we shook our fists at God, when we denied His existence, when we refused to acknowledge His presence, according to Ephesians 2:1-3. Back then we had no peace with God. We were at war with God our heavenly Father. But Paul said that now that we have been justified by the death of Jesus Christ on the cross, we have peace with God through our Lord Jesus Christ. The word *peace* comes from the Greek word *eirene,* which describes harmonious relationships. It is interesting to me that the word *harmony*, so popular in music, is used to describe this peace. Harmony in music is attained when a variety of voices—bass, tenor, soprano, alto, and others— are synchronized to give a sweet, smooth, attractive sound. This implies that as in music, it is the rich mixture of a variety of tones that makes harmony; so in relationships, even with God, the different tones expressed in agreement brings peace. Humanity's tones are temporarily dulled by sin, but when added to the clear, perfect tones of the Trinity, they become the peace that is the reward of justification by faith. This peace is not just feelings of assurance, security, and confidence. This peace with God comes from the fact that we have been reconciled with Him. Paul said:

> *For while we were still helpless, at the right time Christ died for the ungodly. For one will hardly die for a righteous*

man; though perhaps for the good man someone would dare even to die. But God demonstrates His own love toward us, in that while we were yet sinners, Christ died for us. Much more then, having now been justified by His blood, we shall be saved from the wrath of God through Him. For if while we were enemies, we were reconciled to God through the death of His Son, much more, having been reconciled, we shall be saved by His life. And not only this, but we also exult in God through our Lord Jesus Christ, through whom we have now received the reconciliation. [Through whom also we have obtained our introduction by faith into this grace in which we stand. We have been reconciled with him] (Romans 5:6-11).

We are not just at peace, in harmony with God; we are *reconciled* to Him! The word *reconcile* comes from the Greek word *katallasso*, which means to change or exchange, especially referring to money. If I travel to a foreign country, say to Japan, and I convert my dollars into Japanese yen, I would receive about one hundred of theirs for one of mine. That's the idea of reconciling, to be changed or exchanged for much more. That's what God did in Jesus Christ for all believers. He took us when we were worthless slaves to sin and changed us into coinage worth much more so that we can spend and expend ourselves on the kingdom. We can be partners in faith who work for its expansion as we become ambassadors for Christ, taking this good news of reconciliation to those who are still slaves to sin (see 2 Corinthians 5:20).

When the early scholars, such as Jerome, author of the Latin *Vulgate*, began to translate the Bible from the Greek Septuagint into everyday, popular Latin, they had difficulty explaining the concept of reconciliation in one word. Thus they coined a new word borrowed from three of their common words, thereby adding to the English language another important dimension to the meaning of *reconcile*.

This is not the first or only time they borrowed words to describe difficult theological concepts. For example, when they translated the word *hilasmos,* found in 1 John 2:2 and 4:10, they borrowed the Latin word *propitiation* that describes the heathen rites for winning the favor or averting the anger of the gods. Why? Perhaps because *hilasmos* was also originally used by pagans to describe their sacrifices to appease their gods and gain their goodwill. If it did not rain and their crops were being destroyed, some heathen worshipers would begin with a simple sacrifice, and the longer it took to gain the favorable attention of their gods, the more they would sacrifice. Finally, in desperation, some sacrificed their first-born sons (see the prohibition in Leviticus 18:21) to appease the wrath of their gods.

From the foundation of the world, the members of the Godhead formed a plan for the salvation of the race they knew might fall into sin, should they exercise their freedom of choice. In His great love, God's wrath (His holy recoil from sin) necessitated a divine initiative if death, the curse of sin, were to be reversed. God the Father gave His only begotten Son as a sacrifice for sin, and the Son willingly laid down His life, taking the curse upon Himself. To explain this amazing act of grace, the apostle John used the pagan word *hilasmos.* According to Vine, the verb form *hilaskomai,* related to *hilasmos* the noun, "is foreign to the Greek Bible, with respect to God, whether in the Septuagint or in the New Testament. It is never used of any act whereby man brings God into a favorable attitude or gracious disposition."[9]

While discussing this matter, it is important to note that even though the Septuagint and the New Testament used these words, they never used them in the sense that man offered a *hilasmos* to God. Rather, it is *always* God who offers the *hilasmos* to bring about the reconciliation of lost sinners to a holy God. To adequately convey this important concept, the early church fathers employed the word *propitiation* to rightly indicate that "it is God who is propitiated by the vindication of His holy and righteous character, whereby, through the provision He has made in the vicarious and expiatory sacrifice of Christ, He has so dealt with sin that He can show mercy to the believing sinner in the removal of his [her] guilt and the remission of his [her] sins,"[10]

After that "mouthful" of a very theological explanation, I hope you can understand why the early church fathers felt constrained to find simple words to convey those very important concepts. When they encountered the word *katallasso,* they were faced with this similar dilemma. They solved it by creating the word "reconcile," composed of three Latin words, *re* which means "again" to show that what is about to happen existed before and is about to be repeated; *con* which means "with" and the word *cella,* which means "cell". The idea they wanted to convey was that we were once in the great Cell who is none other than God Himself according to Genesis 1 and 2. But there came a separation, a falling out of the Cell (Genesis 3:1-10), and God, in His bountiful love and compassion, through the cross of Jesus Christ our Lord, put us back in the Cell to be together with Him again (2 Corinthians 5:21). This is the heart of the gospel from a human perspective, while John 3:16, 17 unveils it from God's point of view.

Throughout his writings, the apostle Paul emphasized the fact that we are reconciled to God (i.e., 2 Corinthians 5:17-21), as he does in Romans 5:11. He said we have peace with God because we have been reconciled, implying that one can be at peace with someone and not be reconciled. I have experienced some of those relationships, but, thank God, He's still working on and with me through them. The good news is that we have both peace and reconciliation with God. This is only possible through Jesus Christ our Lord, who paid the penalty in full for our sin with His death on the cross. We can believe this! How? Because *"God demonstrates His own love toward us, in that while we were yet sinners, Christ died for us."*

What caught my attention here was the comparison and contrast.

For example, one would hardly die for a righteous or just person, like Joseph, Mary's husband, whom the Bible described as a "righteous man" (Matthew 1:19). According to the biblical meaning of the word, one who was "righteous" was careful to perform all of the duties required by his religion. He was also distinguished for his integrity of conduct yet was not amiable, not known for personal friendship, and often appeared to be without sympathy. And even if one would dare die for a good man, like Jesus (see Matthew 19:16)— one who is beneficent, righteous, kind, winsome, always glad to do favors for others—while we were still sinners, shaking our fists at God, hostile, antagonistic, plotting something harmful and deadly against God and His kingdom, He sent His only begotten Son to make peace with us. Not just to make peace, but to reconcile us, to put us back in a relationship—an intimate, friendly, fatherly relationship with God.

Oh, that is so powerful and precious to me! Not only is there this state of friendship and union with God, but there is much more, according to Romans 5:10, 11. There Paul said that while we were enemies of God, pious pretenders of faith, making a lie against the truth (see James 3:14), we were reconciled to God through the death of His Son; and much more than that, we shall and are being saved by His life.

This thrills me. I'm excited about this glorious truth that you and I are not only at peace with God and are reconciled with Him because He's God and He's good, but also we are saved already and are being saved now. No matter what is going on, no matter how you feel about yourself, this salvation is not dependent on you. Whether you are Jew or Gentile, rich or poor, male or female, this salvation is for all and it is free. All we have to do is say, "Yes, Lord!"

I'm excited about this! Do you know why? Because I remember the days when I was an enemy and didn't believe there was any hope for me. I can't believe that God has given *me*, of all the undeserving people, life—eternal life, that precious gift through the death of

Jesus Christ. And not only has He done that to me, but God also saved some of the men in my past who hurt me and messed with my mind. The greatest revenge that God has taken against me and those who are still shaking their fists at Him, is that He reconciled us to Himself and saved us so that we must now live with one another as brothers and sisters, and with Him as our loving heavenly Father.

This is exciting news to me, but that's not where it stops. The Word says that we have peace with God. There are some who have no peace with God. They don't know that they are saved. They don't understand that this transaction has nothing to do with a denomination, a local church, or anything like that. We've said "Yes" to God and we've been justified and that's so in the records of heaven. Therefore, it behooves us now to believe it and act on it by living as though we are saved.

I used to live in Boston, where the winters were so cold and icy I needed thick coats, gloves, and galoshes to protect myself against the weather. Now I live in California and don't need those thick, heavy winter coats anymore. When God has given us salvation, we don't need to wrap ourselves in human-made coats of fig leaves and fake feathers to protect us from the cold, horrible state of sin because we have the righteousness of Christ. His robe, though invisible, is wrapped around us and keeps us warm, whole and healthy.

Second, the results of justification by faith that cause us to *"exult in hope of the glory of God"* (Romans 5:2b). This is how I understand it. Romans 3:23 says *"all have sinned and fall short of the glory of God"* and all of us have felt that. There has never been a day that passes during which I did not feel like I have come short of the glory of God. But thank God for the cross of Jesus Christ that reminds me that salvation has nothing to do with how I feel about myself, but what God has done for you and me. For *"while we were still sinners"* falling short of the glory of God, Christ died for us and *"much more then, having now been justified by His blood, we shall be saved from the wrath of God through Him."*

Can you see how many times the apostle Paul has been trying to impress upon us that we're saved? Do you believe that you are saved? I am a saved woman. I may be lost to the world, but I am saved to Jesus Christ! If you believe and accept Him, you are saved. It says in Romans 5:2 that we should exult in the hope and the hope is that which we cannot see. We've been consumed by the carnal nature, which is the root. It has produced acts of sin, bearing fruit in us. But according to the amazing words in this passage, while we were still sleeping with the enemy, while still bearing the fruits that are the result of sleeping with the enemy, Jesus Christ died for us.

Amazing grace! God died in our place to save us from the second death because He loved us so much. What kind of love is this, O my soul, O my soul? What kind of love is this that someone would die for me when I was at my worst, when I can hardly find someone to live with me when I'm at my best? It is amazing grace! It does not matter what your nationality or rationality, because this hope is for all of us. If you've ever doubted or felt uncertain about God's love, remember this, He loved you when you turned from Him, so how much more is He going to love you now that you have turned to Him? That's what the apostle Paul was trying to communicate, then and now. If God could send His Son to die for us while we were His enemies, imagine what He will do for us now that we are His friends! He will live for us! He will overcome the second death and resurrect Himself from the grave so that He can live for and with us. That's how much more He will do. Awesome. So how much more will we exult in hope? We may not be able to see it or understand it, but we can believe it and live in a state of exultation for the hope He has given us.

Third, the resources of justification by faith that empower us to *"also exult in our tribulations, knowing that tribulation brings about perseverance; and perseverance, proven character; and proven character, hope, and hope does not disappoint, because the love of God has been poured out within the hearts through the Holy Spirit who was given to us"* (Romans 5:3). What an amazing amount of resources to sustain us and maintain our fledgling faith until Jesus comes!

Let me try to put this in perspective by painting a word picture of our condition before we received the gift of justification by faith, so that we can truly appreciate the resources we have been given since the change or reconciliation took place. To accomplish this, let us reflect on the statement "For while we were still helpless, at the right time Christ died for the ungodly." The Greek *asthenown*, translated as helpless, literally means sick, feeble, weak, diseased, impotent, under the power of sin. Can we get any worse than that? This means that while we were more helpless than anyone can imagine, at the right moment, at the right time appointed by God, at the time foretold by the prophets of old, at the foundation of the world when God foresaw our condition and was overcome with compassion, Christ died. For the good? Absolutely not! Christ came into the world when we needed Him most and died for the ungodly. Jesus died for the irreligious, the impious, the infidel, the reprobate, the disobedient, among whom we were all numbered as *"we too all formerly lived in the lusts of our flesh, indulging the desires of the flesh and of the mind, and were by nature children of wrath, even as the rest"* (Ephesians 2:3). Jesus Himself said, *"I did not come to call the righteous, but sinners!"* (Matthew 9:13b). Is that hope or what?

I don't understand divinity. My upbringing says we look out for the bright and beautiful in a society that gives their best to the good, the healthy, and the strong. But my God and yours comes while we are weak, feeble, and helpless to put His holy hands under our lives and lift us up to heavenly places where He alone rightfully belongs. Then He gives us the Holy Spirit, the Ultimate Resource, so that we may rejoice, exult in our tribulations, knowing that it brings about perseverance, proven character, and hope. Let us look at each of these words to find the fullness of meaning that the apostle Paul provided in this passage.

The word "tribulation" or "trouble" is a very familiar one to this generation. Jesus said that in the last days of earth's history, *"there will be a great tribulation, such as has not occurred since the beginning of the world until now, nor ever shall."* As a result of that prophecy, citizens of both the religious and secular societies have been bracing themselves for that unimaginable, cataclysmic event. In fact, as I look around my world, I am haunted by these words of William Shakespeare: "By the itching of my fingers, by the pricking of my thumbs, something wicked this way comes." Paul promises that this experience will be multipled when he said "tribulations." This literally means pressures, crushing experiences, trouble and trials, oppressions and afflictions of the emotional, physical, and mental kind. In fact, the only people who are not experiencing some kind of tribulation right now are the dead ones.

When we are insulted, verbally abused, falsely accused, persecuted for the sake of righteousness (see Matthew 5:10, 11), that's tribulation. The apostles, the ambassadors of the early Christian church, rejoiced that they were counted worthy to suffer the tribulations, according to Acts 5:41. The Bible tells us that in these last days, believers are going to suffer tribulations, but because we are justified by faith we can rejoice, exult, and glory in and through our tribulations! We can grit our teeth and say, "The world may kill this body, but Jesus Christ has already preserved my soul!"

Paul is saying to you, ambassadors (see 2 Corinthians 5:21) and apostles, *"rejoice, exult, glory"* in your tribulations because you have been justified by faith through grace! Exult, knowing that tribulation brings about perseverance. This is not a passive sitting back, wringing your hands while every kind of indignity is done to you. The Greek word *hupomone* is almost invariably rendered as patience that grows out of tremendous trials. It also means endurance under undeserved chastisement and afflictions.

Not long ago I experienced what I was to later put in this category of tribulation. One member of my pastoral team, Pastor Larry Christoffel, began to have some very successful Sabbath seminars.

He came up with the idea of utilizing the expertise of lay leaders to present seminars on parenting, spiritual gifts, dealing with difficult people, low self-esteem and many more. To our surprise, many attended these seminars the first quarter. The second quarter, he decided to expand the presentations to Sundays, using the same philosophy that appeared in the brochures for the Sabbath seminars. He changed the day to Sunday on the front of the brochure, but forgot that there was a reference of Sabbath in the philosophical statement. The brochures were printed and passed out before he noticed the error.

One Sabbath, a visitor came to Campus Hill Church when these Sunday Seminar brochures were included in the bulletin. This person is a member of the ultra-conservative, legalistic branch of "anything you can do I can do better" religious right in our denomination. She took the brochures, spent her money to photocopy and do a mass mailing to other hysterical Adventists, pointing out that I was promoting Sunday as the Sabbath. Not one phone call was made to verify the information before it was plastered over the Internet, along with some other slanderous statements.

I was very hurt when I went to speak at a camp meeting that summer and was set upon by a bunch of zealous people who lacked the facts but demanded to know by what right I had done such a terrible thing. I was verbally abused by this angry mob that refused to give me an opportunity to explain the simple error which was the basis of their consternation.

I was able to survive that occasion and later experiences of hurt because I remembered that Jesus said, *"An hour is coming for everyone who kills you to think that he is offering service to God"* (John 16:2b). This is the *"patience of the saints"* who keep the commandments of God and their faith in Jesus Christ (Revelation 14:12). They come by it honestly, one day at time, and they rejoice through their tribulations that God counts them worthy to partake in this privilege which brings about patience.

Patience brings about proven, tested character. Romans 8:28 says, *"And we know that God causes all things to work together for good to those who love God, to those who are called according to His purpose."* Our characters are being tested by the persecutions and problems we encounter. If we break under them, we realize that we have been sleeping with the enemy instead of resting with our forever Friend, Jesus Christ our Lord. It was through the testing of his faith that Abraham's character was proven. When God commanded him to take his only son, his beloved boy Isaac, and make a sacrifice of him (see Genesis 22:2), Abraham was faced with a pressure greater than any human being had experienced. He did not consult with human flesh, his own insights, or the sympathies of others, which would have convinced him that he was crazy to think God would ask such a thing of him. He obeyed immediately. Like Christ, Abraham patiently endured this test of his faith and was found faithful by God. Oswald Chambers, in his book on Genesis entitled *Not Knowing Where*, said that the very nature of faith is that it must be tried, for faith untried is only ideal while faith tried is actual and real.

Patience brings hope. The Greek word for hope is *elpis*. The very sound of it is promising. It means favorable and confident expectation relating to the unseen and the future. It describes the happy anticipation of good things. The most frequent and significant usage throughout the New Testament expresses that Jesus Christ is our hope. Added to this meaning is the Old Testament's meaning, to wait on tiptoes, which I'm convinced the apostle Paul was pondering as he penned this irresistible promise that hope does not disappoint. Because we have been justified by faith, and believe that while we were still sinners—sick, helpless, angry with God—He saved us, we can look with great expectations and assurance to be delivered out of the tribulations and mistreatments, out of this planet that is being consumed by sin. He has rescued us out of the destructive world of sin so we can look with hope for the ultimate deliverance at the second coming of Christ. The good news is that this hope does not and will not disappoint.

I consider myself a wordsmith. In fact, some of my friends often describe me as such. I believe I am that, not only because I love to make old, dead words come alive with new meaning but also because I do not take even the simplest word for granted. I spend an inordinate amount of time studying the history of words, particularly those that are used in the Bible. The technical word for the study of words is etymology, and I smile with pleasure as I address myself as an etymologist. You will note that I like to take words and break them down to the original meaning so that we can appropriately extrapolate meaning for our time and day.

I have said all this to say that I could not pass by the word *disappoint* when I read it in the Greek, because the apostle deliberately used the word *kataischuno.* It is composed of two words, *kata*—"out of" or "pertains to," among other things, and *aischuno*—"to shame" or "to have feelings of fear".

The idea in this promise is that, just as your justification was surely accomplished at Calvary with the death and resurrection of Jesus Christ and you have accepted it as a done deal by faith, so also you may glory in your tribulations when they come. For in the same way Jesus rose from the dead and ascended into heaven in the sight of more than five hundred witnesses, He will come again (see Acts 1:11). We can rejoice, knowing that our hope will not be put to shame. It will not be dishonored or confounded. We should not be ashamed of our sufferings, no matter what form they take. They may be unexpected illness, betrayal by family or friends, disunity in the body of believers, or loss of dignity by leaders in your denomination. Our hope, Jesus' promise that He would be with us always, even to the bitter end of this evil age (Matthew 28:20b) will not be dishonored or cause us shame. The *agape,* unconditional love of God has been poured out within our hearts. The Holy Spirit was given to us to assure us that everything will come true as promised! (see 2 Corinthians 1:19b, 20, 22).

The Holy Spirit is poured out majestically, magnificently, and magnanimously within our hearts. This reminds me of a story I heard about a man who went shopping in a commissary on the army base. While he was shopping he picked up two or three items for himself. When he went to the cash register to check out his items, he saw behind him a lady with several children dragging her down, pulling at her with their diverse and various needs. She pushed an overladen cart toward the register. He noticed that she was checking her few dollars in an old, dirty, soiled-looking purse as she examined her overstocked cart with that look I used to have when I was in college and penniless. (That look that says, "I need all of these things, but I don't have enough to pay for it. Which one will I take out before I'm embarrassed by the cashier, who has to subtract what I can't afford and hold up those who are behind me in the line?") As the stranger stood there, feeling compassion for the mother, the cashier told him that there was a bowl of tickets and the winning ticket would pay for all the groceries. He looked at the mother with the overfull cart and thought he should give her the chance to try for that blessing, but the cashier insisted that he take his turn first.

So he reached in and reluctantly pulled out a ticket and to his surprise, he had the winning ticket. Here he was, with only three items, and there was that lady with all her bedraggled, hungry, crying children and she would not get a chance to have her groceries paid for. So thinking on his feet, the stranger turned to the lady and said with an engaging smile, "Honey, you're not going to believe it, we won! Darling, come, hurry and help me put the things on the counter so that the cashier can take care of them! We won! We won!"

That poor lady was amazed, but she did not stop to argue that he was a stranger. She quickly accepted the gift and got all of her groceries paid for by the generous gesture of a stranger. When she went out into the parking lot, she covered him with kisses of gratitude. To every believer, it is the same with justification by faith;

we can't pay for it. It's a free, undeserved gift from God.

We have our baggage of original sin (the root), compounded by the innumerable resulting acts (or fruits), and it's too much for us, we can't pay for it. We don't have enough resources. But the Son of God appeared, a stranger to us, for we were still the enemies of His Father. Even though He had no sin, He was the winner (see Philippians 2:5-11). He paid our debt—in full. After His cruel crucifixion, He overcame the great enemy, the second death, and could be heard shouting to the universe that victorious cry, "*Tetelestai,*" which means, "paid in full." Or to us who are justified by faith, "Honey, we've won!" We can exult, we can glory, we can rejoice!

---

1. Archibald Thomas Robertson, *Word Pictures in the New Testament* (Baker Book House, 1990), 494.

2. Ibid.

3. Ibid.

4. Oswald Chambers, *Not Knowing Where* (Discovery House, 1989), 72, 73.

5. Ibid.

6. Ibid.

7. Ibid., 77.

8. Ibid., 129.

9. William E. Vine, *Vine's Expository Dictionary of Old and New Testament Words* (Thomas Nelson, 1997), 223.

10. Ibid.

Chapter 4

armed and extremely dangerous

The late Corrie Ten Boom was a woman of small stature who stood tall in the power of God. She not only had the distinction of surviving the brutality of the dreaded Ravensbruck death camp in Nazi Germany, but she returned to that place to share the love, forgiveness, and acceptance of God with some of the very guards who tortured her and took the lives of many members of her family.

In one of her testimonies, she told that while a prisoner at Ravensbruck, she and her sister were forced to live in barracks infested with lice. It was such a bad infestation that even the most vicious guard was afraid of entering their cells. One night, as other prisoners were being dragged to their deaths, the sisters were being mercilessly bitten by an incredible swarm of lice. Corrie Ten Boom tried to pray but could not concentrate because her body was burning with the bites of the swarm of lice. They were like a pestilence. Through all this, her sister was thanking God for the lice as she sang praises of gratitude. Finally, in frustration, Corrie asked her, "Why are you thanking God for these lice? They are sucking the life out of us!"

"If we didn't have these lice, the guards would have already come and taken us to our death," her sister replied. When she heard that, Corrie immediately began to sing and thank the Lord for the lice. She realized that the Lord had graciously sent the plague of lice to protect them from the gas chambers.

Sometimes God uses the weirdest armor to preserve our lives and protect us from death. Sometimes, He uses armor that we think may be taking our lives, but is really protecting us from the devil's diabolical and destructive ways. The apostle Paul was in a similar situation when he wrote the book of Ephesians, which many scholars think of as more like a sermon than a letter. Paul wrote this and the letter to the Philippians, known as the love letter to the church, while he was a prisoner in Rome. There, he was chained to a soldier most of the time because of his reputation of miraculously unfastening his chains (see Acts 16:22-30). While he was so detained, instead of whining and complaining, the aging apostle sang psalms and penned this powerful letter of exhortation and encouragement about God's promised redemption. Paul especially underscored the greatness of the purpose of God, the glory of Christ's high calling, the gift of eternal life to those who follow Christ and adhere to His standards for personal and public living, and the importance of healthy relationships in Christ. At the end of that strong support for those who follow Christ, the apostle reminded his readers that because of the spiritual warfare being waged by Satan this life cannot be lived without the power and presence of God.

In Ephesians 6 he ends his letter by saying:

Finally, be strong in the Lord, and in the strength of His might. Put on the full armor of God, that you may be able to stand firm against the schemes of the devil. For our struggle is not against flesh and blood, but against the rulers, against the powers, against the world forces of this darkness, against the spiritual forces of wickedness in the heavenly places. Therefore, take up the full armor of God, that you may be able to resist in the evil day, and having done everything, to stand firm. Stand firm therefore, having girded your loins with truth, and having put on the breastplate of righteousness, and having shod your feet with the preparation of the gospel of peace; in addition to all, taking up the shield of faith with which you will be able to extinguish all the flaming missiles of the evil one. And take the helmet of salvation, and the sword of the Spirit, which is the word of God. With all prayer and petition pray at all times in the Spirit, and with this in view, be on the alert with all perseverance and petition for all the saints. . . . (Ephesians 6:10-18).

Be strong in the Lord, not in yourself, but in the strength of His might! Remember, we're told that it's *" 'not by might nor by power, but by My Spirit,' says the Lord of hosts"* (Zechariah 4:6), that we are able to accomplish these things and overcome the world that would destroy us. Be strong in the Lord and stop walking around as though the devil is the only one on earth with power and unlimited abilities against which we are helpless to survive. I believe that God is really tired of seeing us cringing in the presence of evil, whining, "O, the devil is on my back." Satan can only be in one place at one time, and that bad old boy has bigger figs to pick than us. But supposing that were not the case. Have we forgotten that Jesus Christ has given us power and authority over the devil and his evil compatriots?

Let me begin with what I call the undergraduate commencement ceremony for His disciples, before they began their ministry, as reported in Luke 9:1, 2:

And He called the twelve together, and gave them power and authority over all the demons, and to heal diseases. And He sent them out to proclaim the kingdom of God and to perform healing.

When I wrote my dissertation for the Doctor of Ministry degree, I did an entire chapter on this much-overlooked concept of authority versus power in practical Christianity. I was amazed at how many books and articles have been and are being written on this subject, yet in twenty-one years of organized religion, I had never heard a sermon on the topic. For example, the word *authority* comes from the Greek word *exousia*, which means the ability to perform an action. It is usually used to describe the inalienable right to legally exercise power and strength. John used this word in his Gospel, when he said, *"But as many as received Him [Jesus], to them He gave the [legal] right [authority] to become children of God"* (John 1:12). This is particularly interesting and important since he added, *"even to those . . . who were born not of blood, nor of the will of the flesh, nor of the will of man, but of God."* Have you ever asked yourself, as I have, why was it important to be born again and also be given legal adoption (as in Romans 8:15), to be a member of the family of God?

One day I was reading through an out-of-print book on Roman jurisprudence regarding the trial of Jesus. The author proposed that in the time of Jesus, freeborn children could be sold into slavery if their parents should lose everything and need to use them as collateral. When the Roman Empire took over the governance of Judah, the Romans instituted a law that prohibited a slave who had been freed, or the slave's children, from being sold into slavery again, rare as that might be. To ensure that this was adhered to, the freed slave would be given a certificate of adoption, the *exousia*, by the one who gave him his freedom. This meant that the former slave could not be sold again.

John borrowed this concept of adoption, also popularized by Paul, to explain how doubly blessed believers are. Not only are we born again by the Spirit of God (see John 1:12, 13), but also, just in case the enemy tries to convince us that we may be sold into his slavery again, we receive the *exousia*, legal right, the certificate of adoption, to be part of our heavenly Father's family. When the accuser tries to convince us otherwise, we can say, "Forget it, buster! For when the Son has set you free, you are free indeed!" (see John 8:36).

Authority is a gift from God that cannot be secured from a religious institution or from a great family heritage. It cannot be caught or bought. It cannot be earned or learned. It cannot be grasped by greedy people or won by works of righteousness. It is as unique as salvation. God-given authority, when received and in operation, is awesome. Jesus was always being asked by His detractors, *"By what authority are you doing these things?"* (Matthew 21:23).

Contrary to some popular beliefs, authority is not self-confidence. It is a profoundly deep, inner sense that one is the daughter or son of God with all the rights and responsibilities. Paul said it best in Romans 8:14-17:

> *For all who are being led by the Spirit of God, these are sons of God. For you have not received a spirit of slavery leading to fear again, but you have received a spirit of adoption as sons by which we cry out, "Abba! Father!" The Spirit Himself bears witness with our spirit that we are children of God, and if children, heirs also, heirs of God and fellow-heirs with Christ, if indeed we suffer with Him in order that we may also be glorified with Him.*

Power, from the Greek word *dunamis*, the source of our word *dynamite*, means being able to do or be capable of something. It is noteworthy that one can have power without authority. When power manifests itself without authority, it is always extrinsic, manipulative, repressive, and oppressive. On the other hand, the power that is the natural outgrowth of the charismatic (Holy Spirit–given) gift of authority is always compassionate, liberating, edifying, and redemptive.

Not only did Jesus give His disciples power and authority at the beginning of their ministry, but also after their return from their first mission without Him, He reminded them of this. He said, *"Behold, I have given you authority to tread upon serpents and scorpions, and over all the power of the enemy, and nothing shall injure you"* (Luke 10:19). At the end of His life on earth, Jesus again reminded His disciples that He had given them this gift. In His final instructions to them He said, *"All authority has been given to Me in heaven and on earth,"* implying that He was giving that authority to the disciples when He continued in the same breath to give them the great commission in Matthew 28:18-20.

Just in case someone may argue, saying, "Well, that gift was only given to the twelve disciples," please note that John repeated it for the believers who would suffer the trials and tribulations of the last days. Under the directives of God the Son, with the inspiration of God the Holy Spirit, the beloved apostle was instructed to write to those who would live in the last days, when the devil would come down like a roaring lion, *"having great wrath, knowing that he has only a short time,"* to remind them that they have God's authority and power. Note the following in Revelation 12:10:

1. Salvation (*soter*) is the spiritual and eternal deliverance granted immediately by God to those who accept His conditions of repentance and faith in the Lord Jesus Christ, in whom and through whom alone it is to be obtained. The word *soteriology* describes the study of this salvation. This salvation comes from God alone, as opposed to *sozo,* which describes the material and temporal deliverance from danger, suffering, and ill health. The New Testament writers sometimes used *sozo* to describe salvation. This word was originally used to describe someone who was in good health and conveys the concept of salvation being wholistic, in that those who are saved are transformed in every aspect of their being.

2. Power (*dunamis*), as we have learned, is an external demonstration of one's connectedness to God as son or daughter, so that we may dare to do what our Elder Brother, Jesus Christ, did when confronted with demons (see Mark 5:1-20). This power is given to believers so that we may stand firm against the wiles of the devil.

3. The kingdom (*basileia*) of God describes the sovereignty, royal power, and dominion of God's reign and realm. God's kingdom, now invisible, operates in such a manner that those who belong to it are in the world but are not of the world. One day soon, when Christ comes and inaugurates this literal empire of God, we will have the privilege of living with Him forever and ever, as obedient citizens unshackled from the power of sin.

4. Authority (*exousia*), the legal right from Jesus Christ that makes us know without a shadow of doubt that we are children of God with the rights, privileges, and responsibilities to so live. Because of this, even if we are intimidated by the strong man known as the devil, we will still be able to stand firm against the principalities and powers and evil elements of the air.

When Paul said *"be strong in the Lord,"* he knew of what he spoke. He knew that we have inherited that authority and power which not only gives us the privilege of calling God "Daddy" [Abba], but also we have been given confidence in the face of evil because we are Abba's sons and daughters.

Put on the full armor of God. Paul was chained to Roman soldiers for three years, and many times they would be dressed in only half of their armor. He soon discovered that half-dressed soldiers tended to have a false sense of security. Because of their training, they thought they were as invincible when half-armored as when fully dressed for battle. Believers who approach the enemy half-prepared often run the same risk. Thus the command to put on the *full* armor of God. The enemy can see when we are partially prepared. He knows our vulnerable points, our Achilles' heels, having observed us for thousands of years. He will shoot his arrows to paralyze or kill us. Thus, in order to be strong in the Lord, we must put on the *full armor of God.* We cannot have one foot in the world and the other in Christ, for that is being half-dressed. We cannot decide what portion of the assigned armor is OK to leave off or to wear. No soldier in an army would dare say to his or her commander, "I don't feel like wearing this or that today." They would be put in the brig! Yet, day after day believers say to our great Commander-in-Chief, by their neglect or rejection of His holy instructions, "I can get through the land mines of the day without prayer." We are kidding ourselves! The sooner we obey this instruction, the better life will be for all who are called by the name of Jesus Christ, who never leave home without His full armor.

Be strong in the Lord that you may be able to stand firm. Standing firm is not just repeated (verse 13), but in the word coined and popularized by the victorious Chicago Bulls basketball champions, is "threepeated" (verse 14). The Old Testament writers, such as Isaiah, are famous for their poetic parallelism, in which they would use a word with a slightly different sound that had the same meaning to emphasize or highlight a point. Paul wants to make sure that we do not miss the point he is making in the passage, so he "threepeats" the phrase "stand firm."

"Stand firm" was a Roman military order. They could not back down or retreat, even under threat of death from their adversary. If a soldier stood firm and a whole legion stood firm, they were invincible. The enemy could not break through. The Roman Empire advanced by this tactic. Imagine the advance of God's kingdom if His army would "stand firm."

There is no other generation that needs to hear that message more than this Teflon-coated, morally degenerate group, whose passion seems to be the indulgence in the ongoing orgy of transgression. We fall for just about anything, and as a result we stand firm for little or nothing. So Paul is reminding us that we need the full armor of God in order to be able to stand firm and not slip, though the heavens fall. When we meet unexpected obstacles of temptation, or a rough theological or religious terrain created by the devil through human agents that would cause others to fall, we stand firm. If the evil agents of the devil should come and threaten to take away your children unless you deny Jesus Christ as your personal Savior, you can stand firm.

When I first became a Christian, I was ablaze with that fiery first love. I remember reading a book by June Strong called *Project Sunlight,* which gave some vivid details about the trials and tribulations to be encountered by those living in the final hours of earth's history. Even though it was fiction, it seemed so real to me that I internalized it. My dreams were influenced by nightmarish images, and my waking hours were filled with fear or paranoia. The fear became so intense that on one occasion I took my son aside and held him tightly in my arms, whispering how much I loved him as I covered him with kisses. Even though he was about seven years old, he must have felt that something was wrong, because he kept asking me if everything was all right as he tried to wriggle free from my tight grip on him.

Finally, I held him on my lap and looked intensely in his eyes as I said, "Mommy wants you to be sure that she loves you. Do you know that I love you with all my heart?" His little head bobbed up and down in the affirmative as tears began to roll down my cheeks. I said, "I'm really glad you know that I love you, for there is going to come a day when some wicked people will try to take you from me. They might even put a gun to your head to force me to deny Jesus Christ. So I'm telling you now that I love you so that if and when it happens and I don't deny Christ, you will remember that it's because I love you and Jesus."

Wow! That was some heavy conversation for a child. I must have been out of my mind. Please don't try this experiment with or without a mature adult present! I would surely handle things differently now that by grace I am a more mature Christian. The point that I want to make is that in those early years, I was trying to stand firm, crude though the effort was. Today, I'm even more determined to stand firm, and the only way I know how is to put on the full armor of God so that we may be able to resist the devil.

Be strong in the Lord that you may be able to stand firm against the schemes of the devil. The word *scheme* means a method, craft, deceit or wile of the devil. We are not to stand firm against each other, but against the deceitfulness of the devil that comes to us in myriad forms, the most pernicious of which are our own sympathies, passions, and lusts, according to James 4:1-3.

I can' t help noting that Paul said we should put on the full armor of God and stand firm, not fight. It is important to note the difference, for too often some of us seem to believe, by our choices and actions, that the great controversy is between us and the devil, when the Bible teaches that it is between God and Satan or good and evil. Therefore, when the devil begins to shoot his bullets, we are covered in the armor, and even if we should be hit, we may die, but we will not perish, for the armor is Christ's righteousness, which is sin-proofed against anything the enemy may throw at us.

One of the most successful schemes of the devil is the need we Christians have to vindicate ourselves when accused or attacked. We forget that God does not try to vindicate Himself against the accusations of Satan. He also said, *"Vengeance is Mine, I will repay"* (Romans 12:19b). This has helped me immensely as I remind myself that believers have eternity and can wait for God to take care of our accuser. That does not mean that we just lie down like wimps and let the devil and his army of evil spirits walk over us. Absolutely not! We must remember that the battle isn't ours but God's. Let us do what King Jehoshaphat did in the story reported in 2 Chronicles 20.

The ancient enemies of Israel, the Ammonites and Moabites, descendants of the two incestuous sons of Lot and his daughters, came to make war against Jehoshaphat, the King of Judah. When the king heard that *"a great multitude"* was coming against him, he became very afraid, and instead of forming alliances with the other heathens around him, he did what we must in our times of crisis. He *"turned his attention to seek the Lord; and proclaimed a fast throughout all Judah"* (2 Chronicles 20:1-4). After the king prayed, the Lord sent the following message: *"Listen all Judah and the inhabitants of Jerusalem and King Jehoshaphat. Thus says the Lord to you, 'do not fear or be dismayed because of this great multitude, for the battle is not yours but God's.' "* God replied to His people then as He is imploring now, "Tomorrow go down against them. Don't sit at home feeling sorry for yourself, wringing your hands and wishing you had never been born. Get down on your knees, then get up and go see what I'm going to do on your behalf!" Then God said something amazing. He said, *"You need not fight in this battle; [just] station yourselves [where you can get a good look], stand and see the salvation of the Lord on your behalf . . . do not fear or be dismayed; tomorrow go and face them, for the Lord is with you"* (2 Chronicles 20:15-17).

When did God act on His promise to win? When the people started praising, in advance! God inhabited the praises of His people, and He poured out salvation on them for their simple faith. Joyful anticipation leads to victory. The battle isn't ours or about us. We need not fight in this battle. All we have to do is to put on the full armor of God and go out into the world, and get involved in it without being part of it. God knows that we are a neck-craning generation. We cannot pass an accident without satisfying our curiosity, which is often stronger than our compassion. God knows believers are a bunch of people who love to gape and gaze like the rest of the world. He knew that if He told us to put on our full armor and go sit in the sanctuary, we would get very frustrated. No soldier gets dressed in battle fatigues to sit in the commander's office.

He or she prepares to stand and fight on the front lines. So God said, put on the full armor and go out and stand, and watch and see the salvation the Lord is going to bring on our behalf.

I love that kind of stuff. I don't have to fight; all I have to do is what I used to do when I was in high school. Back then I was an instigator, which should surprise no one who knows my temperament. If I saw two children fighting, I would hide behind the biggest, tallest person and scream directives like, "Punch him harder!"

Nowadays, since I've been saved by grace (and it took *a lot* of grace to save me), I hide behind Jesus. When the devil comes, instead of getting into a brawl with him, I call upon Jesus. When Jesus comes, and He always does, I hide under the shadow of His wings (see Psalm 91), in the cleft of that Rock (see 1 Corinthians 10:4), and I shout, "Hit him, Jesus, punch him and knock him out! Bite him—and not just bite his ears off, but his head off!"

Believe me, before it's over, I have an amazing sense of relief, for I know these two things: one, that the battle is not mine, but God's, and two, Jesus Christ has already won the fight and it's finished. I would be foolish to get in a huddle with the one whom the referee has already counted out. No one is more vicious than a loser who has already been counted out as Satan has.

For our struggle is not against flesh and blood, but against the rulers, against the powers, against the world forces of this darkness, against spiritual forces of wickedness in the heavenly places. The word for struggle also means to wrestle and describes two contenders wrestling until one hurls the other to the mat and pins him there, as I saw demonstrated on television. Now I am the *most* frustrating person to watch TV with. I am nosy and need to know everything that is happening on the other stations, so I sit with the remote control and, every few seconds (not minutes), flip through the channels. Thus, I watch a variety of programs and none. One day as I was surfing the channels, I happened on a World Wrestling

Federation program, and I saw a huge masked man pick up an even bigger opponent high above his head, spin around with him, slam him to the mat, and fall on him. It was a gruesome sight of fat and flab wrestling for freedom from the fall. It came to me then that that is the word, to struggle or wrestle, the apostle Paul chose to use to remind us that we are not in a fight or wrestling match with flesh and blood, with our own sin-filled flesh or that of others. We are up against the cunning devices and wiles of Satan and his evil angels, the one third that fell from heaven (see Revelation 12:4). They hate God's people as much as they hate each other. In their intense competition to outdo each other, they throw storms, hurricanes, and other natural disasters as well as diseases that injure, cripple, and kill people, including believers. But God said, "Don't be afraid of the devil's overwhelming manifestations of power. You have unlimited, eternal, divine authority and power over the devil and his demons' limited, soon-to-end principality."

Notice that the apostle repeats himself. He says that we must *take up the full armor of God [he may have been reflecting on Isaiah 59:17], that you may be able to resist in the evil day, and having done everything, to stand firm"* (verse 13). Paul tells us to prepare to be armed and extremely dangerous, in case the devil's volleys, aimed at God, hit us. To convey this, Paul borrowed the imagery from his daily experience of being chained to the soldiers. He listed not only the armor, but also the way in which we should put it on, in the exact order in which the soldiers put on the various parts of the panoply, so that we can be believers who are known to be appropriately armed, and extremely dangerous.

Stand firm, therefore, having girded your loins with truth. In the Greek, this literally means to "take your stand therefore, having girded around your own loins [not that of your brother or sister, president or preacher, but your own personal loins] with truth, with the facts that cannot escape notice."

Nowadays, most people wear girdles to hide unwanted ruffles

and cover up undesirable ridges that seem to multiply around the middle with each passing month. In antiquity, the girdle had many purposes, such as a fastening for women's undergarments or as a large belt or cummerbund wrapped tightly around the waist to hold up men's long outer garments like the ones Peter wore (see John 21:18). Roman soldiers also wore long outer garments as part of their ordinary, everyday clothes. They girded themselves, then pulled the long tunics up over the girdle until it was about knee high, to restrain the garments and give them freedom of movement so they would not trip over them when running.

In the natural sense, the loin is the hips and pelvic region, which is so delicate we bestow abundant honor upon it (see 1 Corinthians 12:23), yet it is also specially regarded as the seat of physical strength and generative power. Metaphorically, as used in this text, according to *Vine's Expository Dictionary of Old and New Testament Words*, it is "bracing up oneself so as to maintain perfect sincerity and reality as the counteractive in Christian character against hypocrisy and falsehood."

Wow, that's a mouthful! But I'm sure you get the idea as to why the spiritual loins, that place capable of producing or creating the offspring called authority or power, the spiritual gifts, needs to be girded about, wrapped tightly around with truth. What is truth? Is it merely personal honesty? No! It is one honest Person(Jesus Christ our Lord) who announced, *"I am the way, and the truth and the life; and no one comes to the Father, but through Me"* (John 14:6, emphasis added). The apostle was saying that we are to wrap ourselves tightly in Jesus Christ, the living truth, so that we will not trip over the flowing robes of our right doctrines, as do so many legalists who fail to fall at the foot of the cross.

And having put on the breastplate of righteousness. The breastplate was a corselet, or suit of light armor, that protected the body on both sides from the neck to the middle. Our English word *thorax*, the chest part of the body between the neck and abdomen where the heart and lungs are contained in a bony cage of vertebrae, ribs, and sternum, is also the Greek word for breastplate. It was the second piece of armor put on by the soldier, and was commonly called the heart guard, because it covered the heart, the most vital human organ.

Earlier Roman soldiers wore very broad leather and linen doublets fastened to the back of their tunics to avoid a spear-thrust into their hearts, but those were very uncomfortable and ill-fitting, and they made it difficult to move about adroitly. When Rome took over the governance of Judah, the Roman army lost many officers, killed by dagger-wielding freedom fighters. The soldiers were confronted with such an aggressive force of guerrillas that they had to redesign the breastplate to provide the same protection but in a way that conformed more to the shape of the body. It was made of metal or iron studs carefully and closely attached to the leather base that they affectionately revered as the heart guard.

The guerrillas of Judah were fierce and zealous. One of them even managed to join the twelve disciples of Jesus. No, it was not Simon the Zealot. He belonged to a political party of extremist Pharisees who were bitterly antagonistic toward the Roman government, including all of its representatives in Judah. But the Zealots plotted the political undermining and elimination of their enemies.

The guerrilla was Judas Iscariot. Some scholars suggest that he belonged to the Sicarii party, so designated by the Romans as the extremists in the Zealot movement. "Iscariot" was not his surname. It means, "man from Kerioth," the city from which he originated, believed to be in Judea, as well as "the assassin" or dagger carrier. These hated freedom fighters are mentioned by Josephus, the Jewish historian, as robbers and assassins. They carried a short, curved, and very sharp dagger, still popular with the Bedouins today, called the *sicarii*, well hidden under the folds of their cloak. Upon meeting the person targeted for assassination, usually a high-ranking person in the Roman army, the Iscariot would graciously greet the unsuspecting person with the customary kiss, and while kissing him on both cheeks, would deftly pull out the dagger and stealthily stab their opponent in the chest. It took a few seconds for the victim to collapse and die, giving the assailant enough time to slip away, undetected, in the bustle of a pilgrimage, feast, or gathering of a group of people. The Iscariots, as they were called by the Jews, and Sicariis by the Romans, shared an oath to commit suicide before divulging the secrets of their organization, if they were caught.[1]

When I discovered this information, it became clear to me what happened in the Garden of Gethsemane the night Judas appeared with the great multitude with swords[2] and clubs, provided by the chief priests and elders. Judas Iscariot kissed Jesus to betray Him to the Jewish officials. When he saw Judas kiss Jesus, Peter immediately drew his sword (see Matthew 26:47-56). Peter did that perhaps because he knew that Judas, being an Iscariot, was betraying Jesus and would pull out the sicarii and stealthily stab Jesus, so he quickly drew his sword to protect his Master. But when Jesus saw what Peter had done, he spoke firmly and rebuked his impulsive disciple, saying, *"Put your sword back into its place; for all those who take up the sword [as a weapon of murder] shall perish by the sword"* (Matthew 26:52).

The apostle Paul, in using the metaphor of the breastplate, was saying that we Christians need a heart-guard of righteousness by faith, a gift provided by none other than our caring Commander-in-Chief, Jesus Christ our Lord, who knew how the enemy assassin, Satan, targeted the hearts of His soldiers. We must put on the breastplate of righteousness so that we can guard our affections against the onslaught of temptations on the Internet and other opportunities on the increasingly high-tech information highways and byways; in the print and electronic entertainment media; but more than anything else, against the lusts of our own hearts (see James 4:1-3).

Having shod your feet with the preparation of the gospel of peace. The word *shod* means to furnish with footgear or to bind something, like sandals, underneath. Roman soldiers walked about barefooted in their homes, but when on duty or going into battle, they put on low half-boots (leather sandals with a strong sole and long straps that wrapped around their calves like greaves to steady their steps and allow unimpeded movement as they walked over the rough, uncertain Judean terrain).

The word *foot*, besides its literal meaning, is used here, by metonymy, to indicate motion and direction. This reminds me of Isaiah 52:7, which says, *"How lovely on the mountains are the feet of him who brings good news, who announces peace and brings good news of happiness, who announces salvation, and says to Zion, 'your God reigns!'"* How lovely is the movement and direction of those wearing the divinely furnished footwear, the gospel, as they traverse the rough and uneven mountains of this world, or the valleys of the shadow of death so uncertain and dangerous, yet they are steadily standing firm in Jesus Christ, whose gospel gives strength and support.

The gospel has taken on new meaning in this generation. The increasing interest in the gospel is evidence of the truth that our greatest need is the hope expressed in the gospel. Yet, if you should ask a group of Christians what is their definition or understanding of the gospel, most would be uncertain. Many would not be able to say what the gospel is, and the rest would give vague answers. So what is the gospel? The Greek word *evangel* is made up of *eu*, the prefix that means good, and *angello* to bring a message, news, or proclamation.

In an editorial in the June 1999 issue of *Christianity Today*, David Neff noted that "preliminary research showed that the gospel of justification by faith still has a high commitment among CT readers: 100 percent declared that it was 'essential for an evangelical to believe' that 'those whom God saves he justifies by faith through grace alone.'" Because of the findings of such a high commitment to the gospel, an article entitled "The Gospel of Jesus Christ: An Evangelical Celebration," drafted and confirmed by some of the leading evangelical scholars and leaders, was also included in the issue.

Notice the following excepts from the preamble that sum up some contemporary thought leaders' definition of the gospel.

> *The Gospel of Jesus Christ is news, good news; the best and most important news that any human being ever hears.*
>
> *This Gospel identifies Jesus Christ, the Messiah of Israel, as the Son of God and God the Son, the second Person of the Holy Trinity, whose incarnation, ministry, death, resurrection, and ascension fulfilled the Father's saving will. His death for sins and his resurrection from the dead are promised beforehand by the prophets and attested by eyewitnesses. In God's own time and God's own way, Jesus Christ shall return as glorious Lord and Judge of all (1 Thessalonians 4:13-18; Matthew 25:31, 32). He is now giving the Holy Spirit from the Father to all those who are truly his. The three Persons of the trinity thus combine in the world of saving sinners.*
>
> *This Gospel sets forth Jesus Christ as the living Savior, Master, Life and Hope of all who put their trust in him. . .*

The Bible defines the gospel from God's perspective and for man's understanding. First, God's perspective is announced and summarized in John 3:16-21 and reiterated in 1 John 3:16. There we are told that God's unconditional love for the universe (which needs to be brought or put in order or adorned), led Him to freely give His unique, unparalleled, incomparable Son, so that whoever (Jew or Gentile, oriental or occidental, rich or poor, male or female) is persuaded (by the offering of Himself as a sacrifice for sin) to place their confidence, trust and reliance in Him, should not perish (not die the death of sleep which we may all experience before the second coming of Christ) but not experience that permanent separation from God called the second death because of the gift of everlasting life.

Jesus Christ's life, death, resurrection, ascension into heaven, and His continued appeals to sinners and advocacy for saints, is the living gospel. The apostle Paul was and still is the greatest exponent of this truth. Therefore, to gain an understanding from a human perspective, we must turn to his summation of this most precious gift in 2 Corinthians 5:11-21. Look particularly at verse 21: *"He made Him who knew no sin [to be] sin on our behalf, that we might become the righteousness of God in Him."* Therefore, according to Romans 8:1, there is *now*—not yesterday, which has come and gone, or tomorrow, which is not promised to anyone—*"now no condemnation for those who are in Christ Jesus."* (Condemnation, remember, is the punishment of death demanded by the criminal law and the disability or handicap one carries through life as is designated by the civil law operating in the definition of sin.) Simply paraphrased, this is saying, "Now there is no second death for those who are in Christ Jesus. He took our punishment upon Himself."

The word translated as "preparation" has a secondary meaning in this context. The primary meaning is "readiness," and the secondary meaning is "firm footing or foundation," to which I think Paul was alluding when he wrote that we should have our feet shod with the preparation of the gospel of peace. What I understand him to be conveying to us is that having or being in readiness with the Gospel is the *only firm footing or foundation* that will make the believer's walk worthy of the testimony of Jesus Christ and help us *stand firm* on the side of God in the midst of the great controversy between good and evil. This will be evident by the restful wholeness, in Christ, of that person who is a work of salvation in progress, and the harmonious relationships they have with all others.

In addition to all [the above], taking up the shield of faith with which you will be able to extinguish all the flaming missiles of the evil one. The *thureos,* translated "shield," originally described the large stone that closed the entrance of a cave. Later *thureos* was used to describe the long, oblong, four-cornered shield that covered the whole man like a door to protect every part of his body. Lighter, smaller, oval-shaped shields were generally used at home, while large but thinner metal shields were used in parades. The one described in this text was the oblong shield of the Roman legionary, which was made of two wooden pieces glued together for curvature and covered with linen and calf leather. When soldiers came under missile attack from arrows or spears, they took cover as one unit, with shields together like a tortoise shell, thus repelling the deadly missiles.

We are in the midst of an unholy war, and the only way to survive is to take up, or receive to oneself, the shield of faith. Now, for some it may seem impossible to be expected to take up such a large object, but remember that it is done by faith, and to every believer God begins by giving a measure of faith (Romans 12:3). Then, as we grow in grace, the Holy Spirit generously lavishes spiritual gifts, which also include faith. It's like a bank doubling our money without us having to do anything. Now this shield of faith is not given to us to walk around boasting that "we have the truth," or to point out how wrong other believers are about things pertaining to justification, sanctification, and righteousness. The apostle said we should take up the shield of faith so that we will be able to extinguish and keep on extinguishing every volley of the flaming missiles fired at us by the evil one.

Now we must never forget how smart is the evil one. He operates like the opponents of the soldiers the apostle was using to describe this full armor we are to put on. When they went to war, they would build temporary housing—shacks of straw and wood gathered in the region. On many occasions, when they were on the front lines facing the enemy, they would fire volleys of flaming darts over the heads of the soldiers into their temporary barracks. These were arrows with a bituminous head that was lit and shot into the barracks so that they would instantly ignite roaring flames. The moment that happened, many of the soldiers would leave their positions of defense, and the protection of their shields, to run and put out the fire to save their barracks. As they ran, they became excellent targets for the enemy, who would shoot them in the back.

The devil is out there shooting some flaming darts at us, and we don't know where they're coming from or see them until they hit us. Sometimes he fires them into our places of safety and security, such as relationships with spouses, family, and friends. Other times he shoots us with the flaming darts of rumors into our places of employment or even our church congregation. When we see them going up in flames, we react in fear by abandoning our posts of protection behind the shield of faith to try to put out the raging fires. But the apostle assures us that we should not worry about those flaming missiles, because the Holy Spirit has built a garrison or a fort around us and is standing guard (see Philippians 4:7). No matter how bad or how tough the situation, no matter how straight the devil shoots, he cannot destroy your hope in Christ Jesus. Satan may be able to kill the body, but he cannot injure the soul that is placed in the hands of God (see Matthew 10:28).

In addition, this defense weapon we call the shield of faith has a miraculous property that allows it to reach up or out, as far as the fiery missiles fly, to extinguish them. I know that this works, because the enemy has tried to shoot my foundations and friendships full of flaming missiles. He almost succeeded, when I remembered one of my favorite old television programs, "Wonder Woman."

Now I am sure you're wondering how reflecting on Wonder Woman could save me from the flaming darts. Well, years ago, in the seventies, when this program was at its peak in popularity, I watched it faithfully, not because I was seeking or gaining any socially or spiritually redeeming values, but because I enjoyed it. I loved that Wonder Woman and dreamed of being like her, and guess what, now I am better than she could ever be! And so are you who take up the shield of faith.

Not only could Wonder Woman leap over tall buildings, fly through the air without wings, but she also could hold a baby in one hand with the telephone at her ear while she cooked and cleaned with the other. She was not only a foxy woman, but she had one great quality I dreamed of emulating. When she was sprayed by rapidly repeating bullets, she crossed her hands at the wrist, and her oversized bracelets would act like a shield so that the bullets would ricochet without harming her. She would face the bullets without fear, as she stood firm and unmoved by the power of their sounds whistling through the air toward her.

When the devil begins to shoot his flaming darts of temptations, I just stand up like Wonder Woman. Sometimes I even cross my hands at the wrist in the shape of the cross under which I take refuge from the volleys of the enemy. I take up the invisible shield of faith, and on every occasion those flaming missiles are extinguished.

The shield of faith sometimes functions like a fire hose that gushes out the waters, those regenerating showers of the Holy Spirit (see Titus 3:5), to put out the fires of illness, death, divorce, and despair already started by the flaming missiles. As long as I stay under the protection of this shield, I am never burned, even if I'm bruised, and neither is my hope destroyed. Yes, I have been bowed low, brought to my knees. I've fallen flat on my face from the impact of the flaming missiles of selfishness, doubt, fear, the enemy of faith, disappointment, and all those that burn and destroy. But I can testify authentically, with great joy, that I have never been broken, for I am safe in the arms of Jesus. So go ahead and shoot me, Mr. Devil, for I am Wonder Woman when I take up my shield of faith. In fact, I don't leave home without it!

Take the helmet of salvation. The Roman soldiers were given bronze helmets that provided protection for their neck, cheeks, and chin. These were slung on a strap during marches and were put on only at the beginning of a battle. But when they took over the region of Judah, the freedom fighters, who were very familiar with the terrain, would wage guerrilla warfare by ambushing the soldiers. They sometimes hid on the brow of the hills and as the soldiers marched along the ravine, they would throw rocks on their heads. They killed hundreds of soldiers until the army began to wear their helmets for ordinary patrols.

Notice that Paul said we must take up and receive to ourselves the helmet (which covers our head) of salvation (*soter,* which comes from God alone). The head is the place where our minds, the seat of decision, is located. We need the mind, which directs the life-choices we make, covered with salvation. We must accept and wear the helmet, for it is a gift. We don't have to make our own. It is part of the divine panoply graciously provided for every believer. The helmet of salvation protects us from the power, presence, and penalty of sin.

And [take up] the sword of the Spirit which is the word of God. The word for sword denotes the small dagger discussed above. I might add that this dagger was also used by the men of that day for personal grooming such as clipping the nails and cutting the hair and beard. It was also used for the skinning of animals so that the pelts could be used for coats and other items of clothing. The sword as the Word of God is better explained in Hebrews 4:12, where we are told that *"the word of God is living and active and sharper than any two-edged sword [small dagger or knife], and piercing as far as the division of soul and spirit, of joints and marrow, and able to judge the thoughts and intentions of the heart."*

When I first read Jesus' declaration to His disciples, *"Do not think that I came to bring peace on earth; I did not come to bring peace, but a sword"* (Matthew 10:34), I was very disturbed by it. I had a hard time with such a violent statement from the One Isaiah described as the Prince of Peace, the One whom angels sang praises to at His birth, promising the beginning of peace on earth and goodwill among men and women. For a long time I wondered what this statement was doing in my Bible and why Jesus said it, until I learned about the dagger used as a symbol of the Word and its many powerful utilitarian purposes. In essence, the Word of God functions like the sharp dagger to clip away unwanted growth, to skin away the garments of sin, and to cut off unhealthy parts to preserve, by grace, whatever is good for God.

I know of four Greek words that are used for "the word of God." There is *logos,* which denotes the active expression of thought, not just the mere name of an object that is used as embodying a conception or idea such as in John 1:1. *Graphe,* often translated "Scripture," primarily denotes the Written Word of God (see 2 Timothy 3:16). *Gramma,* which means "a letter of the alphabet," is also used, but in some versions is translated as "sacred writings" (see 2 Timothy 3:15). *Rhema,* which describes the spoken word of God, is here used by the apostle, and I cannot help hearing the echo of Romans 10:16-18 in this instruction to take up the spoken word of God.

In the beginning, God created the world, *ex nihilo,* out of nothing, when He spoke and the world was called into being (Genesis 1 and 2). The prophet Isaiah said that just as God causes the rain and snow to come down from heaven and not return there without watering the earth, *"so shall My word be which goes forth from My mouth; it shall not return to Me empty, without accomplishing what I desire, and without succeeding in the matter for which I sent it"* (Isaiah 55:11). If that is not assurance enough about the power of the Word of God, particularly the spoken word, then listen to this. When Jesus was led into the wilderness, after His baptism, where He stayed for forty days without eating and was tempted by the devil to turn stones into bread, He said, *"It is written in Scripture, 'Man shall not live on bread alone, but by every* spoken word *that proceeds out of the mouth of God'"* (Matthew 4:4, emphasis added). John the beloved disciple described Jesus as the Word that became flesh (John 1:1, 14). Jesus, a few years after His successful overcoming of the tempter, declared *"I am the bread of life; he who comes to Me shall not hunger . . ."* (John 6:35). There it is, the secret of success: to put on the full armor of God and take up, or receive, the spoken word of God which cuts two ways, to condemnation and salvation, separating the unwanted acts of sin so that we might live a truly righteous and fulfilling life in Christ.

These parts of the armor already described are the defensive weapons. When we put them on, we are armed but not extremely dangerous until we add the last and only *offensive* weapon, prayer.

With all prayer and petition pray at all times in the Spirit, and with this in view, be on the alert with all perseverance and petition for all the saints, and pray. There's a distinct difference between a prayer that calls on God comprehensively and a prayer of intercession. The difference is best understood when one examines the answer Jesus gave to His disciples after He cursed the barren fig tree. He said, *"Truly I say to you, if you have faith, and do not doubt, you shall not only do what was done to the fig tree, but even if you say to this mountain, 'Be taken up and cast into the sea,' it shall happen. And everything you ask in prayer, believing, you shall receive'"* (Matthew 21:21, 22).

When Jesus *"went off to the mountain to pray,"* He often spent the whole night groaning and petitioning God (see Luke 6:12), interceding for lost humanity in His day, and down through the ages to our time to you and me. A petition or supplication, though a prayer, denotes the seeking or asking for a concrete request that is the result of a lack or need. Supplication describes a specific appeal such as when Jesus prayed that Peter's faith be strengthened in Luke 22:32. So be on the alert with all perseverance because "part of the spiritual warfare which the Christian has to wage in daily life is the prayer which must be constantly offered in faith. The particular admonition is that in this prayer we are to see to it that along with intercession for all saints (and for the apostle) who are engaged in this battle there should also be endurance or perseverance in prayer. Prayer knits together the church militant with a firm bond. The bond should not be broken. Indeed, it should become increasingly close. The roots should go deeper and deeper into the sphere of God's life and power. To this end, there is need of persistence."[3]

I once read that "if Satan sees that he is in danger of losing one soul, he will exert himself to the utmost to keep that one. And when the individual is aroused to his danger, and, with distress and fervor, looks to Jesus for strength, Satan fears that he will lose a captive, and he calls a reinforcement of his angels to hedge in the poor soul, and form a wall of darkness around him, that heaven's light may not reach him. But if the one in danger perseveres, and in his helplessness casts himself upon the merits of the blood of Christ, our Savior listens to the earnest prayer of faith, and sends a reinforcement of those angels that excel in strength to deliver him. *Satan cannot endure to have his powerful rival appealed to, for he fears and trembles before His strength and majesty. At the sound of fervent prayer, Satan's whole host trembles.*"[4]

Can you believe the power of prayer? Satan trembles when he sees even the weakest saints on their knees. James said, *"The effective fervent prayer of a righteous man [person] avails much"* (5:16b, NKJV). Prayer really works. Remember, it put air conditioning in the fiery furnace and changed the fate and future of three Hebrew men when a pagan king thought he could kill them. Prayer works! It put muzzles on the mouths of hungry lions when Daniel was thrown in their den. Prayer works! It moved the mighty hand of God to write an unforgettable message of judgment on a wall during the feast of a wayward king. Prayer works! It turns losers into winners and makes saints out of sinners.

Ask Beverly. She was raised in a Christian home, valued by her parents, valuing herself. She was educated with a master's degree and became a successful teacher. She was married for sixteen years, during which she gave birth to a beautiful baby boy, who grew up to be the pride and joy of his mother. When she discovered that her husband was a secret alcoholic, she felt so betrayed that she divorced him when their child was still a baby. She stayed single for several years, raising her child on her own.

Then Beverly fell in love with a stranger. She loved him so much that against the counsel of her family and friends, against the uncomfortable twinges deep in her being, she married him. On the night of her wedding, though she had never seen him drink before, that man, in a drunken stupor, violated her son so viciously that the couple was arrested for sexual abuse of a child. Although she was innocent, she was tried, found guilty, and sent to prison.

The press of public media made Beverly a *persona non grata* in the town where she taught school and had been respected all her life. While in prison, she prayed and petitioned God for a friend, and He answered. He sent her a young woman on her own quest for truth. That college student visited Beverly in prison and was so faithful that it called public attention to that family who took her in and loved her as they solicited the prayers of the saints to restore her and find her employment. Before Beverly died from AIDS contracted from the reprobate husband who took her child, her reputation, and her future, she gave her life to Jesus Christ. Beverly died loving Jesus Christ and living for Him because prayer works.

If you are imprisoned by chains of circumstances, caused by some of your own choices or others set by the enemy, remember that prayer works. Our God is still hearing His people. Prayer works, especially when we persevere in it. Pray without ceasing, for prayer is a most important part of God's battle plan. Pray and don't faint, for supplication is the backbone of our spiritual warfare. Pray and plead on, because prayer really works when we put on the full armor of God and stand firm against the schemes of the devil. Remember, in prayer, we are armed and extremely dangerous.

---

1. Gerhard Kittel, *Theological Dictionary of the New Testament*, vii:278, 279 and George Buttrick, *The Interpreter's Dictionary of the Bible*, 2:1006.
2. The *machaira*, carried in a sheath, was a short knife used at sacrifice to slaughter animals, for cooking, and as a clipping or shaving tool.
3. Kittel, 3:619, 620.
4. *Testimonies to the Church*, 1:346, emphasis added.

Chapter 5

a touch of grace

Good sermon illustrations are a dime a dozen, yet finding one not told or heard before is like searching for a needle in a haystack. The Internet has ruined any possibility of sharing an illustration that is good and new unless you've only just created it. One of my favorite illustrations, the source of which I do not know, is perhaps popular with every preacher and public speaker from here to Timbuktu. But since it's my favorite, pull up a chair, relax and hear it for the first time again.

You've been plugging away at this book for four chapters now, but I want you to pay attention as though this is the first chapter. I don't want you to be like the students whose story I'm about to share. The great physician and professor of medicine at Oxford University, Sir Williams Osler, was lecturing his students on the importance of observing details. On his desk was a bottle containing a sample of human body fluid for analysis. To emphasize his point, he picked up the bottle and said, "Gentlemen" (for in those days women were not yet accepted in schools of medicine) "it is often possible to determine the disease from which the patient suffers by tasting the sample."

The students frowned in disgust. They couldn't imagine that they had worked so hard to be admitted to Oxford University only to be told they had to taste an unknown human specimen. To add action to words, the eminent professor dipped a finger into the fluid and then put it into his mouth as he continued. "I am now going to pass the bottle around. Please do exactly as I did so that we can learn the importance of this technique and diagnose the disease."

The bottle made its way slowly from row to row as each wide-eyed student reluctantly put his finger in the bottle and then gingerly into his mouth. When they had all taken their turn, the bottle was returned to Dr. Osler almost empty. At that moment he stood before the class holding the bottle so they could see that it was almost empty and said, "Gentlemen, now you will understand what I mean when I speak about details. If you had been carefully observing details, you would have noticed that I put my index finger in the bottle and my middle finger in my mouth!" Ouch!

When we first become Christians, we all earnestly pledge to carefully observe the details our Great Instructor, Jesus Christ, gives us in His Word. However, by the time we filter what we hear and read through our history, culture, customs, personal experiences, our Greco-Roman worldview, and Western minds and mouths, we forget the importance of observing the details that come to us through the Hebrew mind, the Jewish worldview and understanding. Too often we read, teach, and preach the text *out of context* and are generally left with just a "con." When we do not notice the details, we read things into the Scriptures. We proof-text the Word of God to fit our doctrinal concepts, to legalistically control others, and to impress ourselves as to how observant we've been when indeed our Great Physician knows and sees that we are not carefully following what He has so patiently modeled for us.

Having said this, it is my privilege to invite you to carefully observe the details in the following encounter of a maid and the Master whose tender touch of grace transformed her experience. The story is reported in the Gospels of Matthew, Mark, and Luke, but as we examine it, we look to Mark's version, which has more details for us to observe.

> *And a woman who had had a hemorrhage for twelve years, and had endured much at the hands of many physicians, and had spent all that she had and was not helped at all, but rather had grown worse, after hearing about Jesus, came up in the crowd behind Him, and touched His cloak. For she thought, "If I just touch His garment, I shall get well." And immediately the flow of her blood was dried up; and she felt in her body that she was healed from her affliction. And immediately Jesus, perceiving in Himself that the power proceeding from Him had gone forth, turned around in the crowd and said, "Who touched My garments?" And His disciples said to Him, "You see the multitude pressing in on You and You say, 'Who touched Me?'" And He looked around to see the woman who had done this. But the woman, fearing and trembling, aware of what had happened to her, came and fell down before Him, and told Him the whole truth. And He said to her, "Daughter, your faith has made you well; go in peace, and be healed of your affliction" (Mark 5:25-34).*

When I became a Christian and joined an organized religious movement, my Puritan cultural heritage that I came by earnestly as a native Jamaican and cultural Briton, was reawakened. As a result, I went quickly from an "if it feels good, do it" secular woman without much moral restraint to a public and private prude bordering on, if not truly being, a legalist. During that first season of my religious development, when I read this story, I would ask myself, "What on earth is this story doing in my Bible?"

Since studying theology at college and seminary, and learning the original language in which the New Testament was written, I say to myself again, "Jesus, don't go there! Don't You dare go there!" But He did.

And because He did, I must. I've got to go where so many preachers today fear to tread. I've got to talk about a subject that is taboo in the Christian church. It's a subject that one could categorize among those unmentionable in public places. It's not mentioned in movies; radio announcers avoid it; printed media will not press it; and television commercials are coy with it. Yet I must mention the secret subject of menstruation, referred to by some physicians as the weeping of the disappointed womb, if I am to do proper justice to this story.

In order to observe the hidden details so that we may learn the important lessons inherent in it, one has to understand the problem that plagued this woman. The first thing I noticed was that the narrative is about a woman who has no name, perhaps to protect her last vestige of privacy because she had to tell the intimate, horrible details of her illness to Jesus, publicly. Some scholars suggest that her name was deliberately omitted because she became a prominent follower of Jesus. Others suggest that it was to avoid making an icon of her in the early church. Whatever the reason, she had to do this in a setting where men were the majority, and they looked down upon, even despised, women who dared to present themselves in these circumstances—especially if they were ceremonially unclean, as was this nameless creature. Yet Jesus insisted that she come forward and tell her story to a group of people who had the legal right, according to their customs, to take her to the brow of a hill and stone her to death for breaking the law that rendered her unclean.

The authors of her story tell us that this woman suffered from an intense, unusual discharge of blood from her lower extremities, for twelve long years. I have been privileged to travel all over the world, and I have discovered one thing all women have in common: we hate the normal, monthly discharge of blood called menstruation. Even though it is for our health and happiness, we despise it so much, we don't want to talk about it to ourselves, to our husbands, to our friends or physicians, and especially not to strangers in a public forum. In fact, we hate it so much that we've become creative with all kinds of names for this normal, healthy, uterine flow called menstruation.

Some people call it "the period" or "the visitor." One person in Washington, D.C. described it as "Red Riding Hood visiting her godmother," while a genteel lady down south said it is "grandpa visiting." I got caught one day at church. I had just returned from a year of living in England and had forgotten some regional terms. On that day I invited some friends to have lunch in my home after church, when one lady nervously took me aside and carefully whispered in my ear, "I can't come. Sister Betsy arrived unexpectedly." Without thinking, I put an arm around her shoulder and blurted out loud enough for all to hear, "C'mon, just bring Sister Betsy with you." This drew the attention of the others who realized by her flushed faced that I had said something embarrassing, and after I defensively repeated what I had said, all laughed heartily. I felt very foolish that day.

My friend blushed because she was experiencing something that even today, with television commercials highlighting sanitary napkins that are dry or can fly, we don't discuss freely. Even though we can walk into drug stores and pick from an array of multicolored sanitary facilities and custom-made articles, and even though we live in a day when we can be so clean we squeak, she was nervous about discussing this issue in public. So how dare I embarrass you by writing about it?

Once when I preached on this passage, an irate, anonymous woman (I know she was anonymous, because she identified herself as such) wrote an angry note saying that I had destroyed the dignity of the pulpit by using the word "menstruation" in public. Even now, some who read this may be feeling uneasy by my openness on this subject, which I will do everything in my power to discuss graciously while maintaining the integrity of the text. Because we are so nervous about discussing this subject, when this passage is generally preached, we breeze over this story, which describes the fact that this woman had a profuse discharge of blood emitting from her uterus.

She was a poor woman, and in those days poor people didn't have houses as we do today. Many didn't even have a bed. What is referred to as a bed was a couch for reclining at meals (see Mark 7:30) or for carrying the sick (see Matthew 9:2, 6). Most of the very poor slept in tents on the hard ground, and those who could do just a little bit better used a pallet or cloth that functioned as a mattress.

The prophet Isaiah, in describing the destruction of graven images used by the Israelites said, they would "cast them away like a menstruous cloth" (30:22, KJV). This suggests that there were sanitary facilities for women in those days and thereafter until one remembers that Isaiah lived in the palace and functioned among the very rich. The poor women of that day and in the time of Jesus did not have that luxury. They owned very little cloth which was used for their clothing. They had to go out into the woods, scoop out a hole in the ground with their hands, and sit in it until this period, three days to a week, was over. During that time they did not see their husbands, children, family or friends. They saw no one. Everyone avoided them because they were unclean. Let us look at a statement about this in Leviticus:

> *Now if a woman has a discharge of her blood many days, not at the period of her menstrual impurity, or if she has a discharge beyond that period, all the days of her impure discharge she shall continue as though in her menstrual impurity; she is unclean. Any bed on which she lies all the days of her discharge*

shall be to her like her bed at menstruation; and every thing on which she sits shall be unclean, like her uncleanness at that time. Likewise, whoever touches them shall be unclean and shall wash his clothes and bathe in water and be unclean until evening (Leviticus 15:25-27).

This passage makes it clear that this unnamed woman was unclean. She had to sit in her hole in the ground for twelve long years. If she dared to mingle with people, to avoid ceremonially polluting the religious leaders, she had to cry out, like a leper, "Unclean, unclean, unclean!" When a woman cried out "unclean," it could only mean one thing—an "issue of blood," as the King James Version describes it. The ceremonial cleansing for this problem was to wash in water, but the dry climate in Palestine prohibited bathing as we know it today. The very poor had no running water or spigots to conveniently provide hot and cold water because water, the most common agent of purification, was so scarce. Unless there was a pool or stream available, this act was very difficult, and explains some reasons why the religious leaders were so careful to avoid being defiled by unclean persons. When they washed their hands (see Matthew 15:2) as part of their ceremonial rituals, it was not done in our Western way. They simply dipped the tips of their fingers in the water, with the palm of their hands turned upward to allow some water to run over their hands before it was dried. No soap and scrubbing of the hands was done. So someone as poor as this woman would be most careful in her encounters to avoid defiling others.

When she becomes clean from her discharge, she shall take for herself two turtledoves or two young pigeons, and bring them in to the priest, to the doorway of the tent of meeting. And the priest shall offer the one for a sin offering and the other for a burnt offering. So the priest shall make atonement on her behalf before the Lord because of her impure discharge (Leviticus 15:28-30).

A woman in this predicament didn't just go in and say, "I'm through with my period," or "the visitor has gone home," or "Sister Betsy has finally decided to leave, and now I'm ready to go home." The priest would not take her word for anything. In those days they believed that all women were liars, because of Sarah, who *"laughed to herself"* when the angel told her she would have a child in her old age and when asked, denied it, saying, *"I did not laugh"* (see Genesis 18:9-15). So the poor woman, whose dignity had already been pressed by the almost indecent ritual requirements, had to suffer yet one more indignity: She had to lift up her long skirt so that the priest could examine and verify that she was not still discharging blood.

When we consider that this woman was unclean for twelve long years and had to be isolated, we realize how dreadful her situation that led her to risk her life to find help and healing. Suppose her ailment came about as a result of giving birth to a baby. Had she touched her baby, it would have been rendered unclean by her. That child would have grown up without having bonded with the mother, without having been suckled and nestled lovingly at her bosom. She would not be able to recognize him, and he would not recognize her as his birth mother. So, mothers, imagine how devastating it would be to give birth to a baby and then be separated from it for twelve years, unable to respond when your baby cried or needed you. And if her child or children couldn't touch her, neither could her husband. We live in times when smart women know the importance of allowing and encouraging their husband's "touch" for sexual intimacies. In fact, Paul was careful to remind both spouses of their responsibility when he said:

> *The wife does not have authority over her own body, but the husband does; and likewise also the husband does not have authority over his own body, but the wife does. Stop depriving one another, except by agreement for a time that you may devote*

yourselves to prayer, and come together again lest Satan tempt you because of your lack of self-control (1 Corinthians 7:4-6).

Religious women had better not be so holy and full of spirituality that they will not allow their husband's "touch" unless they both agree to delay this for prayer. Thus this business of "having a headache" so that you can use this intimacy, this gift of God, to manipulate your spouse or hold one or the other hostage until you acquire your demands is not only unsavory, it is unbiblical. Find some other weapon, but don't use that one! Discover other ways of solving problems, and if that is difficult, consult a Christian counselor or an understanding minister of the gospel, whose compassion and intimacy with God will provide rich resources from His Word (see Ephesians 3:8) to help overcome the obstacles threatening your marriage.

Imagine that this woman had not touched her husband for twelve years; not felt his loving arms around her as she was comforted by whispered sweet nothings. Imagine that if she was single she had not received a holy hug from family or friends for twelve long years. Like babies, adults who are not touched and nurtured also wilt away emotionally and physically. If my friends avoid me and refuse to make even eye contact for the briefest period of time, I go into an emotional tailspin, yet this woman was isolated for twelve long years as she endured much at the hands of many physicians while she waited, anxiously anticipating a cure.

Nowadays we have an expanding medical profession with specialists in every possible area, but in ancient Palestine, it was the priests who were the custodians of medical lore. They played an important role in safeguarding or preserving the health of the community and in time were the only ones who could declare a person cured of an illness, such as is seen in Mark 1:44 and Luke 17:14.

The priests were regarded as the doctors or physicians even if they did not personally diagnose the disease or initiate its cure. What this means, then, is that that poor woman had to go to priest after priest, during the twelve years, and lift up her skirt so that they could examine her. When they found that she was still suffering from her disease, they would discharge her to that hole in the ground somewhere in the wilderness of Palestine.

Some of us can personally relate to her feelings of shame after having revealed an uncomfortable secret to a pastor. We have difficulty returning to worship at that particular church. We are afraid of eye contact because the pastor knows our intimate secret. We are afraid that others in the congregation may be privy to our very private experiences, so we drop out of church as the fears and shame increase along with the self-imposed isolation.

Be real. There are times when I feel such shame from my shame-based past that I don't want my boss to see me. I don't want my members to see me, and I'm even afraid to look at myself in a mirror because I feel so sick inside that I could die. If it wasn't for God's grace, which is the balm for these deep wounds, and my urgent need for healing, some days I would not be able to face anyone. Some have done things or have inherited such a shame-based history that they run from one church to the other, carrying the baggage or the mess to infest and infect each location. God cannot bless that person or place until and unless everything is turned over to Him. There are churches all across this land that are trying every gimmick for growth and still are not experiencing anything because there are people who refuse to trust God, repent, and be reconciled with their families and friends.

This nameless woman, suffering the indignity of her incontinence, went from synagogue to synagogue to show herself to the priests, who gave her little comfort and no cure after she had spent all that she had. The phrase, *"she had spent all that she had,"* seems to suggest that this woman had had money or property to disburse for her medical needs. But we must not force our western,

Greco-Romanized experiences on the text or her position. She was a poor woman and owned nothing. In fact, there are very few stories in the Bible about women who owned property or financial resources. One is a powerful witness to the justice and fairness of God in the story of the daughters of Zelophehad. It was their tradition that only sons could receive their father's inheritance, but this man had only daughters, who appealed to Moses to make an exception in their case. When Moses brought their case before the Lord, He told Moses:

> *The daughters of Zelophehad are right in their statements. You shall surely give them a hereditary possession among their father's brothers, and you shall transfer the inheritance of their father to them. Further, you shall speak to the sons of Israel, saying, "If a man dies and has no son, then you shall transfer his inheritance to his daughter"* (Numbers 27:7, 8).

This instruction was hardly adhered to, so there are little or no records of women possessing property except in the parable (see Luke 15:8-10), which cannot be used as a legitimate reference because it could have been a story coined by Jesus to get His point across as well as a real event being retold.

There is, however, one report that can be referenced, found in Luke 10:38, where we are told that *"a woman named Martha welcomed Jesus into her home."* Some scholars suggest that the sister of Mary and Lazarus inherited her home from her husband, one Rabbi Eleazar, while others claim it was her husband, Simon the leper (John 12:1). All base their theories on the fact that the names Martha, Simon, and Eleazar were found in an old cemetery in Bethany. Be that as it may, it was so significant that a woman owned her own home that it was mentioned in these sacred records. Women owned nothing. They had no money. They themselves were treated as chattel and owned nothing but their own lives.

So when we are told that this woman had spent all she had, it must mean more than money. Perhaps it means all of her dignity, her persona, self-worth, psychological well being, reputation, character, and everything that makes a woman feel worthwhile, not worthless or filled with shame. She had nothing and felt like nothing. She looked like nothing and smelled like nothing with her pale face, bad hair, and poor skin resulting from the relentless loss of blood. She was treated as nothing so that she became another nameless, faceless sick and dying citizen in her community. She had spent everything, uncovering herself to priests who did not have the grace of God not to wince when they saw her, and give her relief from the debilitating disease she suffered. She had spent everything and was not helped at all, but rather had grown worse.

I once heard a preacher say that whenever we come across a "but" in Bible narrative about a person's experience, we should underline it. For, said he, everybody has a "but." Some people's "buts" are bigger than others, but we all have a "but." This poor woman with a chronic disease had exhausted every resource of her day to find a cure, *"but rather had grown worse."* One can't find a bigger "but" than that! The important thing though is to watch what she did with her "but." Did she sit on it and whine? Did she curse God and die? Did she dig a bigger hole in the ground and disappear in the darkness of the grave? Absolutely not! This story has impressed upon me the importance of knowing my personal "but." To name it and claim it. For how we handle our own "but" will determine whether we sink or swim, whether we soar as eagles or slouch as sluggards.

When she landed on her "but," that woman heard about Jesus, and *"after hearing about Jesus, came up in the crowd behind Him, and touched [the fringe or hem of] his cloak."* The word *touch* in the English language means to bring a bodily part into contact with someone or something so as to perceive through the tactile sense the pressure or traction exerted on the skin or mucous membrane. It is a specified sensation that arises in response to stimulation of the tactile receptors.

The Greek word for touch has a similar connotation, but in the Hebrew mind there was an added dimension and the word was often used in a specific context to emphasize this. The added dimension was that to touch something is to extend one's authority over it with the intent of bringing about a significant change in its content or context. A good example of the use of the word with this meaning is found in Numbers 4:15, where the sons of Kohath are cautioned how to handle *"holy objects"* in the sanctuary so that *"they may not touch the holy objects and die."* The story of Uzzah in 2 Samuel 6:1-11 bears out this injunction. Many well-meaning students of the Bible and sincere Christians have had a hard time dealing with God's apparently merciless killing of this man, who was attempting to do something good when he *"reached out toward the ark of God and took hold of it, for the oxen nearly upset it."* I must admit that I have struggled to understand why God's anger *"burned against Uzzah and God struck him down there for his irreverence; and he died there by the ark of God."*

It seemed like an irrational, ungrateful act on God's part until I discovered that the word "touch" also meant to exercise authority over something with the intent of changing it from its original form. No wonder Uzzah's act was described as "irreverence." For in that holy ark was not only Aaron's rod that budded, a cup of manna, the ceremonial laws written and tucked in its side by Moses, but most important, the Ten Commandments written by the finger of God on two tables of stone (see Exodus 31:16).

Some have suggested that because God had instructed the Levites to carry the ark on poles (Exodus 37:5), and David and Uzzah were bringing it on an ox cart, Uzzah was presumptuously trying to save God. Whatever his intentions, God sees into the hearts of everyone and knows our innermost thoughts. When Uzzah touched the ark, he performed an act that looked proper from our point of view, but from God's perspective he did so with the intent of exercising authority over something that God Himself had written on a table of stone. Had Uzzah been allowed to get away with this irreverent act, there's no telling what he might have changed on the Ten Commandments. Perhaps he would have done what some have since done. I have found versions of the Bible where the fourth commandment has been severely truncated to support the human change of God's instruction to remember to observe the seventh-day Sabbath. Maybe Uzzah would have been used by Satan to change the Sabbath of God to another day and declare that he did so as a vice-regent of God. Whatever his plan or purpose, I believe God's response to his irreverence has been recorded as a reminder to all generations thereafter that we cannot abrogate or alter the law of God without serious, personal consequences.

I have shared all this to point out that as a person of Hebrew heritage, the woman, when she determined to touch Jesus, touched Him with the intent that His authority would change something in her and heal her of her long-standing malady. Thus, she bravely ventured out into the crowd to touch the fringe of His garment, risking life and limb to attain her desired healing. She wanted to touch the fringe of His garment. Why? Because in those days the people, especially the poor, believed that if they touched the fringes of the garments of a popular rabbi (see Matthew 14:36), they would be healed by the miraculous propensities of the person filtering through the garment.

All male Jews, including Jesus, were required to wear an outer garment with fringes because of a commandment by God in Numbers 15:32-41. While the Israelites were sojourning from Egypt to the Promised Land, they stopped for a long period in the wilderness of Sin. One day they found a man breaking the Sabbath by gathering wood during the sacred hours. There he was, gathering his sticks in broad daylight, in a community where everyone showed reverence for the day on which God rested—the day He blessed and sanctified, or set apart, as a holy day for all creatures and creation thereafter.

It wasn't the way we live in America today, where everyone is doing their own thing. This was a community in which everyone observed the Sabbath. But this man was so defiant and brazen that he went out and picked up the wood and walked into the camp with it, whistling while he went. Almost daring God to do something about it. So the people who saw him brought him to Moses and Aaron, and the Lord instructed them to put the man to death. This shows us that God means business when He tells us to honor what He has commanded us to do. After the man was punished, the Lord spoke to Moses, saying:

> *"Speak to the sons of Israel, and tell them that they shall make for themselves tassels [fringes] on the corners of their garments. There shall be a tassel for you to look at and remember all the commandments [all ten] of the Lord, so as to do them and not follow after your own heart and your own eyes, after which you played the harlot, in order that you may remember to do all My commandments and be holy to your God"* (Numbers 15:37-39).

Some of the scribes and Pharisees, in the time of Jesus, lengthened their tassels, or fringes, longer than God instructed even as they had added to His Law. But Jesus did not. As He moved about that day, His tassels followed His movements. Seeing Him, the woman with the issue of blood decided that if she could only touch the fringe of His garment, she would be healed. *"And immediately the flow of her blood was dried up; and she felt in her body that she was healed of her affliction."* He took her uncleanness and gave her His virtue. Notice that she touched Him with the intent of changing herself, but it also changed Jesus as she exercised, by faith, the authority He has given to all believers. *"And immediately Jesus, perceiving in Himself that the power proceeding from Him had gone forth, turned around in the crowd and said, 'Who touched My garments?' "*

Most of us go to church week after week, and we are not touched. Some just don't want to be touched. Others are scared to reach out and touch—scared even to touch Jesus. We don't want to touch and be touched, because it demands a response. We want to stay at a safe distance from the real issues that we carry with us when we come to worship. But when God is changing people, He generally does so through human beings, with a touch that transforms. He allows virtue to go out of Himself into His children, so that they may become sons and daughters instead of slaves and servants of sin. When we touch God to change ourselves, it changes Him also. How awesome that the Creator gives us the power to change and affect Him!

So Jesus asked the question, " *'Who touched My garments?'* " and instantly the disciples began to grumble among themselves and said to Him, *"You see the multitude pressing in on You and You say, 'Who touched Me?'* "

In their frustration, they got in His face and said in today's vernacular, "What is the matter with you, Man? Don't you see all these people around you?" They responded impudently, because at that time they did not believe He was God. They believed that He was a good man, or even a great one, but not God. So they followed Him to fulfill their political ambitions, even though He called them to fill their spiritual needs. But being God, "the Savior could distinguish the touch of faith from the casual contact of the careless throng."[1]

While they argued with Him, Jesus *"looked around to see the woman who had done this."* How did he know it was a woman? How did He know which woman? He knew because Providence had planned earlier that day, when she breathed her first breath of hope in prayer after she heard about Jesus, to meet her on the very spot where she stood. She thought she had gone in search of Jesus, but God had come seeking to heal her. So when He turned around, He could look to see *"the* woman," not "a woman" who touched Him.

I believe that Jesus deliberately sought her in the crowd until it was possible for her to touch Him, even though in her mind she may have thought that it was *her* stealth and determination that brought her in contact with Him.

"But the woman, fearing and trembling, aware of what had happened to her, came and fell down before Him, and told Him the whole truth." The word that is translated fearing, comes from the Greek word *"phobeo"* from which we get our word "phobia," an exaggerated, usually inexplicable and illogical fear of a particular person, object, or situation. She was terrified unto death, trembling with fear because she knew if she was discovered she could be stoned to death. But she soon came to her senses. That woman who had the courage and faith to touch Jesus, "finding concealment vain, came forward tremblingly and cast herself at His feet. With grateful tears she told the story of her suffering, and how she had found relief."[2] She did not stick her chest out when Jesus asked, "Who touched Me?" and proudly say, "It was me." Instead, it seems her knees were knocking so hard you could hear the sounds coming through her clothing. Perhaps her teeth were chattering as one exposed in a snowstorm without shelter. She must have broken out in a cold sweat as she did what most of us would have, and cried in her heart, saying, "Please God, whatever You do, don't let this good man make me tell the details of my disease, here, in public."

In spite of the beseeching look in her eyes and the fearful expression on her face, Jesus encouraged her to get up and tell her story. Not the story we write in books and give in public testimonies about how we paid our tithe and when the time came we got our reward. But it was a true story of suffering that lasted more than a decade without God's intervention, for God doesn't always work the way we want Him to, but the way that is best for the process of salvation.

When she told her story, I am sure that the Pharisees, mentioned in Matthew 9:11 as saying, *"Why is your teacher eating with the tax gatherers and sinners?"* took umbrage to her defiling presence. I am sure they protested vociferously, demanding that the punishment of their religious courts of law be meted out to that poor woman. I imagine that when they heard her mention her malady, there was an audible gasp. They may have jumped away from her polluting presence to part a way on both sides so that Jesus stood with her kneeling at His feet, her face turned up to Him, pleading for forgiveness, mercy and grace. Where the crowd had none, Jesus, being God, had graciousness and generosity.

I imagine that some of the religious leaders were fit to be tied, particularly when Jesus made no immediate move to discipline that woman for breaking their religious laws. They may have bent down and picked up stones to throw at her in their anger and religious indignation when Jesus said loudly so all could hear, *" 'Daughter, your faith has made you well.' "*

He called her "daughter," a term of endearment, to convey a message to them that she was not only a biological descendant of Abraham, but also a child of promise who, like Abraham, believed and was counted as faithful. He also wanted to distinguish that this woman was related to Him in a significant way (see Mark 3:35), that they were family, and if the religiously indignant wanted to hurt her, they had to go through Him to get to His (God's) child. His facial features must have said to them, "If you feel like stoning someone today, it's not going to be this daughter of faith and of our Father in heaven. For if you stone her, you've got to stone Me first." He said her faith had made her well for she was healed in the instant that she touched Him. But when He said, *"Go in peace, and be healed of your affliction,"* His words promised and assured her that she would forever enjoy good health and happiness. He was telling her that she might have storms and troubles in her future, and there might be obstacles and disappointments to overcome, but she would forever encounter life's trials and tribulations with the reconciling peace of God. For her affliction was not merely an over-extended discharge of blood, but a sin problem. The bleeding stopped when she touched Him; the sin disappeared when He spoke to her and removed her affliction or plague—sin.

Let me share some lessons I have learned from this story. This is a real and historic event, but I see it as a living parable. In apocalyptic writings in the Bible, the symbol of the church is a woman (Revelation 12:1-6), and I believe that all of the women who were present that day, collectively represent the contemporary Christian church and individually are symbols of the various denominations that dot the skyline of Christendom. Many of the sick touched Jesus and were healed that day. But this unnamed woman in the story has so many characteristics of my own community of faith, I cannot help but draw an analogy with ours—although she could, for all intents and purposes, represent just about any denomination today.

For most of her life she was healthy and thriving, but the last twelve years were composed of a tragic loss of her health and energy. The issue of blood, or hemorrhage, represents life, particularly since the Scriptures say, *"For as for the life of all flesh, its blood is identified with its life. Therefore I said to the sons of Israel, 'you are not to eat the blood of any flesh, for the life of the flesh is its blood; whoever eats it shall be cut off'"* (Leviticus 17:14).

For decades, the life has been oozing out of traditional Christian churches. In fact, there are several signs of this degeneration. First, church-growth experts who labor to find new ways to reinvigorate old, dying congregations. The second is an intense focus on the importance of developing spiritual gifts, discipling and training members for service. The third is the introduction of church doctors who claim to be able to diagnose and treat the profuse draining of life from congregations. And fourth is the increase in non-denominational churches with freer, more contemporary styles of worship, which none had foreseen or forecast even a decade before.

All churches have a life cycle. H. Richard Neibuhr, in his 1937 publication, *The Social Sources of Denominationalism*, suggested that there are three developmental levels: the cult, the church of the middle class, and the denominational phase, which has seven stages in the life cycle of a church.

I have found that what David Moberg, a sociologist who also studies the developmental cycle of churches, proposed in his book, *The Church As a Social Institution*, is more relevant for my own denomination. He said that there are five stages of institutional growth in the life cycle of a denomination:

1. The stage of incipient organization. An important identifying characteristic is that the movement generally rises out of dissatisfaction within the existing "mother" church. Often people from lower classes complain of corruption among the privileged group. This creates social unrest and crisis among the believers, which the church fails to meet satisfactorily. Out of this arises a new sect or cult with a high degree of collective excitement as they seek and move on to form their independent church led by a charismatic, authoritarian, prophet leader. There are usually unplanned and uncontrolled emotions in the group that lead to a sense of bodily possession of the Holy Spirit. Physical reactions are common results.

2. Period of formal organization. In this second stage, attempts are made to develop a sense of unity and common interest. The followers are asked to commit by joining the new group, which is now totally separated from the "mother" group. Goals are formalized to attract new members. A creed is developed to establish orthodoxy. There's a great emphasis on symbolic expressions of differences between the new sect and worldly nonmembers. These symbols may seem trivial to outsiders but are important boundary markers to members. Some of these symbols are slogans, doctrines, or modified behaviors that reflect the new group's thinking and often draw ridicule or persecution. This increases the resolve and strength of the group, leading to bridge-burning activities.

3. Stage of maximum efficiency. Decades have passed, the leadership now has much less emotional emphasis and is dominated by statesmen who psychologically move the group from a despised sect to near equality with the previously recognized denomination from which it emerged. Hostility toward other denominations and fanatical resolutions to maintain sharply different doctrines are relaxed because the first-generation founders have died out. The group moves rapidly toward institutionalization as it experiences a youthful vigor and growth that is rapid, uneven and one in which formal structure of boards and committees are established to perform specific administrative duties and rituals in worship.

4. **The institutional stage.** Formalism saps the group's vitality. Leadership is dominated by bureaucracy and is more concerned with perpetuating its own ideals and interests than in maintaining the distinctive qualities that established the original church. Administration centers in boards and committees, which tend to be self-perpetuating as mechanisms of structure become an end to themselves. Creeds or fundamental beliefs become little more than venerated relics of the past, organized worship develops into rituals that are largely empty of meaning to most worshippers, religious exercises and symbols become meaningless, personalities are suppressed, and the institution becomes the master more than servant of the people. Conflict with the outside world is replaced by toleration and conformity with societal mores. Standards are relaxed and respectability is often the motive for joining members as the church tries to win primarily socially respectable people. Interests once considered secular become major attractions as the church attempts to become the center of activity. Sermons become topical on social issues rather than dealing with sin and church dogma.

5. **With over-institutionalization comes disintegration.** At this stage the church is operated like the original "mother" institution, where patronage and red tape are the order of the day. Many members share the same complaints of the original founders who left the original church. They withdraw into new nondenominational sects or become nonparticipating members, while a majority of those

who remain continue their support out of guilt or memory of their parents. The life is issuing out profusely as leaders attempt to preserve it with new rules and gimmicks, but the institution is seldom if ever healed, for what it needs is a touch of grace.

Today the post-contemporary church is in trouble. It is regarded to be in stage five by many Christian sociologists such as George Barna. Barna underscores the growing trend of smaller groups being gobbled up by multipurpose megachurches. In his sobering book, *The Second Coming of the Church*, Barna uses scientific data to unblinkingly evaluate the state of the church. He reveals the spiritual and moral decline within the body politic and asserts its unpreparedness to meet the demands of the 21st century. He adds that as a result of his findings, "I am convinced that the typical church as we know it today has a rapidly expiring shelf life . . . Despite the activity and chutzpah emanating from thousands of congregations, the Church in America is losing influence and adherents faster than any other major institution in the nation. Unless a radical solution for the revival of the Christian Church in the United States is adopted and implemented soon, the spiritual hunger of Americans will either go unmet or be satisfied by other faith groups."[3]

No church is immune to either the Neibhur or Moberg developmental stages. In fact, in 1962 Moberg placed my denomination, Seventh-day Adventists, at stage three even as we were moving into evangelical circles and were being recognized as a mainline Protestant church and not a cult. For two decades thereafter, we were regularly listed among the fastest growing churches in North America.

As Americans, we have clearly demonstrated by practice and proclamation, that we prefer speed to depth, immediate gratification rather than the slow hand of grace, by failing to facilitate highly personalized and focused ministries that would build and sustain community. By the end of the 1980s, small congregations were suffering the blight that heralds decay and/or death. The life of the church was pouring out. Many young people couldn't wait to graduate and join the increasing ranks of disenfranchised, nonparticipating adults. Some young professionals grew so tired of poor preaching, petty political skirmishes, and the lack of the clear tones of the gospel from some pulpits, that they tuned into the energetic praise worships offered on television and in some of the charismatic, free, nondenominational churches.

Upon realizing her illness, this woman who had long suffered the relentless rigidity of the Law primarily without grace, like her type who was raised under the rules of Judaism, began to seek out a variety of physicians, many of whom used popular gimmicks, to bring about a cure. There was the charismatic physician called the "deliverance ministry." This was the one who claimed to be able to deliver one from a variety of demons that inhibited growth. There were cassette tapes, circuit-riding deliverance ministry operators, and a diversity of opportunities to exorcise demons and revitalize churches. It worked for a while, but when the novelty was gone, so was the cure. This gimmick was so popular that while I was a student in college, a young man came to me one day and said that since I was a theology major, I should be particularly endowed with the Spirit to deliver him from the demon of procrastination. I told him, "Get a life! You don't have a demon; you're just lazy. You don't need deliverance; you need a swift kick to help you accept the discipline of academia. Stop using demons as excuses to avoid getting your papers done on time and prepare for your classes so that you may be intelligently engaged in discussions." I was amazed at how many thinking people followed that physician, and when the church lifted up her proverbial skirt, the life was still flowing out.

The next physician was the contemporary worship style popularized by Willow Creek Community Church, a church that continues to make excellent contributions in leadership training and church growth. But many pastors adopted a contemporary worship with drums and drama as the answer to their dwindling congregations. So they spent thousands of dollars (for some, all that they had), emphasizing small groups or renovating old churches to install video equipment and multipurpose electronic technology to sing praise songs. Others built new monuments of human glory, with pews that are now empty, week after week. Like the children who followed the Pied Piper, many people came and congregations flourished—for a time—as more praise songs were sung at the expense of the proclamation of the Word of God.

Inasmuch as I am in favor of contemporary worships with all the creative concepts that are popular these days, if the emphasis is only on drums and drama rather than on the gospel of grace or God's Spirit and prayer, it will be another flash in the pan experience. And so it was, for that physician could only deliver temporary relief for the woman's malady. Those physicians can never do what the Great Physician is begging us to allow Him to do. He has gone out of His way to meet us so we can touch Him, but too often we avoid Him for the touch of human opinions and ideas.

Finally, in exasperation, when she was about to give up, she heard about Jesus and determined to find Him and touch the fringe of His garments. There were many women, or denominations, which were restored to their former good health, but I am particularly excited about this portion of the story because it is here that she best represents my community of faith in this living parable.

There were many denominations that needed the cure from the continuous issuing of life just as there were many women in the crowd that day who touched Jesus and were healed. But He highlighted this one because of what I consider to be a most important reason. Notice that when the woman in the story touched Jesus, she touched the fringe of His garments. Remember how I pointed out that Moses was instructed by God to put these fringes on the garments of all male Jews throughout their generations to remind them to observe the Ten Commandments? Did you notice that this instruction was given after an Israelite deliberately broke the Sabbath and was punished?

Before our church was organized in 1860, our founders belonged to non-Sabbath observing churches. In fact, Sunday was not only referred to as the Sabbath, it was so recognized, and many rules were in place regarding an adherent's attitude toward its observance. For example, there was a rule, later practiced by early Seventh-day Adventists, that if one was traveling, wherever they were when the clock struck midnight, they had to stop and rest for the night because traveling during Sunday-Sabbath hours was prohibited. One could not make a fire to cook a meal or wash clothing during those precious Sunday-Sabbath hours of midnight Saturday to midnight Sunday. By the 1840s the life was oozing out of the churches as many turned to the circuit-riding preachers who conducted tent evangelism while others joined the holiness movement that was spreading like wildfire. During that time, many of the other itinerant preachers were proclaiming the soon coming of Christ, but only two Protestant churches (the Seventh-Day Baptists and Adventists) reached out and touched the fringes, spiritually speaking, created to restore remembrance of the Ten Commandments, especially the seventh-day Sabbath.

In our old and restless world, people need to be reminded that the rest, memorialized by God in the observation of the seventh-day Sabbath (see Genesis 2:2, 3) is not just a legalistic command kept by religious fringe elements. It is a reminder that the One who instructed us to observe it is the God who directs our contemporary exodus out of spiritual Egypt or sin.

I welcome, embrace, and observe the Sabbath. Just as Karl Barth could find the gospel in every text in the Bible, I find a touch of grace in every aspect of the Sabbath. For example, Hebrews 4:4 says, *"For He has thus said somewhere concerning the seventh day, 'And God rested on the seventh day from all his works.'"* To me this means that the Sabbath is a sign that from the foundation of the world

God completed all His works, every jot and tittle of what is necessary to save humanity. Sabbath observance is therefore a sign that we acknowledge God's gift and agree that there is nothing we can do or add to the finished works of divinity. Sabbath is a touch of grace.

The following are some brief comments in support of the importance of Sabbath observance to the spiritual formation, development, and growth of the contemporary corporate body and every individual believer:

Rabbi Abraham Joshua Heschel was one of the most widely respected and loved religious leaders of the twentieth century. He was an extraordinarily gifted philosopher, communicator, and author, who wrote one of the most profound, scholarly, and beautiful meditations on the nature and celebration of the seventh-day Sabbath, simply entitled, *The Sabbath*. In this must-read book, he notes that the Sabbath symbolizes the sanctification of time, making Sabbaths "our great cathedrals" in which all humans are called to come and worship. He said, "He who wants to enter the holiness of the day must first lay down the profanity of clattering commerce, of being yoked to toil . . . [For] on the Sabbath we especially care for the seed of eternity planted in the soul . . . Six days a week we seek to dominate the world, on the seventh day we try to dominate the self."[4]

Some of the most sublime statements about the Sabbath have been said by this great man. For example, he said, "The Sabbath is not for the sake of the weekdays; the weekdays are for the sake of Sabbath. It is not an interlude but the climax of living . . . The seventh day is like a palace in time with a kingdom for all. It is not a date but an atmosphere. It is not a different state of consciousness but a different climate; it is as if the appearance of all things somehow changed . . . The Sabbath is the inspirer, the other days the inspired . . . The Sabbath itself is a sanctuary which we build, *a sanctuary in time* . . . For the Sabbath is a day of harmony and peace, peace between man and man, peace within man, and peace with all things.

On the seventh day man has no right to tamper with God's world, to change the state of physical things. It is a day of rest for *man and animal* alike."[5]

Walter Brueggemann, McPheeder Professor of Old Testament at Columbia Theological Seminary in Atlanta and one of the world's most respected Christian theologians and authors, is not a Seventh-day Adventist. His contemporaries not only admire his scholarship, but say that he listens to the Scripture and the human condition, and then develops a conversation between the two that is theologically solid, lively and vigorous. One of my favorite books by this author is his 1989 publication, *Finally Comes the Poet*. In it I have found some more of the most profound statements and sentiments on the Sabbath I have ever read. For example, in his commentary on Exodus 20:11, Brueggeman said, "We shall rest because God rested on the seventh day of creation. That is, the rest to which we are summoned is a rest that God initiates and in which God participates . . . The act of Sabbath is an act of remembering the liberation that permitted new life . . . the Sabbath is identified as the crucial act of obedience that qualifies one for God's presence . . . [it] means desisting from the frantic pursuit of securing the world on our own terms." He also said that "Amos 8:4-6 shows that the Sabbath was a great line of defense against exploitation, to permit the humanization of public life [in spite of the fact that] Sabbath practice had become so restrictive and oppressive that it worked against acts and gestures of human caring."[6]

And one final statement that I could not resist including: "Sabbath is a critique of our entire technical way of controlling human life. Ethical reflection on Sabbath concerns yielding, relinquishing, and letting go . . . Thinking about Sabbath invites us into conversation about the deep restlessness that characterizes our common life—our drivenness to have control—a drivenness that invites interpersonal brutality and public policies of destructiveness. . . . Sabbath is an invitation to imagine our life differently. In risking Sabbath, we discover life can be lived without the control that reduces us and leaves us fatigued."[7]

Finally, I have drawn an important, lasting lesson from this story of the woman with the issue of blood. It is about waiting for God's response and action in our lives. In spite of the fact that He graciously *"causes His sun to rise on the evil and the good, and sends rain on the righteous and the unrighteous"* (Matthew 5:45), no one will be healed of the plague of sin until and unless they accept by faith the grace of God and enter into a personal, intimate relationship with Him.

If you will notice, this woman, although marginalized for her gender and economic status, was a Jew, a member of the race of God's chosen people. This means that even though she may have been excluded from most aspects of their national worship, she was at least acquainted with their religious rituals, perhaps even practicing some of its forms, such as prayer, without the spirit thereof. She must have earnestly prayed and pleaded for relief during those twelve long years of her illness and isolation. Yet, in spite of her affiliation with the church and her vocal part in it, her appeals were not answered until she experienced the touch of grace, was healed of her malady, and converted.

Mark, the author of this story, said it was only *"after she heard about Jesus, [and] came up in the crowd behind Him, and touched His cloak,"* that she was outwardly healed and rescued from the pain of sin. It was only after Jesus said, *"'Daughter, your faith has made you well; go in peace, and be healed of your affliction,'"* that redemption worked its miracle deep within her soul to free her from the power and penalty of sin. And when she heard those words, her life source was renewed according to the promise in Isaiah 41:17, 18.

Every time I read this story, I place my name where the word "woman" appears. It's been more than two decades now since I heard about Jesus and dared to touch Him and be healed. He just redeemed me from the power and penalty of sin, but I had to wait, like most Christians, for over a decade, to be healed from the pain of sin.

Here's how I remembered and reported it in my autobiography, *Will I Ever Learn?*

I was so busy with fixing up the Boston Temple and reclaiming former members who had been disenfranchised from the Adventist community (some for 10 years or more, and who now form 60 percent of our membership) that I totally ignored my own brokenness and desperate need for healing. Things came to a head a few weeks after the miracle rededication service by way of a simple mistake that almost no one noticed, but that threw me into a deep depression.

I had invited the Epic Brass, a horn quintet, to provide a musical Sabbath. The plan was that I would not preach; however, at a given signal, I would conclude the service with prayer. Everything was going perfectly when, only 15 minutes into their presentation, I misunderstood the leader's intention at a pause in the musical piece. I stood, prayed, and dismissed the congregation. The quintet was surprised, but followed my lead, concluding what must have been their shortest-ever concert. I was too embarrassed for words.

I still have no idea what happened. Perhaps I was burned out, having not taken even a day off since we started the renovations the previous November. I immediately turned my embarrassment into shame, then guilt, then despair. Whenever I'm totally drained of emotion and energy, I become physically sick, and this time it exhibited itself as a searing chest pain that caused me to cough uncontrollably. Several physicians in my congregation examined me, but no one could find the cause of this problem that became progressively worse until I became bedridden.

After two weeks in this state, I remembered a brochure that had been sent to our office from Gonzaga, a retreat center run by Jesuit priests, announcing an upcoming "silent retreat." I had never been to anything of the sort, but I sensed that the Spirit was directing me to go. My secretary at the time made the reservations, and one cold Friday afternoon I drove to Gloucester, Massachusetts.

Gonzaga is an old castle built so close to the water's edge that sometimes the tide lashes against the outside walls of the dining room. The rooms were small and sparsely furnished with a monk's cot and a table hewn out of rough wood, and we all shared a common bathroom. The lights were always dim, making us feel as cloistered as the monks who once lived there. One could almost hear their chanting echoing through the silent halls. Because it was a silent retreat, I saw only a few of the other participants at mealtime, and we didn't speak to each other, obeying the code of silence.

At sunset I decided to take a walk along the beach. I sat down on one of the huge rocks that jutted high above the water. The sound of waves crashing against them echoed loudly in the dark lagoon below. The sun sank into the ocean, turning the blue water into a gray magnet that seemed to be drawing me into its agitated waves below. I felt overwhelmed with the pain of my early childhood and teenage years. I had been sexually violated by various relatives and often molested by some of the strangers who sat on the verandah of our little grocery store, quenching their thirst from its meager stock of soda. Now those memories threatened to overwhelm me. I was broken by the abuse in my childhood and the promiscuity of my youth, filled with guilt and shame that I hugged tightly, secretly, to my bosom, even though it was squeezing the life out of me. I was so despairing over the lost opportunities and the enormous mistakes I had made in life that not even my intellectual assent to Christ's salvation brought me even a semblance of peace. I have no words to describe my hurt. I threw myself face down on that rock and cried out to the Great Rock of Ages, confessing every known sin and seeking forgiveness, pleading for healing. Day became night, and my warm tears began to freeze on my face in the icy night air.

Hours later I returned to my room, feeling as heavy as when I had left. On top of the despair, I now had to deal with the memories I had stirred up. I could find no peace in the silence that only mocked me, as self-messages swirled in my head, taking on a life of their own. By Sabbath afternoon I felt there was no help to be found in God. While I had been preaching to others about the value of being naked and vulnerable before God, I remained an emotional cripple and a dysfunctional derelict, who had learned to wear fig leaves to cover up life's great hurts. I was so distressed by my situation that even though the snow was falling heavily that night, I stole away from the retreat and drove the treacherous 30 miles back to my home.

I began to feel better the next day. The coughing and chest pains stopped, but the emotional burden still lay heavily on my heart. Nothing inside seemed to have changed as I returned to work. The following weekend I had to return to California for another session of my ninth-quarter Master of Divinity degree requirement for field school. I stayed in a motel nearby, where I shared a room with another female seminarian.

This particular session began with a lecture by a psychologist. No one had said anything to me, but as the questions were asked during the session, I soon realized I had been targeted as the cause, or one of the causes, of a perceived conflict that had been created at the previous session. Normally, when I am under the gun like this, I do one of two things: act defensively and mouth off, or become depressed and suicidal. But when the day ended, I discovered that I had neither of those feelings. What's more, I invited some friends to a restaurant for dinner.

At the end of the meal, I gave the waitress my American Express card. She returned shortly with my card—and a pair of scissors—and proceeded to cut the card into small pieces, according to instructions she had received over the phone. Later, I learned that someone at my bank had forgotten to record my payment and kept my check in his desk drawer for more than two months. Since I hadn't used the card in some time, I was not aware of the situation. It was later replaced, and I received a letter of apology from the bank. But neither my friends nor I knew this information that night. It was one of those embarrassing moments we all hope we will never experience. But I walked away unscathed. I began to think something must be wrong. My old despair button must be out of order.

After my devotional one morning I stepped out on the balcony of our motel that overlooked a mountain not yet browned by the California sun. As I admired its beauty and strength, the Spirit of God began to speak to me. He showed me how I had been healed at the Gonzaga retreat, but I had been so deep in self-recrimination He couldn't begin to work out the healing effects in my life.

The changes that progressively manifested themselves were tremendous, but I walked around waiting for the other shoe to drop. It never did. I have none of the old pain. That little girl in me who had been crying out for acceptance and recognition had been integrated into the adult me. I was no longer fragmented; I was a whole, healed child of God.

It has been almost ten years since I experienced that touch of grace, and every day with Jesus gets sweeter than the day before. Just as no one embraces time like those who have been given a few months to live, and no one appreciates freedom as those who've been imprisoned, so also no one knows relief better than those of us who've been broken or afflicted by the adversities of sin and have had to wait on God for His touch of grace. *"Those who wait upon the Lord,"* on tiptoes or as a servant, *"will renew their strength, they will mount up with wings like eagles"* (Isaiah 40:31) to soar with our Savior, whose touch of grace is always worth waiting for.

---

1. Ellen G. White, *The Desire of Ages*, 344.
2. Ibid., 344, 345.
3. George Barna, *The Second Coming of the Church* (Word, 1998), 1.
4. Abraham Joshua Heschel, *The Sabbath* (Noonday Press, 1996), 13.
5. Ibid., 14.
6. Walter Brueggemann, *Finally Comes the Poet* (Fortress Press, 1990), 91-96.
7. Ibid., 97.

Chapter 6

watching and
waiting

Three apprentice devils were preparing to graduate from training school. Each one presented their professor, Satan, with their ideas for the destruction of humanity. The first one said that he would tell people there is no God. Satan rejected that idea, saying that not only do people have a gut feeling that there is a God, but there's enough evidence in nature to affirm their faith. The second devil said that he would announce that there is no hell, but again, to their surprise, Satan rejected that strategy. He told them that most of the people on earth already live in hell and know that there are consequences for sin, so that idea just would not work. The third diabolical apprentice said that he would tell the people on earth there is no hurry, no need to rush into making decisions and taking action. To this Satan gladly responded: "Go quickly across the earth; you will be very successful in winning men and women by the thousands."

William Barclay's fable is relevant to this hybrid generation of Boomers and Busters, "X-ers" and "Next"-ers with our plans for the year 2000 and beyond. Why? Because one of the most dangerous delusions influencing this multi-labeled, diverse generation is that time will go on indefinitely. There is always "tomorrow" to make decisions even if they have eternal implications. From the day the devil convinced Adam and Eve to believe the lie that they would not surely die if they disobeyed God, tomorrow, *mañana,* has been one of the most dangerous words in the human vocabulary. As a result, even though we rush about to attain some of the desires of our hearts, we have all succumbed to the subtle influence of procrastination when it comes to accomplishing some of the more meaningful demands of life.

The paradox in the world God loves so much is that we are a nation addicted to speed, but we delay important, eternal decisions until the very last minute. The Word of God says, *"Today, if you hear His voice, do not harden your hearts"* (Hebrews 3:7; see 4:7), but so many respond by saying, "I'll give my life tomorrow; it's only a day away."

The seeming contradiction for the church, the bride of Christ—for whom He has gone to prepare the greatest wedding feast the human family will ever experience—is that having made the decision for eternal life, it is called to watch and wait for the promised *parousia.* It's a case of hurry up and wait, particularly for those who do not expect that Jesus Christ can, and will, come again to receive the righteous to Himself and to put an end to evil.

Whether we are ready or not, as you well know, the return of Christ is not only certain, it is soon, not as humans count soon, but as God settles it. When He comes, it will be a powerful, personal, and public end to sin. God's purpose will triumph over human and cosmic rebellion. Ultimately and eternally, good will be victorious over evil. It will be a time of judgment, a separation of evil and restoration of good, when the secret thoughts of our hearts and the innermost character of our person will be known to all. It will be sudden and unexpected, like a flash of lightning in the sky at a time when only God knows. So don't let anyone lead you astray with foolish speculations of specific dates and times when the Lord is coming. Just be ready as you watch and wait, for even God the Son, in His incarnate state, did not know the day or the hour, and God the Holy Spirit has not revealed it to us.

The disciples did not know when Jesus would come again. In fact, they expected His return in their own lifetime (see 1 Thessalonians 4:16, 17; Revelation 22:10). Preachers, no matter how popular, prophetic, and prolific, are also not privy to the time of Christ's return. All we have are signs, such as the abundance of false messiahs, famines, earthquakes, wars and rumors of wars, listed in Matthew 24 and Luke 21. According to George Knight, these are reminders that our faithful, covenant-keeping God is not yet finished with the plan of salvation and will keep His promise to return and rescue us out of this evil age. He wrote: "It appears that these signs and most others in this chapter [Matthew 24] are similar to the sign of the rainbow that God gave to Noah as a remembrance of His covenant after the flood. Thus every time Noah saw the rainbow he would remember the faithfulness of God, who promised to never again destroy the earth by a flood. It was a sign that God was faithful to His promise (Genesis 9:12-16)."[1]

The day and hour of the second coming of Christ is an extremely well kept secret. To help us avoid being caught by surprise, as well as to stem the human penchant for speculation, Jesus spent an inordinate amount of time using five parables in Matthew 23 to 25, charging us to be watchful and ready while waiting. In one place He said, *"Watch therefore, be on the alert, for you know not which day your Lord is coming. But be sure of this, that if the head of the house had known at what time of the night the thief was coming, he would have been on the alert and would not have allowed his house to be broken into. For this reason you be ready too; for the Son of Man is coming at an hour when you do not think He will"* (Matthew 24:42-44).

The following passages in Matthew and Revelation have been most instructive to me when it comes to understanding the long delay of His return and the way in which the people of God are called to watch for and wait on the Lord.

Behold the Bridegroom!

It was a glorious morning! I woke up with a smile on my face and a song in my heart. In spite of the chill in the early morning air from the unusually severe Washington D.C. winter, I threw off the covers with an air of anticipation. I bounded out of bed, landing on the balls of my feet like an Olympic gymnast. The sensation was so great that I continued the rhythm by flinging my arms wide to stretch. My chest seemed to have a mind of its own as it stuck out automatically in the much admired, perhaps poorly imitated, pose of a gymnast. Suddenly I sensed the applause of an approving, unseen host of angels. I gleefully bowed as I imagined the angels raising their scores, one after the other to reveal a perfect 10, 10, 10. I accepted the accolades with childlike glee, and my heart seemed to burst with a cheery song as I skipped to the shower, singing loudly.

Now some people have such great voices when they sing that the sound is liable to break a glass, but when I sing, my voice curls steel. Still, that did not stop me from making a joyful noise that morning.

The truth is, I cannot carry a tune, not even in a bucket. In fact, in every church where I have served, my singing has been the object of funny stories and challenges. Once, when we were running a deficit in our annual giving at my church, during an offering appeal, a member of our finance committee good-naturedly told the congregation that if they did not defeat the deficit that day, he would call on me to sing a solo. We all laughed heartily, but the congregation showed what they thought of my singing when they gave more than we needed. I still threaten to sing. In fact, I even opened a sermon with a few bars of a favorite song, making a joyful noise to the Lord, many decades ago.

That special morning a few decades ago, I sang at the top of my lungs, and the thought never entered my mind to stop singing. It was going to be a great day because I had accomplished a long-awaited goal, to preach in one of the largest, more prestigious churches in the area. It was a *coup* greater than one could imagine in those days, especially since I was a female and a woman of color, being asked to do something no other theology student of any race or gender had ever been asked to do. I gloated privately as I gushed with pride.

I left the shower to carefully lay out my clothes, choosing a semi-silky, beige skirt with tiny pleats running from the elastic waist to the tip of the tiny hem. A matching silk blouse and stockings purchased especially for the occasion topped off the ensemble as I clicked my fingers and sang "color coordinated and I'm feeling fine" to my made-up tune. I dressed carefully, accentuating the beige with a black, waist-length, A-line jacket cut to augment the geometric lines of my then-slender frame, black shoes and a "drop-dead" black hat. As I adjusted the hat in front of the full-length mirror, I couldn't help taking one last, long, lingering look before leaving my apartment. I shamelessly exclaimed, "O-o-o-o-h girl, you're looking go-o-o-od!"

I ran out of the house to the car and drove to the church, singing psalms and songs of praise. I felt really good. When I arrived at the church, I was escorted to a small room behind the platform reserved for participants in the worship. As I waited, I was joined by several white males in their traditional black suits and white shirt. I congratulated myself on adding a little color and variety to spice up the old theme. I was really proud of being the only woman among those men in black.

We prayed together and as we walked through the barely lit, narrow corridor toward the platform, we passed a full-length mirror, tarnished by time so that one could see shadows of patterns formed from the peeling substance on its back, but I couldn't resist one last admiring glance. Actually it was several glances as I tried in vain to resist the urge to stop and stare as I whispered in my heart, "Girl, you look great!" No one seemed to notice and if they did, they were too courteous to even give a sign by word or body language.

I was more than ready for that magnificent moment as we walked onto the platform and knelt for a moment of silent prayer while the organist played the introit. As the others were praying, I busied myself adjusting my jacket, picking invisible bits of lint from my sleeves, brushing my skirt, and straightening my hat. Forgetting the purpose for which I had been called that day, I whispered confidently to myself, in the words of a Brooklyn buddy, "Home girl is gonna blow today!"

Unbeknown to me, my skirt had fallen over my shoes, and the pencil-thin high heel of my right foot was stuck in the hem. As soon as the introit was over, we all sprang to our feet and at that very moment, when I stood, my skirt did not. Because the waist was elastic over a silk blouse, it not only stayed behind, but also slipped almost down to my knees. I fell back to the floor when I realized what had happened. I began to panic as I frantically reached backward to extricate myself and could not. I thought quickly about how I would get out of that potentially embarrassing situation without attracting the attention of the other platform participants or the audience, most of whom were still on their knees, as I shook my right foot vigorously to loosen the heel and dislodge my skirt.

Now I want you to imagine this without bursting a blood vessel from laughing too hard. On my left was the very serious senior pastor, who had taken a great risk to invite me, a student, to his pulpit. And there I was, at the most sacred moment, kneeling on the floor, shaking like a dog scratching its ear with a hind leg as I shook my foot very hard, still unable to extricate myself from that increasingly embarrassing situation.

6—A.

The senior pastor must have thought that I was overcome by an evil spirit, the way he frowned and cleared his throat to get my attention, followed by sharp gestures as he moved closer to me, indicating that he wanted me to stand, at once. I couldn't, so I knelt there with a helpless look on my face as he continued to gesture, his face clouded with a look of disapproval. By then, the congregation realized that something was wrong, and since I was immediately behind the pulpit and could not be easily seen, they were leaning to the right and left, like in the old V-8 television commercials, to see what was happening. The senior pastor finally realized that I was in trouble and knelt down and undid my skirt from my shoe. I quickly tried to regain enough composure to nervously walk backward to my seat to try and recover from that very publicly humiliating situation.

I was crippled with embarrassment by the time I finally sat down. I began to weep inside. I began to implore God, saying, "How could You do this to me, after all I've done for You?" The title of my sermon that day was "An Attitude of Fortitude," and believe me, it took a lot of fortitude to begin and to get through that ordeal. When it was over, I was surprised that anyone had been blessed. I spoke as though I was present in body and absent in mind as I nursed the shame, not only from the moment, but every other shame-based experienced that had risen up to accuse and abuse me that morning.

After the service, I ran for refuge in a stall of the restroom, where I pouted and prayed, "God, I can't go out there and face those people again!" Then the sweet, comforting presence of the Holy Spirit brought me to my senses. Remember how much pride I had when I knelt to pray? "Well," said the Spirit, speaking to my heart, "you were not ready to be a spokesperson for God. You are called, my friend, but you are not ready to serve!"

I will always remember that occasion. Thank God I have grown beyond it and outgrown, by God's grace, the need to behave like that. But I will never forget the many lessons I learned from it. One of the most important lessons was that I was not ready to be the instrument of God that He had told me I would be, because I was attempting to grasp by *works* what He had promised would be mine by *faith*.

I also found an object lesson for the church, the people of God who are anxiously anticipating the second coming of Christ. For in the same way I was caught off guard and publicly humiliated by that unexpected incident, so I believe the world, especially complacent Christians in it, will be caught unawares when the *parousia*, that Mount of Transfiguration epiphany or appearance, unfolds in human history. In order to be really ready, let us consider and learn from the following parable that emphasizes the importance of watching while waiting for deliverance out of this evil age:

"Then the kingdom of heaven will be comparable to ten virgins, who took their lamps, and went out to meet the bridegroom. And five were foolish, and five were prudent. For when the foolish took their lamps, they took no oil with them, but the prudent took oil in flasks along with their lamps. Now while the bridegroom was delaying, they all got drowsy and began to sleep. But at midnight there was a shout, 'Behold, the bridegroom! Come out to meet him.' Then all those virgins rose, and trimmed their lamps. And the foolish said to the prudent, 'Give us some of your oil, for our lamps are going out.' But the prudent answered, saying, 'No, there will not be enough for us and you too; go instead to the dealers and buy some for yourselves.' And while they were going away to make the purchase, the bridegroom came, and those who were ready went in with him to the wedding feast; and the door was shut, and later the other virgins also came, saying, 'Lord, lord, open up for us.' But he answered and said, 'Truly I say to you, I do not know you.' Be on the alert then, for you do not know the day nor the hour" (Matthew 25:1-13).

The more I study the Bible, the more I am convinced that we should return to the teaching methods of our Master, who used real, earthly stories to give heavenly lessons in parables such as this one. These simple tales, often drawn from daily life, paint an indelible portrait of God and His gracious dealings with people. They yield their inner secrets and outer substance only to those who consistently and faithfully study them. They are like islands that offer a place of refuge to those lost in a storm at sea. They are like a ball of yarn with a protruding strand which, when pulled, unravels truths that are a secret source of joy. As they yield their inner, unforgettable secrets, they draw us closer to God and help us discover spiritual truths with practical answers for our lives and times.

Under closer scrutiny, the bride in this parable represents the church (apparently the second Eve), for whom the groom (the second Adam of Romans 4) gave Himself—heart, mind, soul, and body. The messenger symbolizes preachers or teachers of the gospel, called and inspired by the Holy Spirit, who faithfully cry out, regardless of the situation: " *'Behold the bridegroom! Come out to meet him!'* "Those men and women who are divinely *"made a minister"* (Ephesians 3:7) to proclaim the good news that the long awaited Bridegroom, Jesus Christ our Lord, is coming soon, must do so without fear, the inexhaustible enemy of faith, in this the midnight hour of these last days. But notice that as important as the bride and messenger may be to the successful engagement and unfolding of this drama, they are not the focus of this narrative. It is the ten virgins, the bridesmaids, who represent every individual member of the priesthood of believers, whose sole purpose it is to watch and wait, who are under scrutiny in this powerful parable. Here Jesus carefully defines the differences between those who are wise and ready and those who are foolish and not prepared for His anticipated appearance.

The scene of this parable is set against the background of a wedding celebration, one of the most joyous events in the human experience, just as the hope of the Second Coming should be for believers. Whether we've been married or not, all of us have had occasion to share in the exciting, nervous wedding activities that last anywhere up to forty-eight hours from the rehearsal to the wedding reception. As a result, we can all relate to this story, no matter how old or young we may be.

Although it's not necessary to understand every nuance of Jewish wedding rituals, to better understand some of the profound lessons in this story, there are a few details of crucial importance. For example, Jews in the time of Jesus practiced endogamy (marriage within a specific tribe, similar social setting, religious community, or system of beliefs) although a few, generally kings such as Solomon and Ahab, were exogamous (married outside of their religious faith and culture). Weddings in Palestine were also long, drawn-out affairs that lasted a week and involved the entire community. The regular domestic duties and religious obligations were suspended so that the wedding party and all the guests could relish the delight of the event. The high point of the week occurred when the bridegroom came to take the bride from her family's home to the place he had prepared for her. It was an exciting enactment of Solomon's words: *"He has brought me to his banquet hall, and his banner over me is love"* (Song of Solomon 2:4).

The transfer of the bride was an event accompanied by a great deal of preparation on the part of the bride. Some of these began many years in advance of the actual wedding ceremony in a culture where families betrothed their children at a very early age and bartered for the dowry to bind the agreement. But on that final day, there was great pomp and pageantry as the bridal pair was decked out with ornaments, including garlands and jewelry, to distinguish them from the other celebrants. Ten chaste, unmarried maidens energetic enough to endure the rigors of this tradition were selected to wait with the bride and accompany her on that final journey to the home of her betrothed. Their special task was to wait with the bride for the arrival of the groom, then lead the grand procession, accompanied by loud, lively music, to his home, where the final ceremonies were conducted and the wedding feast held. This ceremony usually took place at night to heighten the excitement of the bride and the enjoyment of the participants. The chief responsibility of each bridesmaid was to carry a blazing torch as they led the marriage procession, singing, dancing, shouting glad tidings of great joy about the groom's progress through the streets toward the newlyweds' home. They also functioned as witnesses to check on the bride's virginity in the bridal chamber (see Mark 2:19, KJV) so that they could pass on the "tokens of her virginity" to her parents as the final ritual of the marriage after the consummation.

Now, the fun part of all this was that no one knew the exact time of the bridegroom's appearance. He kept the exact moment of his arrival a secret, even though he was required to send a messenger ahead of him shouting: "Behold, the bridegroom! Come out to meet him!" It was to be a big surprise, as the second coming of Christ promises to be. It was something like the surprise some of my staff and church members gave me when I first arrived in California in 1996.

I arrived on a night flight, so I thought I'd travel as comfortably as I could in my grubbiest jeans. I was expecting to be met only by one of the pastors and his wife. At about 11:30 p.m., when my plane landed at the Ontario airport, I walked off casually, looking for the pastor, when I saw a group of about thirty people waving and screaming, with lots of balloons. At first, I felt like a deer caught in the headlights of a speeding vehicle, because I wasn't dressed and ready for this kind of reception. Fortunately, I was able to recover quickly as I was drawn into the infectious excitement of the surprise. The exuberance of those who greeted me, and the curiosity of some people in the airport, who kept asking if I was a celebrity when I was presented with the balloons, helped me catch the mood of the moment. While the group of greeters, including some of the other pastors and their wives, were busily snapping photos and making videos like the paparazzi, our emotions were stirred to an even higher level when a little boy in the crowd began to cry loudly and uncontrollably. Nothing his father did seemed to satisfy or pacify him until we discovered that he wanted one of my balloons, which I quickly gave him in exchange for a few photos with him. The balloons were beautiful. I was especially delighted with a purple one—my favorite color—with the slogan, "Queen of the Hill." It left such an indelible impression on my heart that when the time came for me to transfer my car license from Massachusetts to California, I chose the letters "QOTH," which, along with the framed balloon in my office, keeps the memory of that special moment fresh in my mind. The entire event was, and still is, one of the most powerful and pleasing surprises of my life. Every time I reflect on that experience, I immediately imagine that the second coming of Christ will be similar, only on a much more gigantic scale.

Unfortunately, many of those who first believed and broadcast the Second Coming have become quite cynical about it, much like I am about Christmas. When I was a child, I loved waiting for Christmas morning to savor and relish the scrumptious tastes of my grandmother's special breakfast that she prepared only at Christmastime. It was not only the food, but it was the only time the entire family seemed able to eat together. Even though we were too poor to provide or exchange gifts, the warmth of the family made it an exceptional time, the waiting for which I sometimes felt would kill me. But I must confess that I no longer wait with glad anticipation for Christmas, not because I'm no longer living at home or the fact that my beloved grandmother has been laid to rest, waiting for the second coming of our Lord. The reason is that I've become quite jaded. The commercialization of Christmas and the emphasis on Santa Claus are too much for me to bear.

Some believers who waited with longing as they watched for the signs of the Second Coming have also become jaded. They were confident that Christ would come in the springtime of their youth. But now, decades later, as they struggle through the terrors of the winter years in a culture where Jesus seems to sell more than He saves, and He still has not appeared to put an end to sin, they have become disillusioned. They are turning their eyes from that glorious hope and are not enjoying the kingdom of God as one ongoing, joyous party, as Tony Campolo put it in his book, *The Kingdom of God Is a Party*. Instead, their lives often echo the words of 2 Peter 3:4: *"Where is the promise of His coming? For ever since the fathers fell asleep, all continues just as it was from the beginning of creation."*

But thank God for Jesus Christ, who is still breaking into the midst of our weary world of waiting with His powerful words of caution: *"Be on the alert [watch and wait], for you do not know which day your Lord is coming!"* Because of this appeal, there are others who draw relevant lessons from this parable, recorded only by Matthew, whose message was specifically directed to the Jews, the ones who felt jaded about the first advent and appearance of the Messiah.

Sometimes we forget that the story of the bridegroom's appearance is about one of the most exciting events in human history, but more often we neglect to notice how much all the virgins were alike. All were invited to participate in the wedding. They were carefully chosen and set apart from the rest of the community to conduct the special task of leading the wedding procession, just as Christians are selected and sanctified by God to lead the unbelieving world to eternal life in the kingdom of heaven. All ten were committed to the cause of waiting and watching with and for the bride. All were virgins, free from impurity, unspoiled by the prevailing passions of the day, unspotted by the seductive sirens of sin, emancipated from "thingdom" to serve in God's kingdom. They had no guile in them and were not polluted by false doctrines or tainted by cheap grace.

All took their lamps. The lamp is a symbol of the Word of

God. The psalmist said, *"Thy word is a lamp unto our feet and a light unto our path"* (Psalm 119:105, paraphrased). This means that they all relied on the Word of God to deliver them out of darkness and lead them through the valleys of the shadows of death. They went out from the world, though they were still in it, to wait for the arrival of the Bridegroom in the sanctuary of salvation.

All had lamps with oil, which I am interpreting as representing the Holy Spirit, the oil burning brighter and brighter until that wonderful day, that unknown time they anxiously awaited when the bridegroom would come and fulfill the joy of their anticipation. The oil functioned in the lamp as the Holy Spirit does in the world— as the true Light (see John 1:9) to convict it of sin (see John 16:8) and help us acknowledge Christ's Lordship (see 1 Corinthians 12:3). His sanctifying presence in the believer helps us to be obedient to God (see 1 Peter 1:2) and to understand the truth of His Word (see John 14:17). He is in the church to guide its operations (see Acts 13:1-4), to equip it with special gifts (see 1 Corinthians 12) and to fill the hearts of believers (see Titus 3:5, 6).

All were paralyzed by prolonged preparation or extended anticipation and got drowsy, so that they slept until they were jarred awake by the midnight cry, "Behold the bridegroom! Come out to meet him!" None of them called on inner resources to stay awake and watch with the bride. Their lethargy is similar to the lukewarmness of Laodicea, the seventh church in Revelation 3, also described by many as the Christian church of the last days of earth's history. This church is so designated because it appears to be sleeping through some of the most significant times of her life. Yet, there is no need for self-recrimination on the part of the saints. There is no need to sit back and wring our hands in despair because we've been tagged as the Laodicean church, for we are only temporarily infected by the problem of being lukewarm.

First, it is a human condition that those who labor long and hard for the Lord will get tired. The ones who never get tired are not doing God's business, but are simply dancing with the devil. They are on permanent vacation from the vision of God for His church in the world. They are the ones who don't mind taking His money but don't want to do His work, complaining that He is a hard taskmaster (see Matthew 25:24). But those who labor will get tired at the end of a long day, and it has been a long, long day of waiting since the promise was made. The difference is whether or not we are all prepared to respond properly when the midnight cry comes to awaken us, saying "Behold, the bridegroom! Come and meet Him!"

The alarms are going off around us. Listen to the news. Look at the litany of abuses and violence around us. Notice how Christians are treating one another. Bible prophecy which foretold that difficult time would come, when the hearts of humans would grow colder and colder each day (see 2 Timothy 3:1-17), is being fulfilled around us. We are living in times when the wake-up call has been made. The signs are all around us, but are we ready to arise and shine and give God the glory by reclaiming our true Laodicean nature?

To a Jew, a name was not just a badge of identification as it generally is in western cultures. The name of a person indicated their nature and character. Since the book of Revelation was written by a Jew and also uses the apocalyptic genre of symbols, it behooves this generation of Christians who claim to belong to the Laodicean church to discover the true meaning of this name and the intent of the author in using it.

The word *Laodicea* is derived from two Greek words—*laos,* which means people at large, especially those assembled for a meeting such as worship, and is the root from which our word "laity" comes. The second word is *dikaios,* which means righteous. Thus Laodicea simply means a righteous people.

Several cities in Asia Minor and one of the seven churches in Revelation were named Laodicea in honor of Laodice, the wife of Antiochus II, who rebuilt that city of Ephesus where the church was located. Legend has it that she was one of the most beautiful, gracious women to have walked the earth. She was industrious, loyal, and loved by the citizens of her world. It is also said that she was an incredibly elegant bride, which befits the name and nature of this last church, the bride of Christ for whom He will be coming soon.

I have never seen a lukewarm bride, one with a nature that was neither hot nor cold. In fact, having conducted dozens of weddings, I believe I can say with some authority that I have never seen a cold bride. All brides come to the altar dressed in everything, on their faces, feet, and body, which will accentuate what God has already endowed them with. Even if they had a cold or the flu from the stress of preparing and getting married, they all seem hot to trot down the aisle to say, "I do."

In view of the apparently hot nature of brides, it seems quite unfortunate to me that the nature of the bride-church of Christ, in these last days, just hours before His arrival, could be lukewarm. It seems evident that this is definitely and only the diagnosis of a malady that is temporary and can be permanently cured. Yet, some people are adamant that Jesus Christ is coming for a lukewarm bride, instead of securing and applying the medication, the gospel of grace, the only cure for lukewarmness. We, the bride of Christ, had better begin to get dressed and ready for the marriage feast of the Lamb announced in Revelation 19:7-9. We must do so by putting on Christ's seamless robe of righteousness as we ready ourselves for the time when He shall come to take us home, to the place He has gone to prepare for us according to His promise in John 14:1-3.

Furthermore, when we consider the true meaning of the name Laodicea, in the context of the Second Coming, one must conclude that the word means a righteous people for whom Christ will be coming, and not a lukewarm group of ineffective, faithless people. The problem is that, right now, we are suffering from a subtle sickness that makes us lukewarm in the church body politic akin to a bad case of influenza that temporarily destroys the good health in a human body.

For example, if your significant other has a terrible bout of the flu, you would not change his or her name to influenza, would you? Instead, you would quickly seek out and find the best medicine or the best physician so that they may be brought back to perfect health as soon as possible. Yet, when God said that the Laodicean church is *"lukewarm, and [is] neither hot nor cold,"* we adopted the nature of lukewarmness rather than accept the character of Laodicea so that the cure offered by our Great Physician in His Word might be our experience. Remember the prescription Jesus offered in Revelation 3:18? *"I advise you to buy from Me gold refined by fire, that you may become rich, and white garments, that you may clothe yourself, and that the shame of your nakedness may not be revealed; and eye salve to anoint your eyes, that you may see."*

Gold refined in the fire is the human life perfected through the agony of defeat and the adversities we experience but, by God's grace, are able to overcome. It is said of Jesus, our sinless Savior: *"Although He was a Son, He learned obedience from the things which He suffered . . ."* (Hebrews 5:8). We sons and daughters of God, are likewise being perfected, but too often we have come to despise the time of preparation for the promised glorification at the end of this evil age. The problem is that many of us have bought into the idea that discipleship means easy street—freedom from illness, trials, and tribulations. We've grown to despise our adversities rather than to embrace and grow through them, in spite of the preponderance of evidence that suggests the opposite.

In describing the cost of discipleship, Dietrich Bonhoeffer cautioned that "the cross is not the terrible end to an otherwise god-fearing and happy life, but it meets us at the beginning of our communion with Christ. When Christ calls a man, he bids him come and die."[2]

Francis Frangipane noted that "our humble state as the Lord's bondslaves is but a preparation for the coming forth of Christ in our lives. Yes, we have been 'chastened' of the Lord. However, the goal of the Lord's chastening is not merely to punish; He seeks to make us *chaste*: pure and spiritually flawless."[3]

When God wanted to save His beloved prophet, Elijah, He sent him to live with a widow in a town called Zarephath (see 1 Kings 17:8). This was a Phoenician town whose name means "furnaces." It was the workshop for refining metal to produce images of pagan gods of fire and fertility as well as excellent glassware made from the sand in that region of Sidon. Although it was also famous for the production of purple dye and olive oil, Zarephath was well known among the people for the constant heat produced by the daily operation of its blazing hot furnaces. Legend has it that when people were angry with each other, instead of saying, "Go to hell" as some do nowadays, they would exhort each other to go to Zarephath. The name became synonymous with the "lake of fire" kind of heat. Yet, when God wanted to perfect His prophet and save him, He sent him to Zarephath.

Sometimes adversities, crises, and hurtful criticisms are hurled at God's people as a tool of the enemy for evil. But God always uses them for good. Jesus said His true disciples would face persecution and privations. He warned that they would *be hated by all on account of [His] name, but it is the one who endures to the end who will be saved"* (Matthew 10:22). It seems like a divine plan that often the only cure for lukewarmness is a fiery furnace where, through Christ, we are made into gold so that in the end we will be safe to save.

All ten virgins knew that it was the privilege and pleasure of the bridegroom to delay his appearance as long after the announcement of his arrival as he desired. Therefore, it was no surprise to them that after such a long delay their lamps had gone out. But when they rose to trim them, there was one small but significant detail that distinguished some from the others. Five were wise enough to take extra oil with them, and five were so foolish that they failed to be ready for what they all knew could be a long, long wait.

If, as I have suggested, the oil represents the work of the Holy Spirit, how can one run out of it? I believe that some genuinely converted Christians run out of the power and presence of the Holy Spirit in their lives because they live only on the drama of their original encounter with God. They do not study the Bible and grow, but spend their time reliving the excitement and passion of that first moment. I once knew a famous entertainer who was miraculously converted. He left the world of entertainment to find solace in a Christian seminary, but while there, the believers sent him around like a trophy, to give his testimony at a variety of meetings. What the church leaders did not realize was that every time he told his story, in order to be authentic, he had to relive a great deal of the emotional experience of what he was trying to leave behind. At the same time, because of the rigorous schedule he was forced to adopt, his prayer and devotional life began to slip away, along with the little discipline he had garnered, being unable to hold him to his commitment to study every day. Soon, he began to slip and slide back into the old false self. He was able to keep his backslidden life a secret for some time, but eventually it reared its ugly head in a very public and humiliating fashion for himself and the church.

The reaction of those who used him, and those who vicariously lived through the sensational testimonies he gave, was appalling. He was branded a fraud and left to the devil and his demise. His conversion was real, but he was not given an opportunity to become fully grounded in the Word and will of God by those who senselessly used him to attract big crowds to their programs and get their names in the public media.

When I first became a Christian, many people attempted to use me in that fashion, but thank God I had seen what had happened to that man. I was able to wait until I was grounded in Christ before telling my story. To avoid the same experience of that famous artist, I had to repeatedly remind myself of these words: *"Do not call to mind [relive] the former things, or ponder [focus on] things of the past. Behold, [God] will do something new, now it will spring forth; Will you be aware of it?"* (Isaiah 43:18, 19). If we insist on dwelling in the past, we will wake up one day to discover that we have run out of the empowering presence of God's Spirit-oil with, and in, us.

Others who are truly born-again believers, depending only on the preaching and teaching of their pastors without finding and feeding on spiritual food for themselves through daily study of the Word and devotions with God, may run out of the Holy Spirit in their lives. They run the risk of waking up to the fact that the original fullness of the Holy Spirit that caused them to dream dreams and see visions, has been expended and they are like the empty lamps of the five foolish virgins.

Before I responded to God's call to the pastoral ministry, I experienced one of the driest spells of my spiritual life. I had been a legalist, a caustic critic of God's people, and an incorrigible complainer about how harsh life in the Lord had become. I did not read my Bible or books by Christian authors, and when I went to church, I spent my time dissecting the sermon and gossiping about the preacher and God's people. It did not take long for my spiritual experience to become as dry as the hills of Gilboa. I was not a nice person to be around then. I was frustrated and paranoid about everything. Thus, it is not very difficult for me to understand believers who come across like that these days, or to imagine the frustrated frenzy, the anxious appeals that followed when the five foolish bridesmaids realized they had run out of oil with none in reserve.

Try to capture the urgency recorded in Matthew 25:8 as they begged the others, saying, *"'Give us some of your oil, for our lamps are going out.'"* Notice that they were not yet completely out, but by then their lamps were fluttering, flickering, with the last drops of oil. Maybe they tried to fake it by sputtering glossolalia like a young man I met at a church I attended with a friend.

In this charismatic congregation the majority of the members spoke in tongues during the worship service. Some of them seemed to be genuinely in ecstasy, but this one young man seemed to be in travail. He was wringing his hands, crying out, and making more unintelligible noises than normal, as though he was trying to outdo others around him. It was such a sad sight as he faked being overcome by the Spirit. I saw him steal glances out of the corners of his eye before increasing the decibel of his shouts. After the service I sought him out and identified myself as a pastor as I invited him to pray with me.

I did not say which denomination I represented for fear of being rejected, so he instantly assumed that I was one of the watchdog members of his church sent to spy out those who were not participating fully in the outpouring of the Spirit. He immediately began to confess that he had been going through a dry spell in his spiritual experience. As a result, he had spent the last few months faking the presence of the Holy Spirit by being more vigorous than those around when he spoke in tongues. He also said that he was afraid of being cut off from the group or of being despised by those who had been blessed by this gift, if he should be found out.

He told how he had never learned nor understood what it meant to be saved, to give one's life to Jesus Christ, but had carried on that charade. As I listened, I felt that God had sent me to that worship service for that single moment. I was able to kneel with that young man, whose heart was truly seeking reconciliation with God, and lead him into a relationship with Jesus Christ. He never returned to that church after we studied the Bible together. I also had the privilege of baptizing him. He continues to grow in grace, rightly exercising the gifts of the Holy Spirit with which he has been blessed.

So what did those foolish virgins do when it became obvious that they had no oil and their lamps had finally given out? They began to beg and plead for a loan of oil from those who were smart enough to have extra oil in reserve. How tragic to come so close and miss the one thing for which they had hoped and planned and longed for. It was their worst nightmare.

It must have been like the young man who wanted desperately to come to America and leave the famine and war-damaged world of his native land. He heard that there was a lottery for one hundred visas for those who could read English up to the standards set by the American embassy. He quickly taught himself to read English and did so well at it that the other villagers came to him for tutoring. He graciously helped everyone and by the day of the lottery, they were all proficient in English, but when the tests were over, many had passed except that young man. He was heard to have said that it would have been better if he had died when he heard the sounds of celebration coming from those whom he had helped, knowing that he would be left behind.

Imagine how frustrated it must have been for the five foolish virgins when they heard the announcement of the bridegroom's arrival and watched the flames flickering out of their lamps, knowing that they had no oil in reserve. There are four lessons I have learned from their ordeal.

First, there is a time and a way to prepare for the arrival of our Lord, and it isn't when we hear the midnight cry, *"'Behold the bridegroom! Come out to meet Him!'"* The time to get ready is now. This is rehearsal time. We will never have a better opportunity to study to show ourselves approved of God (see 2 Timothy 2:15, KJV). There will never be a better time to practice *"pure and undefiled religion in the sight of our God and Father,"* which is *"to visit orphans and widows in their distress, and to keep oneself unstained by the world"* (James 1:27).

Our Christian heritage has left us with an indelible legacy of how easy it is to fall into the folly of the five foolish virgins. Remember Demas? He was a friend and fellow-worker with the apostle Paul (see Colossians 4:14 and Philemon 23). His name apparently means "popular." He lived up to the nature and meaning of his name as his ability to articulate the gospel brought him great acclaim in the early church. Oh how brightly his lamp burned, but it was short-lived when his love of worldly ease and comforts ensnared him and drew him from fulfilling his divine appointment to preach the gospel. According to the inspired testimony of Paul, Demas, *"having loved this present world,"* deserted him, adding more concern to the apostle's increasingly grave situation (he was being held under house arrest).

How about Diostrephes, whose name means "one who is nourished by God"? He was truly like a shooting star, who went high enough to get his name mentioned in the Bible (see 3 John 9,10), but fell so far and hard that he was condemned by the apostle John. His problem, apparently, was that he lusted after preeminence, loving *"to be first."* He refused to even look at the letter sent by John cautioning him about this sin. He circulated malicious slanders against the beloved apostle while exercising a pernicious influence in the church. In the end, he declined to submit to John's directions or acknowledge his divinely appointed authority, so he was let go from among the believers to be succored by his father, the devil. Today he is only remembered for his evil deeds.

Who can forget Judas? He was the treasurer of the first Christian church. His light burned so brightly that many Christian authors have pointed out the influence he had upon the other disciples. One writer pointed out that sometimes they would double-check their instructions from Jesus with Judas. At other times, they sought his confirmation of the teachings of their Master from this man who was secretly a thief and openly a freedom fighter. But alas, in the midnight hour of his blazing ambition he betrayed the Son of God and sold Him for thirty pieces of silver, the price of a common slave in those days.

So then, how do we prepare for this? First, by totally immersing ourselves in the Word of God so that we are not *"conformed to this world, but [are] transformed by the renewing of [our] mind, that [we] may prove what the will of God is, that which is good and acceptable and perfect"* (Romans 12:2).

Second, we must believe in progressive light as human knowledge increases and the lamp of understanding glows brighter on the Word of God each passing day. Listen to this statement by another Christian author: "There is no excuse for anyone in taking the position that there is no more truth to be revealed and that all our expositions of Scripture are without an error. The fact that certain doctrines have been held as truth for many years by our people is not a proof that our ideas are infallible. Age will not make error into truth, and truth can afford to be fair. No true doctrine will lose anything by close investigation."[4]

We are constantly learning and growing in every aspect of human development, but when it comes to the Word of God, we take one of two positions: the fundamentalist attitude which says, "If it is not written in the King James Version of the Bible, it must be rejected." Some Evangelicals say, "God has said all He plans to in His Word and will not speak through any other extra-biblical prophet until Jesus comes." Both sides are equally wrong, for biblical scholarship has shown that although the King James Version is a most exquisitely literary piece, it is nonetheless a paraphrase. God has also spoken and is speaking through prophets He has raised up and through people in every generation. But before we accept everyone's testimony out of hand or reject the prophetic uttering of others without due consideration, we must get back to the Word of God and *"examine everything carefully; hold fast [only] to that which is good"* (1 Thessalonians 5:21).

Third, we must (using something I borrowed from Chuck Swindoll) BRAG about our faith. That means we are to be Biblical, Relevant, Authentic, and Gracious servants of God who believe that this living Word really works. We must be God's friends and have a personal relationship with Him as we wait for the climax of our hope in the Second Coming. We must not only sing "Give me oil in my lamp, keep me burning," but we must feel the presence of the Holy Spirit oil burning in us so that we become hot for God!

Some people are shocked by my appeals to be hot for God. They are generally the ones embarrassed to respond with even an "Amen" in worship because they are worried about what others may think of them. Some of these same people have no problem jumping, screaming, and clapping without restraint when their teams score at a favorite sports event. Someone greater than the greatest sports heroes, the Holy Spirit, is with us. When He comes upon us we should not be concerned about what people think, but with what He is doing in and through us as we wait for that grand occasion, the coming of the Bridegroom. Still people sit in church and when something grand is said about God, they give only silent acknowledgment, with a slight nod of the head. We live in a world where people get hot over everything, even nonsense, yet we feel bad if we get warm for God as though it is below our dignity or is embarrassing to His divinity. This should not be so! I say, if we understand the cross of Jesus Christ, if we understand the sacrifice that He made, if we understand the irrational love that bought us our salvation, we can't be anything but hot for God.

We need to be energetic and ready, or else we will be like the five foolish virgins who are portrayed in a pathetic position, standing outside the door, shouting, begging, pleading, "*Lord, lord, open up for us.*" They were caught with their lamps empty and learned what we must learn, that there will be a time when we will have to say "No" to those who ask us for oil. Right now is not the time, for we must share every bit of what we have gleaned from the Word of God (see Ephesians 3:7-10), but there will be a time when we will have to say "No" to those who come begging. Some people live on the fumes of a former experience with God. They won't come to church regularly and get involved in the fellowship of believers. They refuse to study their Bible and follow the Word and will of God now, saying they are against organized religion, when they are silent against organized secularism. When the time of the Bridegroom's arrival comes, they will be knocking on our doors, begging us to give them some of our oil. Then it will be too late. If we share what we have at that time, we will run the risk of not having enough for ourselves, and it will be too late to go out and get some more.

Fourth, the wise virgins have an eternal invitation to the final festivities—the marriage banquet of the Lamb:

> *And I heard, as it were, the voice of a great multitude and as the sound of many waters and as the sound of mighty peals of thunder, saying, "Hallelujah! For the Lord our God, the Almighty, reigns. Let us rejoice and be glad and give the glory to Him, for the marriage of the Lamb has come and His bride has made herself ready." And it was given to her to clothe herself in fine linen, bright and clean; for the fine linen is the righteous acts of the saints. And he said to me, "Write, 'Blessed are those who are invited to the marriage supper of the Lamb.'" And he said to me, "These are true words of God"* (Revelation 19:6-9).

According to the grammatical tense in which this verse is written, it appears that the moment of holy matrimony had already taken place, but the consummation of the marriage is yet to come. This is confirmed by the fact that the word "betrothed," which, although it means to "woo and win" in the Greek, has the Hebrew root meaning of "a fine," or to "pay the price," as the bride-price the groom would have paid to be given the right of possession of the bride. The word also appears to be equivalent to marrying the bride, according to Deuteronomy 28:30 and 2 Samuel 3:14. This puts a definite dent in the theory that the marriage of Christ and His church will take place at the Second Coming. Spiritually speaking, it took place at the cross on Calvary when Jesus gave Himself up, passionately, and unreservedly, for His beloved bride, the church, according to Ephesians 5:25.

The Second Coming is equivalent to the grand procession (in the time of Jesus on earth), after the arrival of the bridegroom, with all the lights, pomp, and pageantry. Marriage feasts such as this one took place in the home of the bridegroom after the bride was escorted to his home by her entourage of maidens. It was the social event in the life of the two families, accompanied by generous hospitality if you accepted the invitation and attended, and bitter, lifelong resentment if you refused to attend this last public production in the week-long wedding festivities. The consummation of the marriage followed and, as in the literal marriage, the spiritual one has been delayed until after the big banquet spoken of in Revelation 19:9.

I imagine that on that occasion, the voices of the celebrating numberless multitude of wise virgins, those who remained unpolluted by the wine of immorality or false teachings of the harlot of Revelation 17:1-2, will be like the sound of many waters. They will be like the roar of a million Niagara Falls, like the peal of thousands and ten thousands of thunders. It will be greater than the shouts of satisfaction that erupt when my favorite football team wins the game in the final seconds. It will be a shout of victory combined in a mighty roar of joy when we all see Jesus and sing and shout this victory song: "Amen, Hallelujah! For the Lord our God the Almighty reigns!" Oh for a thousand tongues to sing my Great Redeemer's praise, the glories of my God and King, the triumphs of His grace![5]

Let us rejoice and be exceedingly glad!

The Greek word *agalliomen,* translated "exceedingly glad," or "exult," comes from a special word that means the outward expression of inner joy. This means rejoicing greatly! It is derived from the Hebrew word *gil,* which describes the dance the Jews adopted for the bridegroom based on the legend of how Abraham danced after the events experienced and dramatized in Genesis 15:1-19.

According to that story, after God condescended to enter into a solemn covenant with Abram, using the customs of that generation, He walked between the divided halves of the slaughtered animals to symbolize His perpetual obedience to the covenant. He pledged to Abram that if He should break His promise and fail to fulfill His part of the agreement to make Abram's descendants as many as the stars in the heavens, He would and should be halved like the animals between which He walked. Jewish legend has it that in that magic moment, Abram not only believed God, but when he saw what God had done to ratify this covenant, that old man became ecstatic. He broke out in a robust rhythm of praise, snapping his fingers and stomping his feet in a dance immortalized as the dance of the groom and beautifully portrayed in films such as *Fiddler on the Roof* and *Yentl*. Thereafter, according to legend, this particular kind of dancing has been adopted by bridegrooms and performed after their pledge to the bride at the wedding supper.

Incredibly, it is the same dance that Jesus did when He saw Satan fall from heaven. *"At that very time He rejoiced greatly [that same word for the dance of the bridegroom] in the Holy Spirit"* (Luke 10:21). As His divinity flashed through His human form, the inner experience of joy of the divine Bridegroom couldn't be contained and found expression in this cultural phenomenon. To the amazement of His watching, surprised disciples, Jesus performed the dance of the bridegroom under the power and inspiration of the Holy Spirit. And since the members of the Trinity are always involved in events such as these, I believe it also took place under the affirming eye of His Father to whom He prayed at that moment. No wonder He privately explained to His shocked disciples, *"Blessed are the eyes that see the things you see."* He was expressing a part of the joy that was set before Him (see Hebrews 12:2) that would be fulfilled and experienced at the banquet to which all believers are invited (see Revelation 19:9).

Our passionate Savior could not resist the impulse to perform the *gil* when He saw His chief rival, Satan, fail to steal the heart and affections of His woman, the church. When He knew that the object of His affection—His bride, the church—was His for all eternity, my Lord, and yours, "rejoiced greatly," as most versions translate it. He powerfully performed the sacred dance of the bridegroom in His culture, and it is written down to remind us that the mention of our Savior's matrimony, the very thought of it, should inspire joyous celebration in worship. We must rejoice, especially as we savor the sweet invitation to the wedding supper of the Lamb, the Bridegroom, who daily walks and talks with us, whispering sweet "somethings" (not "nothings") in our hearts to reaffirm and assure us that we are indeed His own.

Giving the glory to Him calls for the demonstration of an attitude of gratitude. It evokes devotion and trust in Jesus which culminates in a voluntary, spontaneous, casting of our crowns at His feet in homage and adoration on earth as it was and is being done in heaven—*for the marriage of the Lamb has come, and His bride has made herself ready.*

Jesus deliberately chose the illustration of a bride making herself ready. Have you noticed that it takes us women almost a lifetime to prepare for our wedding? Unlike men, who seem to cope with nervous anticipation of getting married by waiting until the last day before the wedding to get fitted for a tuxedo, get a haircut and maybe a shoe shine, women begin planning and preparing for that great day almost from the day we are born. As soon as Mom and Dad see their little princess, they begin to talk about the coming of Prince Charming. Consequently, from at least age five, not only do we know who we want to marry but exactly what we want to look like on our wedding day. Even if we never get married, we know what our wedding dress and party are to be as we plan for that day by playing with dolls. We plan every last minute detail, down to the rehearsal and reception, long before we even meet the person we're going to marry. In fact, we do this so regularly, and are so accustomed to thinking in this mode that it makes it difficult for many of us to be single when we are grown up and unmarried. It's as though there's a little voice in our heads reminding us that we've planned this wedding all of our lives and we ought to grab somebody and take them down the aisle before it's too late.

After the engagement, we busy ourselves with finding the perfect wedding gown. First, we have to consult catalogs and books for brides, and then we shop till we drop during weeks and months of trekking from store to store to find the shoes, veil, and a special bargain for the best gown. There is fasting and there are fittings, accompanied by buying dresses for bridesmaids with matching shoes, hats, and gloves. Let's not forget the something borrowed and something blue, gifts for groomsmen, flower girls and Bible boys—and the list goes on and on.

The bride's responsibilities increase at such a rate that they require great organization and steadfast preparation. Nowadays, we have to employ wedding coordinators. As a result of all this, women are usually ready to say "I do" long before they stand at the altar.

That's the kind of extensive preparation God wants His people to enter into as they watch and wait for the second advent of His beloved Son. God uses the imagery of a bride making herself ready for her wedding to emphasize the work His bride must do, under the power of the Holy Spirit, for the final festivities. We, the called-out ones who form the church, must begin by diligently shopping in the sixty-six stores and boutiques in the greatest Mall—the Bible—known to human beings. It is so great that no one has ever exhausted its resources, and it is so handy we can carry it wherever we go. We may purchase, at no cost, the beautiful white wedding garment to clothe ourselves so that the shame of our nakedness is not revealed. We must choose the veil of prayer from the boutique of the beatitudes to cover a multitude of misdemeanors. The bride of Christ must select the shoes of salvation designed by grace, not at Payless stores, but "pay nothing," according to the promise of the gospel which tells us that everything has already been paid in full by the Groom.

After we've made ourselves ready by dressing in the wedding garment provided by our Groom, we can walk confidently down the aisle of righteousness into the arms of our waiting Bridegroom, Jesus Christ the God-man and Lord! The beautiful words, "Sing the wondrous love of Jesus, Sing His mercy and His grace!" written by Eliza E. Hewitt (1851-1920) in the popular hymn, *When We All Get to Heaven*, are ringing through the portals of my mind. Oh what that glorious day will be!

And it was given to her to clothe herself in fine linen, bright and clean.

Notice how we secure the wedding garment. It is given. We can't make it ourselves; we can't buy it with our good works; we can't inherit it from our devoted relatives! There's no charge for it. It's a gift! All we can do is accept and wear this garment that is woven with the golden cords of God's love and tenderly described as the righteous acts of the saints.

The greatest news about this is that we don't have to be rich or religious, white or male, powerful or prominent, to receive this gift. It is offered to everyone, even to those who fall, or fit into the diverse categories of the marginalized misfits. Yet, so many reject it to pay the wages of sin with their eternal life.

Finally, this astounding wedding garment is *made from fine linen*. Not just ordinary linen, but *fine* linen. The finest linen, when woven, could not be distinguished from silk without a magnifying glass. Most of us have bought and worn fine linen without ever giving it a thought as to how it was made. I don't know the process in this technological age, but a closer examination of the procedures used by the ancient producers of fine linen reveals a great deal about what God does to make His bride ready.

Linen was made from a slender reed called flax. The most excellent quality linen came from Egypt, where the plants thrived along the fertile, muddy banks of the river Nile. When the stalks of the flax were ripe, they were pulled up by the root, not cut off as a shoot, and tied in bundles. Then they were spread to dry in the blazing sun on a flat roof. Remember how Rahab, the prostitute, hid the spies from Israel under bundles of flax on her flat roof? (See Joshua 2:6.)

After they were dried, the stalks were vigorously shaken to remove the seeds then put in a steeping pond, where they were weighted down with stones. They were wrung out and dried again, but this time in a hot oven before being bleached and cleaned again. Finally, they were pounded with a firm but tender gavel to loosen the fibers, then twisted into strands and carefully combed to separate the short, broken fibers. Now they were ready to be delivered to the spinner to be woven into fine linen. What an incredible process! It seems just like what God puts us through to make us ready for heaven. That's what He's doing to produce the righteous acts in His saints.

More than two decades ago, God found me in spiritual Egypt, that demilitarized zone of transgression, where everything and anything goes according to the lust of the human heart. I was growing wildly on the banks of the muddy river of sin, but God saw the potential for the finest qualities and proceeded to pull me up by the root. He did not cut off the shoots so they could grow again, but yanked me from the roots of my carnal life. Then He dried me under the glaring heat of the Son of Righteousness. He shook me vigorously with the truth, Jesus Christ, to remove all the seeds of sin from my heart. Then He put me to soak in the steeping pond of His Word, where I was secured by the ten stones of the moral law so that the refreshing, regenerating waters of the Holy Spirit (see Titus 3:5) could soften me. After that, He took me out and wrung out the muddy residues of sin, He used the discipline of sanctification to dry me again in the hot oven of adversity (Romans 8:28). Then He pounded out the hard shards with the tender gavel of the gospel and, in the process, also loosened the leftover, short, broken pieces of sin in me. Every time I think I am ready, He points out a blemish that requires the bleach called the blood of Jesus. He's still not finished. He must pass the sharp-toothed comb of grace through my life until every broken shaft of sin and shame is carefully removed before I am passed on to the Great Spinner, Jesus Christ, to be woven into that majestic matrix of fine linen.

Blessed are those who are invited to the marriage supper of the Lamb.

Happy are the wise virgins. Not only will they be clothed in the fine linen, which is the righteous acts of the saints, but also they will be the special guests of God at the marriage celebration of His Son.

Now there's another supper that has been made ready for the foolish virgins. John the Revelator said:

> *And I saw an angel standing in the sun; and he cried out with a loud voice, saying to all the birds which fly in mid-heaven, "Come, assemble for the great supper of God; in order that you may eat the flesh of kings and the flesh of commanders and the flesh of mighty men and the flesh of horses and those who sit on them and the flesh of men, both free men and slaves, and small and great"* (Revelation 19:17, 18).

That's the supper to which I was heading until I accepted the wedding invitation of the Lamb. That's the door open to the foolish virgins who forgot that it is the prerogative of the Groom to linger long after the announcement, "Behold the Bridegroom!" The five foolish virgins could hear the joy of the wedding banquet, the laughter, the music and dancing, all the sounds of celebration and excitement inside, but the door was shut and they were stuck on the outside.

Imagine being on the wrong side of the door and hearing the words, "Too late! You cannot enter now!" After spending all this time in church, not enjoying God and too scared to embrace the world, imagine how devastating it would be to hear the Son of God, our Savior, say the words, *"Truly I say to you, I do not know you"* (Matthew 25:12). Wherever you are in your relationship with God, *today*, while it is still today, is the time to make a decision as to whether you are a faithful bridesmaid or a foolish one.

A few months after the Waco, Texas, conflagration, I saw a young woman on television telling the story of her mother, who was one of the persons devoured by that fire, with her husband and many others. Her mother had followed her new husband to Waco, Texas, and when she got there, she began to realize that things were not as they should be. She had questions about some of the teachings and was increasingly concerned about her husband's devotion to their leader. She went so far as to write to her daughter expressing her fears. In that letter she stated that she would remain with her husband until he came to his senses.

The day came when the conflagration occurred. It is forever impressed in the minds of this nation and the world. The officials who cleaned up came to the back door of the building leading to where some members had planned to escape to a bus. There they found the charred remains of a woman, identified as this young woman's mother, with her hands still stuck to the knob of the door. She was making her final attempt to escape, but it was too late. Too late! Too late!

How many are saying, "We can linger just a little longer. The signs are not completely fulfilled. We still have time to make up our minds about God." How many others are saying, "We've been waiting and watching for so long, and He is still not here"? How terrible it's going to be when Jesus Christ comes to close the door that is now open, and we who toy with this gift He has given us will be found with our hearts and hands holding on, clinging to that closed door. It will be too late! Too Late!

Are you ready? The messenger is already at the door. I can hear his heavy breathing from having run ahead as he shouts, "Behold the Bridegroom!" I pray that all who are watching and waiting will be ready.

---

1. George Knight, *Matthew: The Gospel of the Kingdom (The Abundant Life Bible Amplifier)* (Pacific Press, 1994), 236.
2. Dietrich Bonhoeffer, *The Cost of Discipleship* (Peter Smith Publications, 1983), 89.
3. Francis Frangipane, *Holiness, Truth and the Presence of God* (Arrow Publications, 1986), 139.
4. Ellen White, *Review and Herald*, December 20, 1892, 1.
5. Adapted from the Charles Wesley hymn (1739).

Chapter 7

don't give up!

The courtroom was packed to capacity. I was late and had to squeeze into a small seat next to the press corps with all the paraphernalia used to beam details of this trial along the increasingly busy information highway around the universe. I didn't want to be there, but had to since I was subpoenaed to appear as a material witness for the defense in the universally acclaimed case of *The Principalities and Powers vs. Ordinary Joe Sinner*.

The defense, led by the world-renowned attorney J. C. Son-Oman, regarded as the greatest human rights advocate, was about to call its first witness. At that very moment, the lead prosecuting attorney, Luce F. R. DeVille, stood up to raise loud objections to the list of deponents called "so great a cloud of witnesses" by J. C. Son-Oman. They included the rich and infamous such as Abraham, Jacob, Samson, David, Rahab of Jericho, and a host of women, like Martha and Mary of Bethany, who had their dead returned to them by resurrection. I leaned forward to listen as Luce F. R. DeVille approached the bench where Chief Justice N. O. Mercie sat, and began to speak.

"Your honor," said he, clearing his throat, an irritating gesture for which he was famous as he created dramatic pauses, pregnant with manipulation and unease. He also pretended to chew thoughtfully on one stem of his half-moon glasses that dangled from his neck like a prized trophy on a gold chain. "Your honor," he repeated confidently after an unnecessarily long pause. The chief justice stopped him short of the bench with a stiffly raised hand and a disapproving glance. "Your honor," Attorney DeVille said again, refusing to acknowledge Justice N. O Mercie's nonverbal communiqué, "what great cloud of witnesses? If it pleases the court, I will show the jury that they are no more than a motley crew of murderers, liars, prostitutes, and peeping toms who will crumble under my cross-examination. Take this one who now calls himself Abraham," he said, whirling around to point a long, manicured, bony finger at the gray-haired man whose face I could not see because I was seated too far behind him. I could tell, however, that he was quite old by the bent shoulders and the arms of his relatives on both sides, which were not only resting on his shoulders affectionately but were obviously there to prop him up.

The prosecuting attorney's voice continued to rape the atmosphere of goodness with a voice that resonated with sarcasm. He said: "This old man fathered an illegitimate son by his wife's maid, and when it became public knowledge, he claimed that his old, barren wife, Sarai, gave the maid to him so that they could have an heir for his vast fortune. But mark my words, Judge Mercie, our investigators will produce hard evidence to impeach his testimony. I will also show this court that his wife did not initiate such an arrangement, nor was she pleased with the outcome, for eventually she forced her philandering husband to end that sordid affair and force the upstart, outcast maid and her unlawful son to leave her home and country."

By then, attorney J. C. Son-Oman was on his feet protesting. His objections were overruled by Justice N. O. Mercie, who seemed partial to the prosecution in this case (billed as the Trial of the Centuries). Prosecutor Luce F. R. DeVille continued, his voice dripping with sarcasm. "Your honor, I beg the court's indulgence as I introduce new evidence to prove that this man is a liar and has been since the day he was born." His voice was at a high pitch as he spoke, pointing a bony finger accusingly toward Abraham, his fingernail too long for a professional man. "He even changed his name to avoid being recognized for what he truly is, the original fugitive! When he married his half-sister, Sarai, he was so poor they were forced to live with his father in his modest home at the village of Ur in the Chaldees. Then one day, when he was almost 75 years old, he left without even a 'thank you' to his family, who had been so generous to them for many decades, claiming that God Almighty had instructed him to go—but get this—he didn't know where!"

The sarcasm seemed to slide off his tongue like hot butter in the sun as he said, "For ten long years this liar drifted around the Canaan countryside, dragging his helpless wife, living by his wits and lying lips as a homeless vagabond. Let the record show that in the famine of forty-nine, he wandered into Egypt, begging for food and lodging. He eventually wormed his way into the good graces of Pharaoh and his wealthy household. While there, he lied and manipulated his benefactor until he was caught and deported. Now, today, he wants to take the stand as a faithful witness for the defense, expecting this jury to believe that he knows the truth and has spoken it." His words were slow and deliberate, like a gavel pounding the podium in ridiculous rhythm. He inhaled deeply and yelled, pointing all fingers on one hand at Abraham, who never seemed to flinch under the accusations: "He will lie again. Put him on the stand, and all you will hear are lies spun by this clever man to save his soul-mate, the defendant, O. J. Sinner!"

"Your honor," DeVille continued confidently, "I will show you

7—A.

that this dream team of the defense is a nightmare waiting to waste the court's precious time if they are allowed to call their witness, Jacob, another liar and thief. If the court pleases, I would like to show a videotape." He turned to a court attendant, handed her the video and said, "please mark this exhibit JER 1323," then quickly turned toward the judge as he continued. "This tape was taken by the FBI's (Fact-finding Bible Investigators) undercover agents of Operation Pottage-gate during their investigation of the scandalous deception he carried out against his almost blind father and his hungry brother. They caught this man and his mother in the very act of defrauding his twin brother Esau out of his birthright and blessing. Judge N. O. Mercie and members of the jury, Jacob's poor brother, Esau, was made to feel like an outcast in the family. He suffered from a very rare medical malady called hypertrichosis (excessive growth of hair) which causes the human body to be covered, in part or whole, with an unusual quantity of long hair. In Esau's particular case, it stood out because his hair was red. So, to defraud his brother out of his birthright, Jacob and his mother covered Jacob's neck and hands in goat's hair to trick his aged, almost blind father into bestowing on him the blessing that was legitimately his brother's.

"What great cloud of witnesses, your honor, when it includes the likes of Moses? This son of a slave was graciously adopted by the king's daughter and raised as a prince in her palace in Egypt. But nowadays," said the prosecuting attorney, his face so close to the witness that you could see the witness's face grimace at the stale breath of hatred that he spewed out with each word. "Nowadays when he's too old for anything important, he wants us to believe that he left Egypt for the noble reason of refusing to be called the son of Pharaoh's daughter, because he would rather endure ill-treatment with his own people than enjoy the pleasures of a prince." Deville's voice was still dripping with sarcasm when he said: "Ha! A likely story, your honor, for these documents from Doctors Exodus and Deuteronomy, experts in the ancient forensic law, will show that he ran from Egypt to avoid arrest one night after brutally beating a defenseless soldier to death in the alleys of the capital city. Members of the jury, this witness has been the number-one fugitive on the Egyptian list of ten most wanted for more than forty years. He should be taken into custody and immediately extradited to face his murder trial, after hiding from the law in a Midian mountain these many years."

"Your honor," appealed J. C. Son-Oman, "this man is not on trial! May we approach the bench for a brief consultation as I explain my objections?" Justice N. O. Mercie waived his hand in a gesture of annoyance without even glancing toward the defense attorney. At that very moment he turned and smiled benignly at the prosecutor, urging—no, egging him on in a most despicable demonstration of justice gone awry as the examination of witnesses continued above the protests of the defense team.

"Samson, your honor," DeVille said sarcastically, scarcely hiding his glee that he was favored by the chief justice. "Samson is indeed the freeborn son of two honorable citizens of this region whom I knew personally, but he is a slave to his sensual desires. Let the records show that the first four words uttered publicly by this former judge and disgraced womanizer was not a pronouncement of justice in a case, but 'I see a woman!' So addicted to sensuality and sex was he, that the second four words noted to have been publicly said are, 'Get her for me.' Samson was known to be the strongest man that ever lived. He was so physically strong, he could pull up the giant gates of Gaza out of their sockets. He could carry them like a feather for more than a mile, yet he was so morally weak he could not pull down the skirt of a pretty woman who teased and tempted him.

"As for David, your honor, during his reign as king of Israel, he was a practicing peeping tom who calculated how to kill one of his most faithful fighters so that he could sleep with that officer's wife. And when the woman got pregnant, your honor, instead of taking responsibility and owning up to his actions, he had the poor man put on the front line of the battle so that he was killed. Murderer! Members of the jury, this man is a murderer! So what great cloud of witnesses are these, your honor?"

I was riveted to my seat as I listened and looked at the incredible impression Luce F. R. DeVille was making on the judge and jury, who took copious notes during his discourse. One by one the credibility of each witness seemed to be destroyed. I became worried that their advocate, J. C. Son-Oman, seemed shy and silent. I wanted to help him out of his apparent predicament, but I realized that my own time was about to come. How would I withstand the prosecution's withering cross-examination?

I was mulling over these thoughts when I was summoned to the front, sworn in, and seated in that witness box. I was ordered to sit in the dreaded hot seat between the judge and jury. I was still feeling stunned by the aggressiveness of the proceedings when I heard a voice like an echo from a distance say, "State your name and occupation."

"Mrs. Samuel Salmon of Bethlehem," I replied nervously, bending my shoulders in shame, looking, staring at Attorney Son-Oman for his non-verbal guidance. Then I remembered that I should keep my eyes fastened on him to remain strong in my commitment to the truth, and that all I knew and had learned would be brought back to my mind. So I fastened my eyes on his calm, compassionate face. I could see beams of love shining out of his eyes, and I knew that everything would be all right. So I straightened up and said proudly, "I am the grandmother of His Royal Highness, King David, and the great-great-great-grandmother of Jesus Christ Son-Oman, attorney for the defense." I smiled proudly in a way only a parent could understand. I could see that he was still pleased with me. This emboldened me to let Mr. I-can-tear-down-a-witness-in-a-second DeVille know that I was a sophisticated woman of substance as he stood up to begin his cross-examination with that disgusting, arrogant look of self-assurance.

"Mrs. Samuel Salmon, aren't you really Rahab from Jericho?" he drawled.

"Yes," I replied as nervousness seemed to shoot through my veins and I began to crumple into a shell of shame.

"In the early sixties, did you not own a house of ill-repute by the wall and the main gate of the holiday resort town known as the Desert Palms in Jericho?"

"Yes," I replied, not providing any more information than I was asked, fearing that if I answered what I wasn't asked, I would jeopardize the case against O. J. Sinner. As Luce F. R. DeVille pressed me for more details, I remained silent. It seemed as though it was less than a second that I took my eyes off my advocate and defender, but it was long enough for DeVille to turn to the chief justice and demand that I be declared a hostile witness. My heart pounded with fear. Blood rushed to my head like the sound of mighty waves crashing in my mind amidst the loud objections of J. C. Son-Oman. I couldn't believe it when the chief justice overruled my defender, insisting that I answer the questions as the cross-examination continued.

"Your honor," DeVille sweetly appealed to the judge, "may I approach the witness?" He did not wait for a response but came so close that I could see the red veins in his evil eyes. "Mrs. Salmon," he said slowly, his words piercing through me like a dagger being pulled, painfully, through old wounds in my heart. "Mrs. Salmon— or may I call you Rahab? Please identify these photographs." He quickly turned and addressed the judge with a mellow voice, "Exhibit JER 3434, your honor" Then he turned again to me, resuming his harsh onslaught. "Describe to the court what these photographs portray." He handed them to me. I did not take them. They fell, upturned, on my lap. I didn't have to look at them to describe them. My tongue seemed glued to roof of mouth. My eyes clouded with the mist of tears that were struggling against a floodgate of shame. I must have moved my lips even though I couldn't find the voice to answer when DeVille shouted, "Speak up, Mrs. Salmon, so that everyone may hear you!"

The tears were now streaming down my face as my sordid past rushed up to meet me in a snapshot of a much younger me cavorting with two spies in my house in Jericho. "Mrs. Rahab Salmon," drawled the prosecutor, mocking me with his face contorted in a diabolical grin that words cannot describe, "Were you not in fact a prostitute?" He said that word as though it had a thousand syllables. "Did you not invite two strangers, Hebrew spies, into your bedchamber for a shameless night of orgies? When the police arrived on a tip that you were sleeping with the enemy, did you not lie to them?" His rapid-fire questions culminated by the slamming of one hand, so hard and unexpectedly, on the desk for dramatic effect, I was startled and jumped like a scared cat. "Tell us about that wild night under the bleaching flax on top of your roof, Rahab, *chief prostitute of Jericho*!" DeVille was screaming, almost beside himself with anger and malice.

In that instant, J. C. Son-Oman was on his feet, shouting objections. This time, no one could accuse him of being a wimp. His voice was strong and firm as he spoke. Yet there was a great deal of compassion in it even though he would not be silenced by the noise of the gavel and shouts for order by the judge. At that moment, the court observers behind him began clapping and laughing, adding to the confusion as they hurled obscenities and accusations at him. Simultaneously, some members of the jury began to lean forward, leering with ridiculous smiles and gestures unbecoming of their position. The noise level continued to increase. It reached a crescendo when the courtroom erupted in a buzz of chatter and a flurry of movement as reporters rushed to call their news networks with the juicy tidbits from the trial. The judge stood up. He adjusted his robe, cleared his throat to attract the attention of the noisy courtroom. No one noticed. An angry shadow crossed the judge's brow as he began to bang the gavel on his desk. I could hear the sound of the gavel. I could see the rapid movement of his hands, yet it seemed to be in slow motion. It was surreal. It seemed far away, and then it got louder and louder as Justice N. O. Mercie tried to out-shout my advocate, J. C. Son-Oman. The judge was demanding, commanding, "Order, I say, order in the court! Order! Order! Order in the court!"

The uproar jarred me to my senses. It woke me up, and to my great delight, I discovered that I had been dreaming. Before getting ready for bed that evening, I had been reading Hebrews 12:1-3 for a sermon I was preparing to preach. I did not realize that it was almost midnight, so when I left my study, I turned on the television to catch the late news on CNN. As I nestled in for the night, I noticed with interest that it was the late-night recapitulation of the day's events during the O. J. Simpson trial, but I was too exhausted to stay awake and dozed during the report. During that short nap, my overactive imagination transformed the reality into one of the most fascinating dreams I've ever had, producing the court drama I tried to recapture above.

Therefore, since we have this great cloud of witnesses surrounding us, let us also lay aside every encumbrance, and the sin which so easily entangles us, and let us run with endurance the race that is set before us, fixing our eyes on Jesus, the author and perfecter of faith, who for the joy set before Him endured the cross, despising the shame, and has sat down at the right hand of the throne of God. For consider Him who has endured such hostility by sinners against Himself, so that you may not grow weary and lose heart (Hebrews 12:1-3).

Most of us who are reading this had long expected Christ to come, or imagined ourselves spending the first season of this one thousand years with God, in heavenly places. But in this first part of the new millennium, we must admit that we have a lot in common with this great cloud of witnesses described more vividly, in dramatic details, in Hebrews 11. It is not just that they represent every age, gender, profession or position in life, but that we share a similar shameful history erased by the gift of God's amazing grace through faith in Jesus Christ our Lord. We also share the fact that we have been called to wait for the promise of deliverance made so many centuries ago. Having read about, seen, and heard of so many who waited and did not experience its fulfillment, it is very easy for those still waiting to give up. However, in the famous phrase popularized by Winston Churchill in what is reputed to be the shortest, most powerful speech ever given, "Never, never, never give up!"

"Be brave. Be strong. Don't give up. Expect God to get here soon" (Psalm 31:24, *The Message*). Just wait a little longer on the Lord, if your hope is in Him, for there are significant reasons for the delay of that great and awesome day—the promised second coming of Christ.

As I was reading John 11, I discovered that the story of the death and resurrection of Lazarus is also a parable with eschatological assertions that provide some answers to the long delay. The story begins with the fact that Lazarus, whose name means "the one whom God helps," was deathly ill. His sisters whom Jesus loved (see John 11:5) sent an urgent message to Jesus, who was less than a day's journey away, saying, *"Lord, behold, he whom You love is sick"* (John 11:3).

As a pastor, when I receive an urgent message that a member is sick, especially seriously ill, I try my very best to visit that person as soon as possible and prayerfully support the family. When it is someone that I love, I drop everything and rush to see him or her. For example, a few years ago one of my best friends was seriously ill in a hospital in Las Vegas. I was about to walk out the door to catch a flight to a speaking engagement I had reserved a year in advance when I received the awful news about my friend. It did not take a second to make up my mind as to the direction in which I would be flying. I immediately canceled the engagement, put my life on hold for about ten days, and stayed with my friend and her family until, regrettably, she passed away. That's how I believe all people should respond to their loved ones, so it really bothers me when I read in the Scriptures that *"Jesus loved Martha, and her sister [Mary] and Lazarus"* (verses 3, 5), yet He deliberately delayed His visit in an emergency such as theirs.

John reports that when Jesus *"heard that he [Lazarus] was sick, He stayed then two days longer [than necessary] in the place where He was"* (verse 6). Why would the Giver of life delay until death occurred? Jesus Himself gave the answer and provides a birds-eye view, for me and hopefully for you, of some of the reasons why He has delayed for so long His second coming to this sick and dying world that He loves so much (see John 3:16).

The first reason Jesus gave for His delay was that it was *"for the glory of God, that the Son of God may be glorified"* (verse 4). This is best understood in light of the meaning of the word *glorify*. It means to magnify, extol, praise, ascribe honor and acknowledge Him in His divine being, and His attributes and acts. This was very important in the time of Jesus. He *"came to His own, and those who were His own did not receive Him"* (John 1:11) as the Son of God. It is particularly significant today where He is *"in the world"* that He made *"and the world [does] not know Him"* (verse 10) as He really is.

How was He really glorified? God publicly demonstrated that Jesus was and is the Resurrection and the Life, a member of the divine Trinity, by His being, attributes and the act of raising the dead. God the Father was glorified by Jesus on earth because He accomplished the work His Father had given Him to do (see John 17:4). As joint heirs with Christ (see Romans 8:17) we should also glorify God by accomplishing what He has given us to do, not only with the raising of our hands and voices in worship, but in every facet of our lives. In fact, the apostle Paul said, *"Whether then, you eat or drink or whatever you do, do all to the glory of God"* (1 Corinthians 10:31).

A second reason was that Jesus seized the opportunity to correct one of their greatest erroneous doctrinal and theological teachings.

He deliberately idled away the time instead of going immediately to His beloved friend in Bethany, a place whose name means "house of the poor and afflicted." This name is also a good synonym for planet Earth in the last days, where many of His beloved friends are also afflicted and dying. In explaining His unorthodox behavior, Jesus said that Lazarus's *"sickness is not unto death, but for the glory of God."* But Lazarus did die! Was Jesus lying or didn't know of which He spoke? Neither! He was about to revolutionize their theories on the state of the dead.

The doctrine of resurrection was one of the most controversial teachings in the time of Jesus (see Matthew 22:23-33). It held an important and prominent place in the lives, discussions, and religious instructions of the day. Donald E. Gowan, in *Bridge Between the Testaments*, said, "The subject of life after death was a matter of intense interest . . . with almost every conceivable option being proposed." Beliefs about resurrection were the basis for one of the major differences between the Pharisees, who believed in life after death, and Sadducees, who rejected all ideas of a resurrection. They held strictly to the literal interpretation of the Torah, claiming that the Pentateuch (five books written by Moses) did not teach the resurrection of the dead, but that it was part of the Pharasaical oral Torah to be repudiated. At one stage, the "disputation [between the Pharisees and Sadducees on this issue] led to an alteration in the wording of the liturgy used in the Temple" so that the conclusion of the benediction was changed from "for ever" to a Sadduccean one-world view: "from everlasting to Everlasting."[1] Their often public and volatile debates were also major contributors to a popularized and perverted concept of the state of the dead, based on traditions that had tremendous influence on the lives and beliefs of the common people.

One of these Jewish traditions conveyed the idea that there was a resurrection, but only after a certain period of time, after which not even God could raise the dead person. Many of the religious leaders taught and believed that for three days the soul of the dead hovered over the body, or nearby, in the hope of entering into it again. If the person was a beloved citizen, they hired professional mourners, mostly women, who would weep and make an eerie ululation (howl or wail) with their tongues as is still done in regions of Israel and Ethiopia. They did this to help drive or direct the soul back into the body where it belongs. At the end of the three-day period, when the features were disfigured, the flesh decayed and, in the words of Martha, *"there [would] be a stench for he had been dead four days,"* the soul would depart, never to return again. Those first three days after death were therefore crucial for the family and friends of the deceased. They would visit the tomb and make as much noise as possible, banging drums and beating pans, to scare or entice the wandering soul into the lifeless body so that the dead person might live again.

Jesus was familiar with these erroneous concepts and was about to perform what those who held to this teaching would consider His greatest miracle and reveal His divinity to the world. He was delaying His visit *"for the glory of God,"* to free His disciples from the influence of this false doctrine and to strike a permanent blow against the fallacy of Sadducean theology. So Jesus did not respond with the expected or customary urgency when He was summoned by the sister, in order to arrive at their home on the fourth day and do what His disciples and others then believed was an impossible feat. Throughout His life, the miracles of Jesus could be paralleled with those of Elijah the prophet, but to the Jews who were eyewitnesses of this event, it was His greatest miracle.

He raised Lazarus, who had been dead for four days, by calling him to come forth from the grave! They must have been stunned. They must have concluded that Jesus must be God and gave to Him the praise, honor, and adulation He deserved as such. One of my friends from Australia has said that if Jesus had not called Lazarus by name, all of the dead within proximity of His voice would have come out of the grave when they heard the voice of Him who is the Resurrection and Life. Since this was not prime-time show time, but rather meant for the glory of God, Jesus did not do what He will do at the end of the world and call all who are asleep, in Him, to awaken from their sleep of death to live forever in the new earth.

A third reason for the delay was that Jesus wanted to impress upon the hearts of the disciples what had gone no further than their heads—that *He* is *"the resurrection and the life, [and] he who believes in [Him] shall live even if he dies, and everyone who lives and believes in [Him] shall never die"* (John 11:25, 26). He wanted to confirm to them that He was indeed the Messiah, the "I am," the Life-giver, "the believer's assurance of eternal life" in whom is "life, original, unborrowed, underived."[2]

It appears from this passage in John's Gospel that Martha (and perhaps other disciples listening to their conversation) believed what she said when she said, *"Yes, Lord; I have believed that you are the Christ, the Son of God, even He who comes into the world."* Even so, it may have been a stretch of their imagination and understanding of God to reject the *Shema* they repeated every day and to accept Jesus as the Messiah. The *Shema* said, *"Hear, O Israel! The Lord is our God, the Lord is one! And you shall love the Lord your God with all your heart and with all your soul and with all your might"* (Deuteronomy 6:4, 5). They were not yet able to make the bold leap of faith to recognize Jesus as God the Son, *"the resurrection and the life,"* without having seen Him perform at least one miracle that was greater than their ancient prophets. Thus, Jesus used the opportunity of the death of His friend to demonstrate to His disciples, and those watching with curiosity and criticism in their hearts, that He truly was and is Almighty God as described in their Scriptures.

A fourth reason for Jesus' delayed response to the appeals of Martha and Mary, was that He wanted to demonstrate His divine power over death. The greatest fear of humanity is not the Y2K predicted millennium fever, as public relations propaganda would have us believe. The greatest fear of humanity is death. It exercises dominion over all—the small and great, rich and poor, free and slaves. We are all tyrannized by the death of sleep described by Jesus (see John 11:11-15), but believers are particularly afraid of *"perishing"* (see John 3:16) or the second death from which He came to save us by giving us eternal life. Because of the reign of death, both the first, called sleep, and the second, called perishing, the world then and now needs a Savior with the ability and the raw power to overcome death. Jesus, the God/Man, the Savior of sin-beset humanity, has that power. However, even though He wanted to deliver them and us from the darkness of fear, no matter how many miracles Jesus performed, if He were not able to break the power of death, His life would have been meaningless. Thus, raising Lazarus from the dead was only a prelude, a down payment, on what He paid in full when He died on the cross and was resurrected three days later.

The fifth and final reason was more implicit than explicit: to break down barriers of prejudice. Reporting the events surrounding the resurrection of Lazarus, John said, *"Martha, therefore, when she heard that Jesus was coming, went to meet Him; but Mary still sat in the house"* (John 11:20). Martha's impulsive act was not only a violation of several of the strictest rules governing the role and behavior of women in her day, but it also betrayed the very propriety of decency for single women and widows, all of whom she represented in her present circumstances. The incredible thing was that Jesus openly embraced her, endorsing her behavior in direct opposition to the following customs:

1. Women took no part in and were expected to remain unobserved in public life. To appear in public without the strictest coverings was worthy of divorce, banishment, and death by public stoning. Joachim Jeremias writes, "When a Jewess left her house, her face was hidden by arrangement of two head veils, a headband on the forehead with bands to the chin, and a hairnet with ribbons and knots so that her features could not be recognized. For example, it was said that once a chief priest in Jerusalem did not recognize his own mother when he had to carry out against her the prescribed process [of stoning] for a woman suspected of adultery."[3] Yet, according to John's report Jesus immediately recognized Martha, indicating that she was not wearing the prescribed public head coverings when she rushed from the house to meet Him. Instead of rebuking or reviling her, Jesus welcomed and embraced Martha.

2. *It was dangerous to meet a woman in public after she had been in contact with the dead.* Women were expected to avoid the presence of men, even their closest relatives, during the funeral of a family member. The whole world saw this practice in 1999, when King Hussein of Jordan died. His beloved wife, Queen Noor, who was at his bedside in the hospital and with him up to the end of his life, could not participate in the funeral procession. It was a pathetic sight to see her and the other female members of the family, peering through windows and partially opened doors, with their heads carefully covered by the prescribed veils, as the funeral bier of her beloved husband passed by in the streets below. Both the Pharisees and Sadducees rigidly adhered to this custom, guarding and preserving it with many incantations and religious rituals from their traditions. Some of the formulas were unswervingly followed, since fear of the consequences struck terror in the heart of the common man. Some of the requirements for a man who met a woman, especially a single woman or widow, who had been in recent contact with the dead, were ridiculous. For example, he should "remove four cubits [approximately six feet] from his place" in the opposite direction, "or if there's a river . . . cross it . . . or turn his face away and say, 'and the Lord said unto Satan, the Lord rebuke thee, O Satan.'"[4]

Imagine Martha's relief when she was not rebuked or rejected by her Lord who, without the slightest reservation, embraced her with deep empathy. His actions struck at the heart of this old tradition to set grieving females in their society free to move about in public with a sense of self-assurance and respect. Notice the contrast between Martha and Mary's actions on that occasion. While Martha threw caution to the wind and broke with tradition to rush out and meet Jesus, Mary, who had a very checkered past, clung to the old customs. She "still sat in the house," apparently even after she was told that her "Rabboni" had arrived and was calling her, so as to properly observe their customs. Mary, often described by commentators as contemplative, with a deep store of love for people, sat in the house, apparently reluctant to risk her fragile respect in the community.

3. *The rules of propriety forbade women to meet a man without a proper chaperone.* This particular rule was aimed more at the wealthier families, and although Martha and her family were poor according to national standards, they were wealthier than the rest of the citizens of Bethany, being among the most prominent families in that small locale. This being the case, a deep sense of propriety should have tempered Martha's movements as an example to the rest of the citizenry. If it didn't, Jesus, a respectable rabbi with many followers, should have severely disciplined her and put her in her place in view of their traditional belief's that "it was disgraceful for a scholar [i.e., a rabbi] to speak to a woman in the street."[5] Instead, there's a note of warmth and compassion when they meet, suggesting His strong approval of her action.

4. *It was disgraceful for a rabbi or scholar of the law to speak to a woman in the street.* In their culture, it was "considered preferable for a woman, especially an unmarried girl, in general, not to go out at all." The lawmakers and leaders felt that "market places and council-halls, law-courts and gatherings . . . meetings where a large number of people are assembled, in short all public life with its discussions and deeds, in times of peace and war, are proper for men" only.[6] Rabbis and their disciples (men only) adhered reverently to this rule. But Jesus, who brought about a quiet reformation for

the women by calling them to be His disciples and traveling companions, met Martha and discussed the doctrine of resurrection with her in public.

5. *Women were exempt from the study of the Torah because they were considered inferior to men.* They were treated as mere property with little or no religious rights and rites, except to be the janitor in the temple (see John 18:17) and to exercise those duties graciously extended to them by a loving husband or father. Joachim Jeremias tells of one Rabbi Eliezer (c. A.D. 90) who was a tireless upholder of the old traditions. Apparently, the rabbi had his own mother stoned to death when he discovered that she could quote passages from the Torah. It should also be noted that Jewish women were forbidden to teach and "bear witness because it was concluded from Genesis 18:15 that she is a liar."[7] This relates to Sarah's denial that she laughed when she heard the pronouncement of the angel that she would become pregnant in her advanced age.

Only from this background can one fully appreciate Jesus' attitude and all that He has done to set women free from traditions and customs that would inhibit our complete understanding and partaking in His grace. Not only did He *"proclaim release to the captives"* (Luke 4:18), men and women bound by legalism and false doctrines, but He also eliminated the barriers that prevented them from full participation in the religious and social activities as free-born citizens of the kingdom of God. The freedom from captivity to legalistic religious customs and cultural traditions that Jesus granted to Martha so many centuries ago is available to all women and men today. He continues to call us away from what one of my seminary professors described as "broken cisterns," to drink from deep fountains of spiritual enlightenment and living waters (see Titus 3:5).

Not only have we all sinned and come short of the glory of God, but on closer examination, we are all polluted by erroneous religious and social concepts that are barriers which the apostle Paul said should be and are broken down and destroyed in Christ. Consequently, we are not ready for His second coming because our eyes are still filled with false images of discipleship and servanthood. Our hearts are still lifted up with pride. Our hands are determined to do our own human will, and until we strip away the masks of disobedience and obstinacy and accept the mantle of grace, we will not be ready to welcome the end of this evil age.

Dietrich Bonhoeffer said that the one "who is called must go out of his [her] situation in which [she] he cannot believe, into the situation in which, first and foremost, faith is possible. They must burn their boats and plunge into absolute insecurity in order to learn the demand and the gift of Christ . . . For faith is only real when there is obedience, never without it, and faith only becomes faith in the act of obedience."[8]

How then shall we live? Fixing our faith in Jesus Christ alone can help us to never give up, especially during the times of sickness, trials, disappointment and even death, during these last days. We can reflect on the host of witnesses, from our own times as well as those from the history of Christianity and our community of faith, especially those mentioned in Hebrews 11, a chapter known as the hall of faith (not fame).

The Greek word for witness is *martur*, from which our word *martyr* is derived. It describes men and women who died for their beliefs, to become martyrs for the Master instead of simply being on a quest for spiritual fulfillment or a faith that made them feel good. God is seeking committed men and women who will not only talk but also walk by faith and not by sight, by the Spirit and not worldly power, to be members of this great cloud or host of witnesses. As we face the final conflict that is literally heating up around us between good and evil, there is a way to ensure that we are included among these chosen witnesses. To be counted worthy of this great honor, believers must strictly adhere to the following instructions and orders recorded in Hebrews 12:1-3.

Let us lay aside every encumbrance [weight] and the sin that so easily entangles us.

This statement echoes the activities of a sports arena in the author's day. Imagine the scene at an Olympiad. The stands are packed with thousands of spectators who are watching athletes vie for the golden wreath of victory as the excitement fills the air with anticipation and the arena with shouts of encouragement. Try to see the track and field stars stretching and psyching themselves up for the moment when they will launch into a fierce contest for the prize. How often we've watched such a scene and felt the tension as we waited for our favorite sports person to break existing world records!

Almost two thousand years have not diminished the energy and excitement of Hebrews 12:1, 2, but there are a few differences. For example, contestants in ancient Olympiads trained with weights strapped to their bodies. On the day of the race they laid them aside along with all their other attire, stripping down to their naked bodies, so that they would feel weightless, as light as a feather, as they competed. That was the background for the writer's call to believers to *"lay aside every weight [or encumbrance]"* i.e., everything that hinders us from running the Christian race without restraint.

What are some of the weights constraining Christians today? Certainly not overt lying, stealing, cheating, and adultery although, regrettably, these things are still numbered among us. The majority of us have gone to great lengths to lay aside those weighty things. But we've neglected the little sins that easily entangle us, wrapping their tentacles tightly around our hearts to impede our spiritual progress and rob us of our delight in God. Some of these are too many unconfessed secrets—the lust for material things, and the three religious concubines I've labeled below.

1. *Legalism* is a strict, literal, excessive conformity to the moral law and other ceremonial codes at the expense of grace. It leads one

to believe that she or he can work hard enough to please God and be saved.

The Pharisees whose name means "one who is separate," were notorious legalists who, in their determination to uphold the law, conspired to and participated in the murder of the innocent One, Jesus Christ our Lord. Their legalism appears to have been at its peak during the earthly ministry of Jesus, who taught that He, the Son of Man, was Lord of the Sabbath (see Matthew 12:8) and He had made *the Sabbath for man, and not man for the Sabbath"* (Mark 2:27). During this time, recognized as the intertestamental period, the Pharisees imposed so many restrictions and trivial regulations around the observation of Sabbath, it made this beautiful gift from God a burden instead of a blessing. These rules and regulations were later codified in the Mishnah and were part of the tradition Jesus vigorously opposed throughout His ministry. For example, the Mishnah lists thirty-nine types of labor the people could not perform on the Sabbath alongside hundreds of other minute regulations. For instance, one could not carry a handkerchief unless it was pinned to the clothing; otherwise the person was carrying a load on the Sabbath. One of the best known Sabbath regulations concerned the so-called "Sabbath day's journey" of about two-thirds of a mile, which described the distance that a Jew in the time of Jesus was allowed to travel on the Sabbath without breaking their traditional law (see Acts 1:12). It was also counted Sabbath breaking to look into a mirror fixed on a wall, to expectorate (expel matter from the throat or lungs by coughing and spitting) upon the ground in case a blade of grass was irrigated. They were forbidden to light a candle or fire on the Sabbath unless a Gentile was hired to do so.

Other examples of their legalism are found in Matthew 12. Jesus and His disciples went through a cornfield on the Sabbath day, and His hungry disciples picked some ears of corn and ate them. When the Pharisees saw it they said, *"Behold, Your disciples do what is not lawful on the Sabbath."* Later on in the day when Jesus healed a man with a withered hand (see verse 10), they questioned Him so that they could accuse Him of the crime of Sabbath breaking, saying: *"Is it lawful to heal on the Sabbath?"* It did not seem to matter much to them that the poor man be delivered from his misery and helplessness as long as their artificial regulations remained unbroken. The incongruity of legalism is dramatically demonstrated by the fact that the Jews had no problem in calling for the crucifixion of the innocent Jesus. They even begged that His legs be broken so that He could die quickly because they were adamant *"that the bodies [of Jesus and the two thieves] should not remain on the cross on the Sabbath"* (John 19:31).

No matter what day we worship on as our Sabbath (Saturday or Sunday), Judeo-Christians have inherited some aspects of legalism in the expression of our faith. Some who regard Saturday as the Sabbath and a "high day" on which to concentrate the expression of their love for God, in their zeal may cause those who have not been so convicted to feel like spiritual infidels. On the other hand, some people who worship on the first day of the week as their Sabbath are so dogmatic about some aspects of their faith, such as the defense of their choice to worship on Sundays or speaking in tongues, that it makes me wonder if they plan to live with each other in the same heaven throughout the eternal ages after the second coming of Christ.

2. *Dogmatism,* the second religious concubine, is an arrogant opinion about a tenet of faith without adequate biblical grounds while declaring authoritatively and unequivocally that this is the only way to do things. It is generally fueled by pride, one of the seven deadly sins, and is always accompanied by a judgmental attitude.

Not long ago, I was driving to the airport in Chicago when I tuned into a Christian radio station to hear a popular evangelist, one who also appears regularly on television, berating some Christians for their belief in the importance of observing Sabbath on Saturday. He agreed that this was stated in the Ten Commandments, but pointed out that Jesus rose on Sunday and that's good enough reason for him to worship on that day, even though he could not give any biblical basis for the change in the fourth commandment. He was emphatic in his statement that any day is as good as the other for worship, but he was determined to follow in the footsteps of the church fathers and his family and observe Sunday as his Sabbath. He further declared that "we are now under grace, and if Adventists want to be saved, they had better conform quickly."

As that electronic evangelist continued to berate the beliefs of other Christians who disagreed with his opinion on certain biblical doctrines, I realized that dogmatism is a very pernicious distortion of truth. Those who operate under the banner of dogmatism will be heard to declare, "I'm not argumentative, just making a point. I'm not critical—I just know the original language. I'm not a hypocrite—I just know what is right for you. I'm not intoxicated with self, I'm just humbly pointing out your faults."

Dogmatism is a very destructive tool used by the devil in the hearts of those who *have a zeal for God, but not in accordance with knowledge*" (Romans 10:2). Dogmatic people assume a dogma is right because a church teaches it or their fore-parents have believed it. They thrive on arrogantly putting down others and their beliefs and are busy taking the speck out of the eyes of others while ignoring the beam in their own (see Matthew 7:3).

3. *Traditionalism,* the belief or practice of those who blindly adhere to a set of ancestral teachings that are no longer relevant or important to eternal life or the edification of the body of believers. Their opinions are expressed in the seven most famous words of the traditionalist: "It's never been done that way before!" Some examples are so absurd they are embarrassing.

For instance, during a morning service, a pastor invited the congregation to dedicate their children to God. A couple who were married by a justice of the peace responded by going forward to the front of the church to have their firstborn baby dedicated to the

Lord. After a few whispered exchanges, the pastor announced his refusal to dedicate their child on the basis that their marriage had not been blessed by a minister and was therefore illegitimate. He stated that it was the *tradition* of that church not to encourage the dishonoring of marriage by dedicating such children during the worship service. The young couple, who reported this experience to me, said that they were humiliated in the presence of more than two hundred worshippers, who affirmed the minister's decision with shouts of "Amen." Not only did that leave a permanent emotional scar on the couple, but it also drove them from the bosom of Christianity into a cult that quickly accepted and loved them without regard for such trivial regulations.

If God, who did not approve of polygamy, could look favorably upon and generously bless with His grace those like Abraham, David, and Solomon who practiced it, why then do we sinners, seeking salvation by grace, dishonor God and alienate each other with ridiculous, man-made traditions?

We need to lay aside these weights along with other things that so easily encumber us. The church and bride of Christ, must put on the amour of light (Romans 13:12). It is the *"fine linen, bright and clean"* (Revelation 19:8) that empowers us to run the grace-race and not get tired. It gives us strength to walk the distance for and with God and not become weary as we wait on the Lord (Isaiah 40:31).

When the ancient athletes practiced for the Olympiad, they did not have Nike and Air Jordan brand sneakers. They actually ran barefooted, and sometimes the weeds and little thorns would become imbedded between their toes and in the soles of their feet. If those little thorns were not carefully removed, they would remain and become infected, impeding the runners' ability to sprint as fast as they were able. There is nothing harder to bear than that little shred of a thorn that is often so imperceptible until it festers and causes pain not only in the location where it is imbedded, but also in the entire body. Many athletes who suffered from this problem either had to drop out of the race or limp through to the end out of sheer determination not to quit.

The author of Hebrews used this illustration from the annals of sports in ancient Rome to make a significant appeal to believers. We must make careful self-examination to ensure that there are no hidden thorns of selfishness, deceit, jealousy and so on, imbedded deep in our hearts and lives to fester and cause us to fail in our goals to see Jesus Christ's face when He comes again. All of us wrestle with the small stuff, while sweating the big ones. We are all vulnerable to spurts of bad temper, greed, materialism, religiosity, and selfishness, to name a few.

A few years after I was converted, if I had been accused of being selfish, I would have been highly offended, until the Lord revealed a thorn of selfishness that could have festered into a major problem without His radical surgery. One weekend I was at home by myself. My son had gone off with his friends, and as I was relishing the Sunday afternoon freedom, the doorbell rang. I opened the door, and there was one of my friends whom I quickly invited in to supper. As I prepared supper, I opened the freezer to find the box of burgers almost empty. My son had eaten three of the four burgers and now I had only one for the two of us. I had no problems sharing, but when I cut that burger, the knife, almost on its own whim, cut one side larger than the other. I cannot tell you the difficulty I had making up my mind as to who should inherit the bigger piece of that burger. The internal conflict was overwhelming. I argued with myself that the burger belonged to me, and I therefore deserved the larger "half," while my conscience kept urging me to do what is right and give it unselfishly to my friend. It was only through this struggle that I became aware of the fact that I had gotten rid of the heavy weights of narcissism choking the life out of my world, but the little tender shoots of selfishness had burrowed deep into my soul. Thank God that through the ministry of healing of our beloved Savior, I no longer struggle with that shoot of sin. I have moved on to other areas that even now the Holy Spirit, by grace, is helping me to excise.

Run with endurance the race that is set before us.

In the author's day, as it is in ours, only one runner could win the first prize. The apostle Paul said in 1 Corinthians 9:24-26: *"Do you not know that those who run in a race all run, but only one receives the prize?"* Yet hundreds if not thousands, throughout the ages, have competed to win that golden garland of victory. Therefore, *"run in such a way that you may win. And everyone who competes in the games exercises self-control in all things. They do it to receive a perishable wreath, but we an imperishable. Therefore I run in such a way, as not without aim."* In the Christian race, everyone who completes the course gets the gold.

The problem however, is not our run, but our walk. The prophet Jeremiah said, *"If you have run with footmen and they have tired you out, then how can you compete with horses?"* (Jeremiah 12:5). Those who are able to set aside the weights are those who've graduated from foot soldiers who regularly run an obstacle course into horsemen and women who exalt Christ and are daily empowered to serve Him. One significant way we can be transformed from foot soldiers to men and women of faith is to do what this verse commands. We must peel off every shred of weight of sin and lay aside every thing, whether small or great, that would encumber, restrain, and hinder us from running this awesome race with grace. We must take radical steps to rid ourselves of the obstacles those weights impose on our lives, but we must never forget the little encumbrances so that we may be able to run the race like mature members of our faith.

Just as runners compete against each other, so there is also a tendency among believers to strive to outdo one another for recognition of being more righteous. Instead of competing with each other, we should help each other as a group of special-needs children who were participating in a race demonstrated. They were running a short race when, shortly after they left the starting place, one of the little boys tripped and fell. As he lay on the ground, crying and wailing in anguish, the others heard him and stopped in their tracks. To the astonishment of the spectators, they all turned around, ran back to their friend and knelt around him as they soothed his bruises and helped him up. When they were satisfied that he was all right, they all linked their arms on both sides of the still wimpering competitor and ran together to the finishing line where they gave each other high fives and celebrated their victory. They showed a lack of interest in winning, in being first or best, against each other while they demonstrated the blessing of making sure all finish the race together and are winners.

If we must compete, it should be only against ourselves as we strive, by God's grace, to reach His highest level of performance, knowing that all races have rules and regulations. For instance, just as the runners in athletic sports cannot run or wander anywhere they please during a competition, but must follow a course mapped out for them until they reach the finish line, so also must Christians observe the path assigned by God. We must run according to the path mapped out for us in the Word of God and proven by the great cloud of witnesses who followed in the footsteps of our Lord and Savior, Jesus Christ, the Author and Perfecter of our faith (see Hebrews 12:2). In that way, the world will know not only who we are, but also whose we are.

A race is also characterized by intense preparation before, not on the day that it is run. No marathon is planned the day before it begins, neither do the participants practice for it the morning it begins. Runners train for months and years to gain speed and endurance. Those who do not put in the long hours of preparation needed to endure the rigors of the race not only hurt themselves physically, but also emotionally, when they have to drop out or, even if they finish, fail to win a prize.

The divine, spiritual life can only be maintained by constant, diligent, strenuous effort. It is sometimes perfected through conflict with the world, unexpected adversities, and persecution for an unswerving commitment to God and His Word. There is no room for laziness or indifference in a marathon, neither is there time for those in this tremendous race in which believers are booked by their profession of faith in Jesus Christ.

Thank God, all races come to an end. In athletic races, the first prize goes not to those who enter, but to the one who endures to the end to cross the finishing line before the others. Praise God that all of this is true of the spiritual race, *except* that all who endure to the end, not losing heart in spite of the diabolical attempts to cause us to fail or quit, will receive the golden crown of victory. In addition to that, we will also have the privilege of living with God forevermore!

Fix your eyes on Jesus, the Author and Perfecter of our faith.

To fix means to make firm, stable or steadfast; to hold steady; to prepare; to establish and restore. I have personal experience of what it means to fix oneself to something. For ten days in 1998, I had the privilege to be the devotional speaker on a cruise ship to Alaska that was engaged by radio station KSGN in Riverside, California. It was my very first time on a ship, and it was a fabulous experience. One of the highlights of the trip, and my life, was my first ride on a helicopter to the top of the glaciers and the privilege to walk on them. There are no words adequate to describe the awesome beauty of the blue glaciers, frozen in time and space. Unless one has the opportunity to personally see and touch them, no artist can evoke the imagination to do justice to being there. In spite of the signs of sin, for even there pollution rears its ugly head, it was incredibly, breathtakingly beautiful. In addition to the daily excursions inland along the Alaskan trail at the various ports of call, in the evenings we dressed formally for some of the most deliciously prepared dinners I had yet, or since been honored to enjoy.

One evening as I was getting dressed, a button fell off my favorite evening dress. It seemed as though I would have to find something else to wear when a friend suggested that I could use some of the crazy glue she carried for such emergencies. She warned me to be careful not to get the crazy glue on my skin, but I was in a hurry. Instead of heeding the warning or watching how much I squeezed out of the tube, I recklessly pressed and spewed out more than I needed. I then proceeded to wipe the extra drippings off with my hand and followed up by using that same hand, fingers still wet with glue, to press the button in the socket out of which it fell. It took only a second for me to realize that I was in trouble. I found myself fixed to the button, but the button refused to be fixed in the brass socket out of which it came. Over half an hour later, after trying every shampoo, body lotion, and baby oil I could get my hands on to dislodge the glue, I finally came to the conclusion that I had to cut my way out of that sticky, so to speak, situation.

Ever since that event, whenever I see the word "fix," I have a twinge in my stomach, as my mind is flooded with memories of the awful event. Well, thank God for that experience, for I now know what the Bible means when it instructs us to fix our eyes on Jesus. It means to fasten one's attention relentlessly on Jesus as tightly as crazy glue holds things together. No matter what the attraction or distraction, our eyes should not and must not be moved from looking full in our Savior's face as it is so excellently portrayed in His Word and in nature. So when things get rough as they are bound to do, don't give up. Hang in there, and remember the Scripture says, *"And we know that God causes all things to work together for good to those who love God, to those who are called according to His purpose"* (Romans 8:28). Let us not grow weary in watching and waiting, but fix our eyes on Jesus, the Author and Perfector of our faith.

Over a decade ago, I, along with millions of viewers, was amazed by an event that ended one of the track and field races in the Olympic games. A young man from Britain, touted by the international press as the fastest man in the world, was slated to win one of the races and break the world record. It was a nail-biting event as I watched so many world-class athletes lined up, waiting for the starter's gun. I can still hear the banter between sportscasters as they gave all the young man's vital statistics. After a couple of false starts, the race was off. I must say that the reporters did not overrate that young runner. He moved like a gazelle. To tease our appetites for the race, they showed him turning corners on the track, in slow motion, highlighting muscles rippling in a rhythm that emphasized the discipline, preparation and expertise that brought him recognition. To our delight, he flew past the other contestants around the first lap, indicating to spectators that they were participants in a history-making event. Camera shots showed people in the arena standing, shouting, filling the air with roars of appreciation that sounded like a well-rehearsed choir of praise and adulation.

I remember the chills going through my body as I watched the race and vicariously enjoyed the promise of a world record by standing in front of my television, screaming and urging him on to the finish line. Nothing was more exciting than that race as we watched the runners move into the last lap toward the home stretch. They picked up speed, still chasing that young Brit, but he was not about to be caught.

The young man held his well-established lead, but less than a hundred yards to the finish line, a gasp of horror rippled through the stands. With my eyes still glued on the race, I moved closer into the television set. My nose was almost pressed to the glass as I held my breath and watched. There, before the watching world, we saw the feet of that well oiled human machine buckle under him and he fell to the ground, grimacing in pain while all the other runners sped past him. It happened in a moment, but time passed slowly as reporters anxiously speculated about the cause of that sudden tragic end to the young man's bid to show that he was indeed the fastest man in the world. They talked about how he was well on the way to breaking the old and establishing a new world record for that race.

They repeated his accomplishments and bemoaned his bad luck by repeating his movements in those last seconds, in slow motion, with digital timers counting off the milliseconds on the screen. All that time, he was still writhing in pain where he fell on the track. No one came to his assistance, for the rule was that the other runners could not be distracted before the end of the race.

As we watched, now with disappointment at the sudden fall of our hero, the cameras focused on a man running out of the stands, down toward the fallen athlete. The reporters quickly identified him as the runner's father, who went over to the side of his son and tenderly lifted him from the ground. We could see the intense pain on the athlete's face as the camera's telephoto lenses transported close-ups to satellites that beamed them instantly into our homes to satisfy our curiosity. We could see the lips of the father moving as he put one arm of his son around his shoulder and one of his arms around his son's waist and began to walk the final few yards of the lap. The race was over, the winner declared, but the eyes of the spectators in the stands and the television audience were riveted to the drama unfolding on the field as the father encouraged and helped his son to the finish line. The reporters said that as they walked, the father was urging his son not to give up, saying, "Keep your eyes on the finish line. I am with you, and I won't leave you. Don't give up, just lean on me and I will take you across the finish line!" There were no dry eyes in the audience, at least in my house.

The object lesson from this drama is permanently and indelibly impressed on my heart. To me, the son represents believers and the father is a symbol of God, who promised that He would be with us, always, even to the end of the world (see Matthew 28:20). He also said that before we call He will answer and while we are still speaking, He will hear (see Isaiah 65:24). He whispers the assurance of faith to our weak minds, reminding us that He will see us through to the finish line if we only lean on Him instead of on our own understanding.

Believers are like that athlete, prepared by our profession of faith in Jesus Christ for that long, hard race with all the potential to make it to the finish line, the second coming of Christ. But sometimes we trip and fall by giving in to temptation. At other times we might feel broken and despondent to the point where our spiritual muscles may also give out as we grow weary of doing good (see Galatians 6:9). All of this is possible in a world where some believers (not the non-believers as we often expect), members of our own family of faith, take our words and twist them to persecute us and to ruin our reputation. When these things happen, the enemy is always present to urge us to give up. He is quick to remind us that the pain is not worth the promised reward. He wants us to believe that everything has been going on the same way for centuries and that the trials and tribulations have not been decreasing, but are becoming worse. In those periods, we must remember that these are all his formulas for failure and not give in or drop out, but hold on with Jesus who *"endured the cross, despising the shame."* We must reflect on the emboldening power of the Holy Spirit who picks us up when we have fallen from grace and cannot get up on our own. He, like the father in that Olympic stadium, wraps His holy presence around us and whispers into the portals of our minds saying, "Don't give up! I've got you. I will take you across the finish line. Only lay aside every encumbrance and the sin that so easily entangles and fix your eyes on Jesus, the Author and Perfecter of your faith. *Don't give up!"*

---

1. Abraham Cohen and Jacob Neusner, *Everyman's Talmud* (Shocken, 1995), 357.
2. Ellen G. White, *The Desire of Ages*, 530.
3. Joachim Jeremias, *Jerusalem in the Time of Jesus* (Fortress Press, 1979), 359.
4. *Everyman's Talmud*, 295.
5. *Jerusalem in the Time of Jesus*, 360.
6. Ibid.
7. Ibid., 375.
8. Dietrich Bonhoeffer, *The Cost of Discipleship* (Peter Smith Publications, 1983), 64.

Chapter 8

ambassadors of anticipation

It was one of the fiercest ice storms in the city's history. All of the trees and ground were covered with sheets of sleet that made the streets practically impassable. The rich patron was wrapped in warm blankets by a blazing fire in his home, yet he was not feeling comfortable. He twisted and turned, seeking relief, until he realized that it was his conscience burning with the burden of homeless men and women who would be helpless and frozen in the relentless storm.

Eventually, with a sigh of determination, he shook off the warm blankets and called his chauffeur to bring the Rolls Royce, now filled with blankets and hot bottles. They set off on a quest to help the homeless in the city. They drove along deserted streets, where they found a few shivering women in an empty alley before coming to a street where they could not maneuver the car because of the ice on the road. The rich patron wrapped his expensive cashmere coat around himself, pulling the collar up high as he braced himself against the cold wind whistling between the tall buildings. He stepped out of the car onto the icy pavement. He used his cane to steady his wobbly steps as he ventured out into the still-robust storm. In a few minutes, as he was poking his cane into every little mound of old snow covered by fresh sleet, something moved and moaned in barely audible tones. He stopped at once, threw his cane aside, and with his gloved hands, dug a hole into the moving mound, where he discovered a dirty, disheveled child, chilled to the bones and barely breathing. He bundled up the child in his coat and ran to the car, slipping and sliding as he moved quickly and unsteadily in the sleet. He was barely in the car before he ordered the chauffeur to rush home so that he could try to revive the unconscious bundle cosseted to his bosom.

When they arrived home, he rejected every offer of his servants to care for the child. He was determined to do everything himself. He carefully bathed the young boy, dressed him in his best sleepwear, and tucked him in his own bed, beautifully made up with white sheets and down pillows. He ordered soup and carefully spooned the warm liquid into the child's chapped mouth. He rubbed his feet, warmed his hands, and prayed for his recovery as he gently cared for the little stranger. As he continued to feed him, the little boy began to breathe evenly again.

After a few hours, his eyes fluttered open. When the child looked around and saw the large room with its fancy furnishings, and heard the sound of music playing softly, he thought he had died and gone to heaven. When he touched the white sheets enveloping his body and looked into his benefactor's face, tender with love and compassion, the boy whispered softly and earnestly, "Mister, are you God?" The rich patron smiled affectionately, took the child's hands and whispered, "No my son, I'm not God. I'm His ambassador of hope."

Those who touch others with humane hands and inspire the human heart to overcome obstacles and ride the waves of adversity until they savor the sweet taste of victory, are God's ambassadors of hope. To those who benefit from spiritual books and other rich resources, many of which are inspired by the author's experience in the eye of a storm, the benefactors are like God's fountains, bringing the sweet, refreshing, regenerating waters of hope to their parched spirits.

Today, an ambassador is a diplomatic official, a resident representative of the highest rank, appointed and sent by a president or prime minister to another state on a mission, bearing a message from his or her native land. In the Bible, the word *ambassador* comes from one that means an elder, a person of mature means whose mind is full of wisdom to effectively execute the mission on which she or he has been dispatched. Spiritually speaking, an ambassador is an authorized agent of God, an official representative or messenger of Jesus Christ, who is anointed and empowered by the Holy Spirit to exercise oversight over the church and have spiritual care of those whom God is daily drawing into His kingdom of grace.

In the time of the apostle Paul, an ambassador was one sent to deliver a message, carrying the authority of the one who sent him. He wrote, *"Therefore, we are ambassadors for Christ, as though God were entreating through us; we beg you on behalf of Christ, be reconciled to God"* (2 Corinthians 5:20). Most of the time, an ambassador has to be personally present to deliver the message, but in these last days God is entreating through us via a variety of technological advances. Sometimes God uses unorthodox methods to entreat the unsaved world through his ambassadors of anticipation.

For example, I was once told by a pastor that a year after I had spoken at a conference in England, a man was listening to, and obviously enjoying, a Walkman while traveling on a train. He was laughing, sometimes giving expressions of astonishment, at other times saddened with tears in his eyes, oblivious to the other passengers around him. Sitting next to him was a woman whose curiosity finally got the better of her and asked the man what was so interesting.

The man told her that he was listening to an American preacher-woman. She was not brave enough to ask to listen, but the man, being a member of the army of ambassadors of Christ, ejected the tape and gave it to her, telling her that he had enjoyed it repeatedly and could now part with it. Upon reaching her destination, she hurriedly listened to the tape of Hyveth Williams preaching. After attentive attention to the message on that tape, she not only recommitted herself fully to Christ, but also consented to become a member of His church.

Her son, who told me this story, said that he had tried everything to win his mother to Christ and His church, with no success. But God did what he could not do, through the words and work of two strangers. We are all ambassadors with a message on a mission for Christ, even when we are not aware that we are performing this awesome task, through which God is entreating the world that He loved so much He gave Himself up for the people in it.

Hope, in Webster's dictionary, is defined as a person or thing in which expectation is centered. It means to look forward to a person or thing with reasonable confidence, trust, or belief in the fulfillment of something desired. It means to long for something with high expectation or anticipation of its attainment.

The Bible describes hope as a favorable, confident expectation of things that have to do with the unseen future. Paul who uses the word *hope* more than any other New Testament writer, defines it as faith in things not seen, but longed for and desperately desired (see Romans 8:24). Hope also describes the happy anticipation of good, the confident feeling that what has been promised will come to fruition.

Ambassadors of hope are therefore ambassadors of anticipation, a word extensively defined in earlier chapters. They are new creatures in Christ who are authorized agents and official representatives of God. They are mature in mind and focused in mission. They live with confident expectation of things not seen and happy anticipation of the fulfillment or attainment of good, yet are intimately acquainted with the promise of hope, the pressure of hope and the power of hope.

The promise of hope

This existed from the beginning of Creation and was experienced fully after the fall of humanity into sin, according to the apostle Paul:

> *For I consider that sufferings of this present time are not worthy to be compared with the glory that is to be revealed to us. For the anxious longing of the creation waits eagerly for the revealing of the sons of God. For the creation was subjected to futility, not of its own will, but because of Him who subjected it, in hope that the creation itself also will be set free from its slavery to corruption into the freedom of the glory of the children of God* (Romans 8:18-22).

Until Adam and Eve fell, they were one with God in communion. When they turned from the true course for which God created them, according to Genesis 3, not only was their relationship with God negatively impacted, the entire sphere of planet Earth was affected. Earth came under the divine sentence that *"cursed is the ground"* where *"both thorns and thistles"* would grow and *"by the sweat of your face you shall eat bread, till you return to the ground"* (Genesis 3:17-19). Not only was Paradise lost, but also the whole creation changed from its original state of ministering the joys and blessings of grace to meet man's new condition in the shadow of the fall. Since then, sin has bludgeoned God's creation and everything—nature, the elements, animals and plants, and Adam and Eve's posterity—has been subjected to futility and senseless sufferings. Now we see marks of decay and death in the fury of the elements and the destructive instincts of humans and beasts.

In spite of the power and potential for destruction, nature in the Old Testament, is almost always associated with happiness. The prophets and psalmists have written about floods clapping their hands (see Psalm 98:8; Isaiah 55:12) and valleys, hills, and mountains laughing, singing, and rejoicing before the Lord (see Isaiah 44:23; 49:13). This emphasises one of the characteristics of the Bible. God's Word brings us face to face with life's sufferings and distress, but it also gives us the sense that this is not incurable. When we are faced with suffering and we turn to God, we have a sense that there is a remedy for evil and a way out of our predicament of confusion and despair.

But who can avoid thinking about the unmistakable voice of suffering echoing in nature, not only in the trees that shed their substance each changing season, but also in men and women who walk about, aimlessly, like leaves blown by the wind? There is a groaning of creation evidenced in flash floods, tornadoes, hurricanes, and earthquakes. In the New Testament, the apostle Paul pointed out the realities of sadness and suffering in these last days when he said, *"I consider the sufferings of this present time."* It is obvious in the acts of sinners without conscience who rape one another and pillage the land, the insane actions of those who violate human dignity, in the mass murders by perpetrators of hate crimes, and a litany of other vice and viciousness around the world.

One can hear the pain escaping the hurting hearts of lonely losers and throbbing heads of worried winners in the church as in the world. Our willingness to murder one another by the sword or wicked words makes it appear as though we are "thinking that competition and rivalry are essential to the carrying out of civilized life."[1] Our murderous intentions come from the fact that "the first civilization was founded by a murderer, and the whole basis of civilized life ever since has been a vast, complicated, gilded-over system of murder."[2] Yet, in spite of all this travail and tribulation, none of this is *"worthy to be compared with the glory that is to be revealed to us.*" This promise is so potent that the apostle Paul said creation waits with *"anxious longing"* or earnest expectation for this glory.

I find it very interesting that the word for anxious longing is composed of three Greek words, *apo*—to turn away; *kara*—head; and *dokeo*—pleasure. The apostle was conveying that creation is turning its head away from pleasure in order to fix its focus on what is promised—redemption from its slavery to corruption, and liberation from the ghastly grip of sin. It means that the whole creation is now conducting itself like Moses who, by faith, *"when he had grown up, [that great ambassador of anticipation] refused to be called the son of Pharaoh's daughter; choosing rather to endure ill-treatment with the people of God, than to enjoy the passing pleasures of sin; considering the reproach of Christ greater riches than the treasures of Egypt; for he was looking to the reward"* (Hebrews 11:25, 26).

The creation is turning away its head from earthly pleasures, with earnest expectation, to focus on heavenly promises as it waits eagerly, anxiously anticipating *"the revealing of the sons of God."* The word *apokalupto,* from which the English word apocalypse is derived, means "revealing." It appears that Paul deliberately chose this word to emphasize the eschatological theme of the second coming of Christ in this passage. This is the revealing, uncovering, unveiling of the sons and daughters of God, best illustrated in the act of a parent who buys a promised gift for a child at Christmas time. The child is aware of the purchase, but the parent has hidden the gift out of the child's sight. The pleasure of the child is to daily search for the gift as the day of reception draws closer. At the same time, the doting parent is also enthusiastically guiding the quest by declaring when she or he is getting closer to the place of hiding. That's the idea of the waiting for the apocalypse, or revealing of the children of God.

Paul is trying to engage our attention to start looking, on tiptoes; to keep on searching for the unveiling of the children of God who have been redeemed, paid for in full, by the blood of His only begotten Son. Right now, we do not know who are all the children of God, but when Christ comes, we will all be revealed. John the beloved disciple of Christ and apostle of biblical apocalypse said, *"Beloved, now we are children of God, and it has not appeared as yet what we shall be. We know that, when He appears, we shall be like Him, because we shall see Him just as He is"* (1 John 3:2).

While there's the anxious anticipation, there's also the futility to which creation was subjected since the appearance of sin. The word futility means "to be delivered up to vanity," something that is pointless, aimless, deceptive, and leading to no purpose. It lacks goodness and dissipates expectation. When sin came into the world, the entire creation was put under this futility, hopelessness and frustration, but God says, "Just hold on a little bit longer," because we are about to break free from slavery to that corruption of sin unto death. In fact, I've broken free to become one of the oldest women that ever lived in this world.

I once read that the reason women so carefully hide their age is because a woman who tells her age will tell anything. Be that as it may, I am pleased to admit that I have eternal life, and that puts me among the oldest creatures anticipating life in God's new creation. I have absolutely no intention of cashing this in for any of the cheap thrills or temporary pleasures I used to enjoy, that the world still offers to tempt us away from our commitment and goal. Like the apostle Paul, I am *"determined to know nothing among you except Jesus Christ and Him crucified"* (1 Corinthians 2:2). I intend to keep my eyes fixed on the cross of Jesus Christ and all it portends for believers. I have decided to have my mind focused on the promise that the chains of slavery to sin will be broken and I, who can now only function as an ambassador of anticipation, will one day be liberated by the Son of God to live with Him in heavenly places. No women's movement, no political ploy, no liberation theology can or will be able to set us as free as when the Son has set us free *"into the freedom of the glory of being the children of God."* Note that we are not servants or friends, but children of God.

The idea of truly being children of God is a radical concept. If properly understood, it can preserve us from the excesses of fanaticism, the seduction of libertinism, the pride of isolationism, and the restrictions of conservatism. Paul understood the magnitude of this gift and the potential for Christians to live a new life as children of God in a world overwhelmed by selfishness and greed. As a result, he is one of the greatest exponents of the declaration of the psalmist: *"You are gods, and all of you are sons [and daughters] of the most high"* (Psalm 82:6). Jesus also repeated it in John 10:34: *"Has it not been written in your Law, 'I said you are gods'?"* And Paul explains it in this passage: *"For you have not received a spirit of slavery leading to fear again, but you have received a spirit of adoption as sons by which we cry out 'Abba! Father!' The Spirit Himself bears witness with our spirit that we are children of God, and if children, heirs also, heirs of God and fellow heirs with Christ, if indeed we suffer with Him in order that we may also be glorified with Him"* (Romans 8:15, 16).

Note that it is the Spirit of God (not our denomination, religious affiliation, or confession of faith) who bears witness with our spirit that we are children of God. In his book, *New Testament Theology*, Donald Guthrie said, "Here it is specifically claimed that the believer's filial consciousness is directly induced by the Holy Spirit." The Spirit makes us know that we are children of God. Paul also used the term *"Abba! Father!"* in Galatians 4:6. Guthrie comments again, saying, "The retaining of the Aramaic form [Abba] alongside the Greek in a second passage shows the importance attached to the words, especially in view of their use by Jesus in Gethsemane, according to Mark 14:36. This is all the more remarkable in view of Paul's description of the Spirit as 'the Spirit of His Son.' It is the same Spirit who enabled Jesus at the hour of His agony to cry 'Abba,' who enables all the adopted children of God to approach the Father in the same way."[3]

In considering the theological, if not personal, implication of "sonship," or "daughterhood," inspired by the declaration in Psalm 82:6, I am proposing an idea for which I have been vilified by some who *"have a zeal for God, but not in accordance with knowledge. For not knowing about God's righteousness, and seeking to establish their own, they did not subject themselves to the righteousness of God,"*(Romans 10:2). Thus, with profound humility and careful biblical, exegetical, support for my hypothesis, I am presenting this concept for your reflection and consideration.

I often explain this concept by using the following illustration: When a cat gets pregnant and produces its offspring, we call them kittens that grow up to be cats. When a dog does the same, we name them pups that grow up to be dogs. When humans produce offspring they, by nature and character, are human beings, not kittens or pups. Since sin came into the world we are also burdened with the sinful nature inherited from Adam and Eve, our rebellious fore-parents (see Psalm 51:5). If this is true, then those who are born again by the power and providence of God (see John 1:12, 13) to partake of His divine nature and character, are indeed "gods" (with a small "g") as the psalmist declared and are children of the Most High.

I shared this with a friend, and it totally revolutionized her self-concept and sense of identity. Several months later, I had the opportunity to visit with her and was amazed at the visible change in her demeanor, attitude, and physical appearance. As I expressed my astonishment, she explained that she was no longer self-conscious, intoxicated with her failures and foibles which led her to try to work for her salvation, but had surrendered herself to God. In the process, she was born again and had become a daughter of the Most High— a godling, as another friend declares—and a new creature in Christ.

Later on, as I sat in my office reflecting on our conversation, I happened to glance at my wall, where I kept photos of my son. In one photograph he was almost two years old and is wearing his father's hat that is much too large for his little head. It brought a smile to my heart and my face, not only because he looks so cute, but also because God used that portrait to bring home a practical application of this concept.

Almost every child, at one time or another, puts on his or her parents' clothes. They dress up in the oversized hats, jackets, pants, dress, and shoes. They trudge around the house pretending to be grown up, to be like that beloved parent. They would never do that with a stranger's clothes. It only produces the feelings if the clothes belong to their own parents. Even though sin has made us into spiritual midgets, so also, when we are born again and know that we are truly the children of God—gods or godlings—we are able to *"put on the Lord Jesus Christ"* (Romans 13:14). At first, Christ's robe of righteousness will be ill fitting, but as we study and mature, by grace and sanctification, we grow into it. We will never be able to walk in His shoes, but we will always be able to follow in His steps as beloved sons and daughters of the Most High.

Some may question "how does this theory or concept differ from doctrines promulgated by the New Age movement?" The answer is simple. New Age adherents believe that a person is God and has no need of the saving grace of Jesus Christ expressed in His sacrifice on the cross. They do not embrace any of the tenets of our Christian faith, particularly the fact that Jesus Christ died for the sin of the world so that sinners may be transformed into saints who one day will live with God throughout eternity.

There are those who might argue that the word God is reserved only for the Almighty One. But, upon closer examination, one realizes that the Greek word *theos* translated "god," is by no means restricted to God the Father, Son, and Holy Spirit. It is also used frequently, in the Bible as well as in other literature, to name and describe heathen gods. It occasionally denotes men and women as in John 10:34, where Jesus showed the Jews that "to use this term of men is not inconsistent with biblical thinking."[4]

Those who accept the biblical doctrine of sonship will also

comprehend the tremendous responsibility attached to this gift. It is a particularly significant truth that in order to become a member of the family of God, believers must be bought by the blood of the Lamb. We must also be bound by the chords of His incredible love and blessed by rebirth, as well as adoption by grace through faith in the continued saving work of divine providence.

The birth metaphor in the Bible best illustrates the process of conversion. Jesus told Nicodemus that he must be *"born again"* in order to *"see the kingdom of God"* (John 3:3). This birth into the family and kingdom of God is described in John 1:12, 13. *"But as many as received Him, to them* He gave the [legal] right to become children of God, *even to those who believe in His name,* who were born not of blood, nor of the will of the flesh, nor of the will of man, but of God" (emphasis added).

This means that as many as believe and accept Christ as their personal Savior, to them are given, by rebirth adoption, the authority to partake of the divine nature as children of God. "Human motives and human planning play no part in the birth of which John speaks. It resembles physical birth only in the sense that both mark the beginning of new life (see John 3:3-8; Romans 6:3-5). It is not accomplished through human initiative and action, but is altogether a new creation, wholly dependent upon the will and action of God Himself."[5] John himself also confirmed that statement when he said, *"That which is born of the flesh is flesh, and that which is born of the Spirit is spirit"* (John 3:6).

To better understand this new birth which provides a new nature and makes one a new creature in Christ (see 2 Corinthians 5:17 and Romans 6:11-14), we must re-examine the conception of Jesus. When Jesus' birth was announced to His mother, the angel told her that *"the Holy Spirit will come upon you, and the power of the Most High will overshadow you; and for that reason the holy offspring shall be called the Son of God"* (Luke 1:35). The conception and birth of Jesus, by the Holy Spirit, is a type of the new birth that happens to every believer in essentially the same way. Long before there are any feelings of love for God, the Holy Spirit plants His Seed, Christ (see Galatians 3:16), in the barren, lifeless heart of the sinner, whether they are Jew or Gentile.

The Jews misinterpreted the promise of redemption to all mankind, *"even those who believe"* on the name of God. According to their theology, to be born a son of Abraham was almost certainly a guarantee of admission into the kingdom of heaven (see John 8:33). Non-Jews, they believed, had to be baptized into Judaism and become adopted sons of Abraham in order to be saved. Jesus clearly pointed out a new and disturbing concept to Nicodemus that all human beings, both Jews and Gentiles, must be born again *"by water and the Spirit"* to inherit the kingdom of God.

To explain this radical concept, B. A. Demarest, writing in the *New International Dictionary of New Testament Theology,* suggests that the Hebrew word *zera* (seed) is used figuratively to indicate offspring or progeny either individually (Genesis 9:9) or collectively (Genesis 4:25; 21:13), highlighting the cohesion of the elect community. "Zera in Genesis 3:15 includes the two proceeding ideas: collectively the seed foreshadows the spiritually renewed posterity of Adam who strive with Satan: ultimately refers to Christ the paramount seed who seals Satan's doom. In the Genesis promise texts zera denotes Abraham's spiritual offspring (Genesis 15:5, 17; 7:8; 22:18) who adhere to the covenant of Yahweh. Psalm 22:30 refers to the seed (i.e. spiritual progeny) of the Messiah."[6]

B. A. Demerast also notes in the same entry that the Greek word *sperma* (seed) occurs forty-four times in the New Testament, and in almost thirty texts it is employed in the sense of offspring or posterity. It appears most frequently with the latter connotation in citations of Old Testament promise texts that foretell the future blessings of the descendants of Abraham (see Genesis 12:7; 17:7), Isaac (see Genesis 21:12) and David. Demerast said, "In Paul, *sperma* occasionally transcends the basic physical relation to include the spiritual descendants of Old Testament believers. The common New Testament expression, 'seed of Abraham,' thus is not restricted to the generic house of Israel, but includes all who possess the same kind of faith as the patriarch. New Testament believers are represented as the true seed of Abraham (Galatians 3:29). . . . Paul ultimately interprets the Old Testament promise of seed in terms of Christ, the paramount offspring of Abraham (Galatians 3:16-19; cf. Genesis 12:7)" who is described as the ultimate fulfillment of the divine promise to the patriarchs and later to David according to Acts 12:23, 33.[7]

The divine seed is given a surprising interpretation in a chapter that emphasizes sonship. The apostle John said, "No one who is born of God practices sin, because His seed abides in him; and he cannot sin, because he is born of God" (1 John 3:9). Demarest explains that here "*sperma* signifies the divine principle of life (the Spirit) in the believer, which renders continuance in sin incongruous."[8] John adds that "by this [continuous sin] the children of God and the children of the devil are obvious: anyone who does not practice righteousness is not of God, nor the one who does not love his brother" (1 John 3:10).

As the physical sperma was the generator of life in the natural order of creation (Genesis 1:11 ff.), so the divine sperma becomes the fount and origin of life in the new order of recreated humanity by the presence and power of the Holy Spirit. One of my cherished Christian authors affirmed this idea by pointing out in many of her writings that the Lord puts His own Spirit into the seed. In one place she stated that "the mysteries of the Kingdom of God are to be read in the growth of the seed." God designed that nature should be to man a lesson-book to guide him from the path of disobedience back to God . . . under the guidance of the Holy Spirit."[9]

Jesus described the effects of the Spirit on the one who receives Him as coming "from the innermost being" (John 7:38b). Here the Spirit is referred to as an internal experience of a person's deepest spiritual nature. The Greek word for "innermost being" is *kolias*. It comes from the word that means "belly, abdomen, stomach or womb." Jesus used the same word for womb in His conversation with Nicodemus (see John 3:4) in a figurative sense, to represent the area of the Spirit's dwelling in a person where the new spiritual life is generated, and out of which it issues forth into practical experiences with God and people. By this, it appears that He intended for us to understand that conversion is a real and personal experience, similar in many ways to the natural baby in the womb of its mother, as well as its development after birth.

"The germination of the seed represents the beginning of spiritual life" where, "as its growth is silent and imperceptible, but continuous, so is the development of the Christian."[10] During this period of gestation or germination, "the Spirit works upon man's heart, according to His desire and consent, implanting in him a new nature."[11] This miracle of grace adds the divine nature to the person's existing carnal nature to transform it daily via the process of sanctification, into its original, pre-sin character we call the human nature.

After the period of gestation, birth occurs. A new being is born, not of the corruptible, carnal seed (see 1 Peter 1:23), but of God, a holy offspring who is also given a new name (see Revelation 3:12). At that time, "the old nature is not improved. By faith the believing one is made a partaker of the Divine nature."[12] (Also see 2 Peter 1:4.) While we cannot understand the method by which God works this miracle of a new creation, we can know the effects of it. Paul said, *"Because you are sons, God has sent forth the Spirit of His Son into your hearts, crying 'Abba, Father.' Therefore you are no longer a slave, but a son; and if a son, then an heir through God"* (Galatians 4:6, 7).

Henry Drummond said that "the new birth wrought by the Spirit in man dead in his trespass and sins like the inanimate soil into which the animate plant sinks its roots, transmutes to it life, takes it up into its living organism, and thus transforms its being and nature."[13] Charles Webb Carter notes "likewise the living and life giving Spirit of God penetrates the spiritually inanimate nature of man, imparts to it new life from God above, takes that nature up into His living self, and transforms it into a new being."[14]

Peter confirmed this when he wrote:

> *Grace and peace be multiplied to you in the knowledge of God and of Jesus our Lord; seeing that His divine power has granted to us everything pertaining to life and godliness, through the true knowledge of Him who called us by His own glory and excellence. For by these He has granted to us His precious and magnificent promises, in order that by them* you might become partakers of the divine nature, *having escaped the corruption that is in the world by lust* (2 Peter 1:2-4, emphasis added).

"The change of heart by which we become children of God in the Bible is spoken of as birth. Again it is compared to the germination of the good seed sown by the husbandman. In like manner those who are just converted to Christ are 'as newborn babes,' to 'grow up' to the stature of men and women in Christ Jesus. 1 Peter 2:2; Ephesians 4:15. Or like the good seed sown in the field, they are to grow up and bring forth fruit . . . So from the natural life, illustrations are drawn, to help us better to understand the mysterious truths of spiritual life."[15] That is just awesome. *"See how great a love the Father has bestowed upon us, that we should be called children of God; and such we are. For this reason the world does not know us, because it did not know Him. Beloved, now we are children of God"* (1 John 3:1, 2a).

When God inspired the psalmist to write, *"You are gods, and all are children of the most High"* (Psalm 82:6), He was communicating the totality of the new person and the enabling work of the Holy Spirit to reflect His image, physically and spiritually, in His children.

Because we do not understand "God language," anthropocentric terms are necessary to describe God as a concrete and physical being in whose image we are created. Our Greek heritage that gives us the idea of the body/flesh combination prohibits our acceptance of the Hebrew concept of the image of God (*Imago Dei*) as one who had both physical form and spiritual attributes.

To the Hebrew, God is not an abstract principle. If He did not exist physically, He could not exist spiritually. The Bible communicates this concept in Genesis 9:6, where God said that men should not kill each other *"for in the image of God He made man."* This injunction implies that man is made in God's physical, mental, and spiritual likeness, as a unique, mysterious, irreplaceable, invaluable being. Therefore, to kill a person is tantamount to deicide—killing God. It is therefore not foreign to the Hebrew understanding of God and His relationship with His chosen people or children that they should be called "gods" and it should not be so to believers this side of the cross of Calvary.

There was general acceptance of the idea of sonship in Jewish belief and theology. According to the records of John, the disciple whom Jesus loved, the Jews accused Jesus of blasphemy. They said to Him, "You, being a man, make yourself out to be God." Jesus responded to that charge saying, *"Has it not been written in your Law, 'I said, you are gods?' If he called them gods, to whom the word of God came (and the Scripture cannot be broken), do you say of Him, whom the Father sanctified and sent into the world, 'You are blaspheming,' because I said, 'I am the Son of God?'"* The whole force of Jesus' reasoning showed that the idea of sonship was by no means foreign to the revelations of the Old Testament or to those hearing His response to the charges. It is also significant that Jesus confirmed the statement by adding that *"the Scripture cannot be broken."*

Sonship or daughterhood places a great responsibility on the believer. For "it is one thing to know we are children of God, [but] it is another to act like children of God, with full awareness of utter dependence on and love for God as Father."[16] The implication is that as the natural person inherits the human nature from their parents, so should the born-again child of God exhibit the characteristics of his or her heavenly Parent in nature and attitude according to Philippians 2:5. There should be both the physical, genuine humanity that Jesus modeled as well as spiritual evidence of the life under the divine guidance of the new birth that He puts in the heart, mind, and soul of the believer. His statement, *"I can do nothing on My own initiative. As I hear, I judge; and My judgment is just, because I do not seek My own will, but the will of Him who sent me"* (John 5:30) demonstrated that Jesus did nothing but the will of His Father and so should the sons and daughters of the Most High. In fact, *"everyone who has this hope fixed on him purifies himself, just as He is pure"* (1 John 3:4).

When God inspired the psalmist to declare, *"You are gods, and are all children of the Most High,"* it was a challenge for all who profess to be so to exhibit the character, compassion and family features of our heavenly Parent. In this waiting to break through to the fulfillment of the promise period of human history, we can hear, we can feel that something is about to happen. In the words of William Shakespeare as I've said before, "By the itching of my fingers, by the pricking of my thumbs, something wicked this way comes." Since we have the sense of a life-changing, world-reshaping cataclysmic event, every believer should *"be imitators [followers] of God, as beloved children; and walk in love, just as Christ also loved you, and gave Himself up for us an offering and sacrifice to God as a fragrant aroma"* (Ephesians 5:1). Even though some of us may not be recognized for our good deeds, we must live a godly life. It is also a commonly recognized fact that the sons and daughters of God are not now clearly known (see 1 John 3:2-4), but after every wicked something there is always a revealing, and they appear to be just like their Elder Brother—kind, compassionate, and faithful.

We are a people in waiting, ambassadors of anticipation, who must also be watching for the signs God gave as a guide to those who are alive in these last days. Jesus said, *"Watch therefore, be on the alert or lookout, for you do not know which day your Lord is coming . . . For this reason you be ready too; for the Son of Man is coming at an hour when you do not think He will"* (Matthew 24:42, 44, paraphrased). It appears, from this passage, that there will be no major upheaval. Jesus is just going to come. That's why He gives us signs.

The Bible addresses two types of signs—one that says He is near and the other that shows He is here. Those that point out that He is near include the appearances of false messiahs, famines, earthquakes, wars, and rumors of wars. However, we discovered earlier that they are reminders, like the rainbow was to Noah, that our covenant-keeping God is not finished with the plan of salvation. These are signs of the birth pangs spoken of by Paul: *"For we know that the whole creation groans and suffers the pangs of childbirth together until now"* (Romans 8:22). They are reminders that sons and daughters of God are being born again every moment of every day and the devil is angry, so he throws tantrums to disrupt the ebb and flow of our human relationships as well as our equilibrium with nature. Every falling star, every eclipse, every betrayal of trust, every cooling of love is a sign that Christ will keep His promise to come again. They are not concrete signs by which we may begin the countdown. They are just signs to tell us that He is near and that what He promised will absolutely come to pass.

While we are watching the signs, we must always remember that Jesus said, *"An evil and adulterous generation craves for a sign; and yet no sign shall be given to it but the sign of Jonah the prophet; for just as Jonah was three days and nights in the belly of the sea monster, so shall the Son of Man be three days and three nights in the heart of the earth. The men of Nineveh shall stand up with this generation at the judgment, and shall condemn it because they repented at the preaching of Jonah; and behold, something greater than Jonah is here"* (Matthew

12:39-41). He was telling them that just as Jonah came out of the belly of that big fish after three days and was able to transform the lives of thousands of people with his resurrection appearance and preaching, so also after His death and resurrection, many people will be converted. The sign of Jonah is not only his burial in the bowels of the earth for three days, but is also the conversion of non-believers through the preaching and teaching of the gospel of Christ's death, resurrection and mediatory ministry in heaven. This sign of Jonah was fulfilled in part at Pentecost and also every day when a sinner turns to the Savior. It is also being fulfilled when non-believers come out of the darkness of sin into the marvelous light in Christ Jesus to be born-again sons and daughters of the Most High.

Ambassadors of anticipation are also the midwives of God, assisting with the delivery of His newborn babies. When a midwife is in the act of delivering a baby and a tornado comes, she doesn't say to the mother and child, "Just rest here while I go underground for protection." Instead, she hovers over the infant until it is delivered, then she tenderly, even if hurriedly, wraps it to her bosom and runs with it for cover. That's the business we are in, delivering spiritual children, and when we see the signs we hasten, not to run for cover, but to preach with power and conviction the good news of the imminent return of Jesus Christ.

There are a few concrete signs of the end. For example, *"Just as the lightning comes from the east, and flashes even to the west, so shall the coming of the Son of Man be."* In addition, *"the sign of the Son of Man will appear in the sky, and then all the tribes of the earth will mourn, and they will see the Son of Man coming on the clouds of the sky with power and great glory"* (Matthew 24:27, 30). If we are alive to see this, be assured that it is not countdown time, but is the end! It will not be time to deliver babies. Jesus said it would be the hour of gathering *"together of the elect from the four winds, from one end of the sky to the other"* (verse 31). Until then, we live *"in hope that the creation itself will be set free from its slavery to corruption into the freedom of the glory of the children of God"* (Romans 8:21).

The liberty of the glory is the knowledge that in Christ we experience freedom from the presence of sin in our personal, spiritual life such as temptations, trials and tribulations that the devil throws at us daily. Perhaps that is why Revelation 12:12b said, *"Woe to the earth and the sea, because the devil has come down to you, having great wrath, knowing that he has only a short time."*

In the past, whenever I read this text I would worry whether or not I would be able to withstand the onslaught of the devil during these last days. Then I read these comforting words: *"Humble yourselves, therefore, under the mighty hand of God that He may exalt you at the proper time, casting all your anxiety upon Him, because He cares for you. Be of sober spirit; be on the alert. Your adversary, the devil, prowls about like a roaring lion, seeking someone to devour"* (1 Peter 5:6-8). Every time I read the last sentence of this text, I laugh to myself. It is humorous. I am sure Peter intended it in order to draw our attention to a very significant fact, that lions never growl while they prowl.

Over the years as I have watched the Discovery Channel and National Geographic programs on television, I have learned a lot about lions. That's where I learned that the lion does not roar when it is prowling. In fact, the male lion is the one who generally prowls or stalks the prey. While the female is hidden in a certain location, the male stalks the prey, allowing itself to be seen only enough to intimidate and push its prey into the direction of the waiting female. At the appropriate time, the male lion roars loud enough to scare the prey into scampering into the trap where the female is waiting.

The devil is so anxious to destroy the people of God that he forgets the important fact that he should not be roaring while he is prowling. For when he does that, the children of God can hear him coming at a distance and, empowered by the Holy Spirit, are able to escape and *"resist him, [by] stand[ing] firm in [their] faith, knowing that the same experiences of suffering are being accomplished by [their] brethren who are in the world"* (1 Peter 5:9).

Second, we also experience freedom from the power of sin or the calamities and hostilities of this evil age that attempt to intimidate or coerce us into rebelling against God. I believe that the fallen angels, sometimes called demons, hate each other. They do not know what it is like to love and forgive as the children of God do. As a result, they are in a constant battle to outdo each other. Often, we are pawns in their hands and at other times, are caught in the middle of their rumbles against each other and against God. Sometimes a legion of demons may throw tornadoes that destroy homes, ending the hope and lives of people. Others might try to outdo that by creating bigger hurricanes. Their hostilities are also evident in the senseless murders reported in the daily news, sometimes to kill God's precious children because it's their way of killing God Himself.

The sister of a friend was viciously and tragically murdered a few years ago, by a young man who was attempting to hijack her car by holding her hostage at gunpoint. She had just completed her physician's training and was shopping for things to take with her on her medical missionary tour. She returned from the store, opened her car and got in. A stranger came and asked her to get out of the car. She tried to quickly lock the doors, but he pulled out a gun and shot her point-blank in the face. She died instantly. He was apparently only sixteen years old. She was one of the most dedicated, faithful Christians one would ever meet. While some of her classmates studied on Sabbath, she worshipped God and served His people. To this day, I shudder over the loss of such great potential, but I also know that it is the enemy who has done this. So I live in anxious anticipation, eagerly waiting for the day when God will come and put an end to sin and death.

In the meantime, we do not have to live as though we are helpless while Satan and his hosts of evil angels, knowing that their time is short, rage against us. God in His great providence has, through the power of the blood of Jesus Christ, liberated us from the power of sin. The Son has set us free so that even if the enemy shortens the life of a loved one, even if our homes get blown down and our hearts are broken, we may be bent but never broken, because we are no longer under the power of sin.

Third, we also experience freedom from the penalty of sin, the second death. Before Jesus died on the cross, His final statement was, *"It is finished!"* This is a phrase that comes from the Greek word *tetelestai* and is also translated "paid in full." To best understand the freedom we have from the penalty of sin, I must share with you a story from which this word is believed to have originated. Scholars suggest that while He was growing up in Palestine, Jesus may have witnessed many transactions in which this word was used and that He deliberately chose it as His final testimony to the power of the sacrifice He was making for humanity.

In the time of Jesus, Jewish families who were going through hard times and could not afford to pay their bills would often forfeit their property and eventually, as things got worse, sell themselves and their families into slavery to cover their debt. The caveat was that only a relative, recognized as the *goel,* could purchase them and redeem them from slavery. Legend has it that one day a family, composed of mother, father, sister and brother, were being sold in the marketplace by a merchant who had acquired them as slaves for unpaid debt. As he called out the cost of the family, like our modern auctioneers, a stranger came into the marketplace. He did not look as though he could afford to purchase those slaves, yet he walked confidently up to the auctioneer and asked the price of the family.

The auctioneer sneered, noting that the stranger did not appear able to afford the slaves, then continued shouting to attract other investors. The stranger urged the auctioneer to humor him by giving him a price for the family, to which the auctioneer quoted, let's say, thirty pieces of silver each, the price of a slave in that day. Without arguing, or engaging the auctioneer in the usual bartering to reduce the price, the stranger reached into the folds of his flowing garments and pulled out a bag of coins and counted off gold coins well in excess of the cost of the family. In fact, he was so liberal that the auctioneer had to stop him, protesting that he was paying much more than they were worth; but the stranger did not stop until he had emptied his purse. When he placed the last coin on the table, he slammed his hand over the money onto the table and shouted triumphantly, *"Tetelestai!* Paid in full." This action attracted the attention of all the other shoppers and merchants, who were amazed to notice that upon securing the slaves, the stranger graciously gave them their freedom.

We have all been sold into the slavery of sin. But Jesus Christ, our elder Brother, the *goel* (kinsman redeemer), came and bought us back with His life and blood. As He gasped His last breath on the cross, He shouted, *"Tetelestai!* Paid in full," so that the observing principalities and powers, the evil elements of the air, plus all the human participants at the foot of the cross, would know that He had purchased us back and paid it in full. He redeemed us for Himself by pouring out His greatest treasure—His life—so that we may be graciously set free from the penalty of sin. That's why, even though I can't carry a tune in a bucket, according to a friend, I always sing lustily, "Jesus paid it all, All to Him I owe; Sin had left a crimson stain; He washed it white as snow."

The pressure of hope

In spite of the gift of freedom from the presence, power, and penalty of sin, even as we are proclaiming and partaking of the promise of hope, we are also confronted with the pressure of hope. The apostle Paul said:

> *For we know that the whole creation groans and suffers the pains of childbirth together until now. And not only this, but also we ourselves, having the first fruits of the Spirit, even we ourselves groan within ourselves, waiting eagerly for our adoption*

as sons, the redemption of our body (Romans 8:22-23).

Paul must have witnessed the birth of a baby on one of his missionary journeys, because he used the vivid, dramatic language of birthing to describe how creation groans and suffers the pains of childbirth. Imagine the power of this metaphor that pictures nature in the pang of childbirth. The sufferings around us are sometimes so unbearable that *"we hide, as it were, our faces from it."*

All of us who have given birth are intimately acquainted with the pain. It amazes me that in spite of this indescribable pain, women continue to bear children. In television dramas about childbirth, invariably the mother curses the father, at the peak of her agony, for putting her through the pain of childbirth. Yet, as soon as the little bundle of joy is placed in her hands, she forgets all of the pain and is almost anxious to repeat the performance.

Mothers-to-be are encouraged to attend classes to prepare for the birth of their baby. They learn how to push down hard so that they can help the baby pass quickly and safely through the narrow birth canal. Living through the last days of earth's history is sometimes akin to passing through that tiny passage. Nature recoils from it, but is forced through it. Even we ourselves are groaning. Many can't stand the pain and are giving up. But I can almost hear the Holy Spirit coaching God's ambassadors of anticipation, saying, "Push! Push harder! Don't give up! We're almost there!"

Saints, it won't be long before the birth of the hope that is set before us happens. We sense that it won't be long because the birth pangs are coming faster and harder. We who are waiting eagerly (the Greek says "craning the neck") for our adoption as sons and daughters are anticipating the arrival of the Son of God, bursting through the clouds of heaven. When we see Him we will be rejoicing like a mother holding and kissing a brand new baby. We will be so happy to see Jesus we will forget the pain of the past as we shout with joy, "We would do it again! Lord, we would do it again for You!"

This expectation constitutes the inspiration and cheerfulness of the Christian ambassador's heart. The prospect of future glory is absolutely certain, for we have Jesus' word on it: *"Let not your heart be troubled; believe in God, believe also in Me. In My Father's house are many dwelling places; if it were not so, I would have told you; for I go to prepare a place for you. And if I go and prepare a place for you, I will come again, and receive you to Myself; that where I am, there you may be also"* always (John 14:1-3, emphasis added).

The Greek word for "adoption" in Romans 8:23 picks up this theme. It is composed of two words, *huios*, a son, and *thesis*, a placing, which in this context, signifies the place and condition of a son given to one to whom it does not naturally belong. This word, used by the apostle Paul only, indicates that when the sons and daughters of God are revealed, they are and will be placed in a position of sonship at the right hand of God. Our waiting and watching, our faithfulness as ambassadors of anticipation will be richly rewarded at that time. That's good news to me, not just the position of all positions, but the being with God and His being with us (see Revelation 21:3b). It gives me goose bumps when I think about it! For, it is unthinkable that a person of color, a woman, a poor person from the ghettos, a handicapped person, and all the others who are marginalized by secular politics or other barriers in the world, can dare to hope, alongside the rich, strong, and well-endowed, for this kind of liberty and promotion. This brings me to the final fact that keeps the joy flourishing in ambassadors of anticipation.

The power of hope

The same passage that vividly depicts the pressures of hope, equally emphasizes the power of hope in the following verses:

For in hope we have been saved, but hope that is seen is not hope; for why does one also hope for what he sees? But if we hope for what we do not see, with perseverance we wait eagerly for it (Romans 8:24, 25).

Salvation, the power of hope, is the essential element that must never be omitted from our contemplation of what the Christian life means. It is experienced by faith that looks backward and upward, with hope that looks onward and outward because of the unlimited gift of God's unconditional love.

Faith accepts everything and is concerned only with Christ while *"in hope we have been saved"* to expect the good things promised when He comes again, such as the end of sin and the destruction of the devil. Faith helps us appropriate the righteousness that is ours by grace, while hope anticipates the fullness of salvation at the second coming of Christ. But, praise God, it is love that lives in our hearts every moment of every day to bring us through to what we anxiously anticipate—to see God and live. The power of this expectation is proclaimed in the New Testament as the "blessed hope" that we live by and labor for. The power of hope is always centered on Christ, on the resurrection of the dead, on the reunion of family and friends, on the transformation into the likeness of Christ when we are delivered from sin, and on the final revelation of the sons and daughters of God who are ambassadors of anticipation.

While we are watching and waiting for the Great Event, we must also be working. Jesus said, *"We must work the works of Him who sent Me, as long as it is day; night is coming, when no man can work"* (John 9:4). He used the word "must," meaning there is no other option—we must work. It is compelling. It is necessary. I hear Him saying that salvation by grace given to us demands that we work for the salvation of others. We cannot work for our own salvation, but we have a responsibility to labor for others. This is the only salvation by works that is mentioned and accepted in the Word of God—that we do nothing for ourselves and everything for others. Salvation by grace is not an invitation to laziness. We must come to rest in Christ, as we work for and with Him. There's a sense of urgency. We must do so right now because the time is passing.

The day is slipping away. The moment is almost gone.

This passage had a local meaning as Jesus referred to His own day and the short time left for Him to spend with His own people until His return to live eternally with us. He was referring to His own impending death and departure from this world. It also has meaning for us in these last days when the time is short between now and the second coming of Christ, which the apostle Paul reminds us is nearer than when we first believed (see Romans 13:11). We have a job to do, and we have to stop our navel-gazing obsession and, in the words of the popular Nike commercial, "Just do it!" We must pull our heads out of the doctrinal sand where we are desperately trying to prove that we are right and others are wrong, so that we may experience the privilege of telling people that Jesus came and died so that none should perish or endure the second death.

In His day, Jesus said, *"Behold, I say to you, lift up your eyes, and look on the fields, that they are white for harvest"* (John 4:35b). Today I say, "We don't have a lot of time left and we have many babies to deliver, so let's get on with it!" There are people in prisons of concrete walls and iron bars, and there are people in prisons without walls in the world, captives of childhood experiences and past foolish choices. They all need to be delivered from their sufferings, and there's only One who can set them free—our soon-coming Savior, Jesus Christ our Lord! Here is a story about a woman who, like me, was rescued from both the real and surreal prison in which many of us are trapped.

One day a Christian woman was impressed, in prayer, to take twenty roses to the women's prison in upstate New York, about thirty miles from her home. When she was through praying she argued with God that the instruction did not make sense, since it would be a waste of money to take fragile flowers to the hardened criminals in that maximum-security prison. The next day, she was again impressed with the same instruction. This time she argued that she would not be able to gain entrance because it was a maximum-security prison. She had no idea where to begin to gain access and approval for what she was beginning to realize was really a directive from God. By the third day, she was so overwhelmed by the strength and power of the impression that she ran out of her home to purchase the roses. She made her way to the prison, protesting every mile that drew her closer to it.

Upon her arrival, the corrections officer looked at her as though she was a lunatic, but remembering his own mother's strong faith in God, decided to humor her and send her into the senior officer on duty. He tried to discourage her by vividly describing the worthlessness of the prisoners, but she insisted that she must obey God and give the flowers to the women. Finally, the officer had her taken into a room where she was searched and made ready to enter the large holding center of the prison to which the women had been taken.

She nervously gave each one a rose and prayed with them, but as she was being escorted out by the chief himself, to the sounds of some of the most unappreciative invective from the prisoners, she realized that she had one rose left. She asked the officer if she had missed anyone, to which he quickly and firmly replied, "No!" He seemed to be rushing her out with a gentle but firm push toward the great iron bar doors. But under the influence of the Holy Spirit, that generally timid lady stood her ground, insisting that if God told her twenty roses, then there had to be twenty women to receive them. The officer realized that she was not going to go away quietly, so he relented and admitted that there was indeed one more prisoner. He said that the prisoner had murdered her husband and was sent to prison more than a decade before. She was filled with such bitterness and spewed out so many expletives that the other criminals could no longer tolerate her profanities and bad attitude. She had become so violent and unruly that they had isolated her from the others and finally placed her in solitary confinement, where her only visitors were those who fed her.

The woman with the roses graciously asked if she could see her, to which the officer agreed but with a condition. He told her that he would take her to the cell with that poor miscreant, but he would not open the door. She had to drop the rose in the cell without seeing the prisoner. They walked silently down the long corridors to the cell, where they could smell the stale odor from that unkempt, disheveled, bedeviled woman. As soon as the chief slid open the slot through which her food was shoved into her cell, a horrible, blood-curdling sound came through the small opening. They both jumped back as though someone had dashed a pail of dirty water over them. The woman with the rose quickly dropped it in the cell and took off down the corridor behind the officer, who was running so fast one would think his life was in jeopardy!

After they left, the prisoner, still screaming at the top of her lungs, finally looked at the rose. In the darkened cell it seemed to take on a life of its own. The rose appeared to be glowing in the dark, beckoning her to pick it up. She did so and couldn't resist lifting it to her nostrils. The fresh scent awakened memories she had buried in her subconscious mind. She recalled how when she was a little girl she used to go to Sunday School, and on her way she often stopped to admire the rose garden in front of the church. She reminisced about Vacation Bible Schools where she memorized Bible verses, some of which began to come to her mind again. She held that rose to her bosom and began to cry as she remembered John 3:16, 17: *"For God so loved the world, that He gave His only begotten Son, that whoever believes in Him should not perish, but have eternal life. For God did not send the Son into the world to judge the world, but that the world should be saved through Him."*

As she remembered, she began to whisper the words, then to shout them through her tears. She pulled the petals of the rose, saying, "God loves me, God loves me, God loves even me," and there, in that foul-smelling cell, she committed her life to Christ. The next morning, when the food was shoved into her cell, there was silence instead of the usual foul language and bitter diatribe. The guard thought that she might have died during the night, so he quickly called the officer, who rushed to open the cell door. He found the prisoner sitting on her heels in a corner, her hands wrapped around her knees, the petals on the floor around her, as she clutched the stem in one hand. She was rocking herself, still saying in a singsong voice, "Jesus loves me, Jesus loves even me," as more tears filled the rivers that had been running down her face through what seemed like a decade of dirt.

She was so unusually calm and gracious that the officer removed her from the cell and sent her to be washed and cared for. Her fingernails had grown long like claws; her dirty, graying hair was a long, tangled mess that had to be shaved, since none of it could be saved. She was plagued with a terrible cough, so they placed her outside in the warm sun. When nothing helped to stop the cough, a doctor was called in, but he discovered she had developed a virulent strain of tuberculosis that was quickly choking the life out of her. She was given about six months to live.

One day, a wealthy Christian patron heard her testimony at the church of the woman who had given her the rose and had watched her grow into a model prisoner and believer in Christ. The patron was so moved by her story that he rented Carnegie Hall and invited the public to come and hear this woman's incredible testimony.

In the audience that Sunday night, well over three-quarters of a century ago, was a seventeen-year-old lad from the farms of Nebraska who was himself on a quest to find Christ. He was so moved by the testimony of that woman who told of her hope to be one day reunited with the God who had forgiven and given her eternal life, that he gave his life to the Lord. He grew up to be an ambassador of hope himself, and one day served as one of my professors in college. That great man, who so profoundly influenced me, is now asleep in Christ, waiting for the fulfillment of his desire. However, before I graduated, he shared this story with me when I was so discouraged I was about to quit preparing for the ministry. He told me that I had been called to a great army of ambassadors for Christ, that I am no longer a part of the sea of people who refuse to respond to this high calling, of whom Jesus said, "No one, after putting his hand to the plow and looking back, is fit for the kingdom of God."

My professor was an ambassador of hope to me, and even though he did not have the opportunity to write a book before he passed away from the scene of this great mission, he prepared me to give testimony of the hope we all have in Christ. Without being aware of it, we've all been strung together by God, to be ambassadors of anticipation.

I hope that this book will be a rose dropped into the pressured world in which you may be trapped. I hope that it will be a sweet fragrance of joy that inspires you to dream dreams and see visions. I hope that it infuses you with courage to reach for the stars and grab them. I pray that it will ignite the fires of love, peace, and grace as you serve out your calling as an ambassador of anticipation.

Keep on waiting, on tiptoes, for the Lord as you continue the glorious adventure of being an ambassador for Christ, through whom He is always entreating the world. He's coming soon! I can almost hear the choirs of heaven singing

"Soon we shall with Jesus reign, and never, never part again."

Grace to you, ambassadors!

---

1. Oswald Chambers, *Not knowing Where* (Discovery House, 1989), 26.
2. Ibid.
3. Donald Guthrie, *New Testament Theology* (InterVarsity, 1981), 554, 555.
4. Gerhard Kittel, ed. *Theological Dictionary of the New Testament* (Eerdmans, 1964), 3:104.
5. *Seventh-day Adventist Bible Commentary*, 5:901.
6. Colin Brown, ed., *The New International Dictionary of New Testament Theology* (Zondervan, 1986), 3:522.
7. Ibid. 3:523
8. Ibid. 3:524
9. Ellen G. White, *Christ's Object Lessons*, 64.
10. Ibid., 65.

11. Ibid.

12. Herbert Lockyer, *The Breath of God*, 54

13. Henry Drummond, quoted in *The Person And Ministry of The Holy Spirit: A Wesleyan Perspective*, 118

14. Charles Webb Carter, *The Person And Ministry of The Holy Spirit*, 118

15. Ellen G. White, *Steps to Christ*, 67.

16. *New Testament Theology*, 555.

If you enjoyed this book, you'll enjoy these as well:

Jesus For the New Millennium

Ken Wade's *Jesus For the New Millennium* examines key evidence from the life and words of Christ and provides fascinating and fresh answers to the question "Is Jesus coming or not?" If the commencement of yet another century is beginning to chip away at your faith in a "soon"-coming Savior, this book will give you ample reason to hope again.
0-8163-1761-5. Paperback. US$8.99/Cdn$13.49.

The Gift

Kim Allan Johnson. An unforgettable look at the sacrifice of Christ. *The Gift*, by Kim Allan Johnson, will put you back in touch with the God who would rather go to hell for you than to live in heaven without you.
0-8163-1768-2. Paperback. US$11.99, Cdn$17.99

Stand at the Cross and Be Changed

This powerful book by E. Lonnie Melashenko, speaker/director of the *Voice of Prophecy*, and John Thomas McLarty, revisits the greatest event in human history through the eyes of those gathered at Golgotha and through the last words of Christ.
0-8163-1384-9. Paper. US$8.99, Cdn$13.49.

Order from your ABC by calling **1-800-765-6955**, or get online and shop our virtual store at **www.adventistbookcenter.com**.

- Read a chapter from your favorite book.
- Order online.
- Sign up for e-mail notices on new products.